YAMAHA

WORKSHOP MANUAL

MINI ENDURO JT1 AND JT1L

MINI ENDURO JT2 AND JT2·MX

1971 - 1972

A Floyd Clymer Publication
This edition published in 2020 by
www.VelocePress.com

All rights reserved. This work may not be reproduced or transmitted in any form without the express written consent of the publisher.

INTRODUCTION

Welcome to the world of digital publishing ~ the book you now hold in your hand was printed using the latest state of the art digital technology. The advent of print-on-demand has forever changed the publishing process, never has information been so accessible and it is our hope that this book serves your informational needs for years to come. If this is your first exposure to digital publishing, we hope that you are pleased with the results. Many more titles of interest to the classic automobile and motorcycle enthusiast, collector and restorer are available via our website at www.VelocePress.com.

NOTE FROM THE PUBLISHER

The information presented is true and complete to the best of our knowledge. All recommendations are made without any guarantees on the part of the author or the publisher, who also disclaims any and all liability incurred with the use of the information contained in this manual.

TRADEMARKS

We recognize that some words, model names and designations, for example, mentioned herein are the property of the trademark holder. We use them for identification purposes only. This is not an official publication.

INFORMATION ON THE USE OF THIS PUBLICATION

This manual is an invaluable resource for those interested in performing their own maintenance. However, in today's information age we are constantly subject to changes in common practice, new technology, availability of improved materials and increased awareness of chemical toxicity. As such, it is advised that the user consult with an experienced professional prior to undertaking any procedure described herein. While every care has been taken to ensure correctness of information, it is obviously not possible to guarantee complete freedom from errors or omissions or to accept liability arising from such errors or omissions. Therefore, any individual that uses the information contained within, or elects to perform or participate in do-it-yourself repairs or modifications acknowledges that there is a risk factor involved and that the publisher or its associates cannot be held responsible for personal injury or property damage resulting from the use of the information or the outcome of such procedures.

MEASUREMENT & VALUES

The metric system is the primary measurement method used in both the manufacture of these motorcycles and this reproduction of the Factory Workshop Manual. As such, the reader is urged to verify that the conversion of those metric measurements to other forms of measurement is correct. All measurements and values are made without any guarantees on behalf of the publisher.

WARNING!

One final word of advice, this publication is intended to be used as a reference guide, and when in doubt the reader should consult with a qualified technician.

FOREWORD

The new YAMAHA MINI ENDURO, though small in size, is a fully functional motorcycle in the Yamaha Enduro vein. The 60cc engine, four speed gearbox, tubular frame and fully functional suspension combine to provide an ideal vehicle for the younger rider.

Its rugged design and excellent performance also make it an intriguing diversion for older, more experienced riders as well.

This service manual has been prepared in order to provide all Yamaha dealers and their service technicians the repair instructions and technical information required to keep the MINI-ENDURO in top condition We hope that you will find this manual most helpful and valuable in carrying out this goal.

IMPORTANT

The reader is encouraged to review the 'Parts and Service Bulletins' located in the appendices prior to performing any repairs or modifications as they contain additional data and information that is supplemental to the contents of this manual.

MODEL IDENTIFICATION

This manual was originally printed for the JT2 Mini-Enduro. It has been edited to include information for the JT1, JT1L and JT2M models.

Generally speaking, there were no major changes to any of the Mini-Enduro models since the JT1 was released for the 1971 model year. The JT1L (1971½ release) was a JT1 with lighting kit. The JT2 had various internal engine changes to improve reliability and carburetor changes to improve performance. JT2 lights were upgraded in intensity. The JT2M was styled after the JT1 for those people who wanted a Mini-motocrosser without lights. Additional identification information is given in the table below.

MODEL	YEAR	IBM ID NUMBER	STARTING ENGINE NUMBER	IDENTIFYING COLOR
JT1	1971	288	JT1-000101	Desert Orange
JT1L	1971(½)	338	JT1-200101	Desert Orange
JT2	1972	288	JT1-050101	Mandarin Orange
JT2M	1972	288	JT1-300101	Competition Yellow

CONTENTS

CHAPTER 1 GENERAL 1
    1- 1 Profile 1
    1- 2 Features 2
    1- 3 Specifications and Performance 3
    1- 4 Performance Curves 5
    1- 5 Tools and Instruments for shop service 6

CHAPTER 2 YAMAHA AUTOLUBE 7
    2- 1 What is Yamaha Autolube? 7
    2- 2 Features of Yamaha Autolube 7
    2- 3 Handling the Oil Pump 7

CHAPTER 3 ENGINE 11
    3- 1 Engine Removal 11
    3- 2 Cylinder Head 15
    3- 3 Cylinder 16
    3- 4 Piston Pin 17
    3- 5 Piston Ring 18
    3- 6 Piston 19
    3- 7 Flywheel Magneto 20
    3- 8 Crankcase Cover (R.H.) 21
    3- 9 Clutch 22
    3-10 Primary Drive Gear 27
    3-11 Kick Starter Mechanism 27
    3-12 Shift Mechanism 29
    3-13 Rotary Valve 31
    3-14 Drive Sprocket 33
    3-15 Crankcase 35
    3-16 Transmission Assembly 36
    3-17 Crankshaft 38
    3-18 Bearings and Oil Seals 41
    3-19 Carburetor 42
    3-20 Air Cleaner 44

CHAPTER 4 CHASSIS ... 46
    4- 1 Front Wheel ... 46
    4- 2 Rear Wheel ... 49
    4- 3 Rear Wheel Sprocket ... 53
    4- 4 Tires and Tubes ... 54
    4- 5 Front Forks ... 54
    4- 6 Rear Shocks ... 57
    4- 7 Gas Tank ... 58
    4- 8 Rear Swing Arm ... 58
    4- 9 Steering Head ... 60
    4- 10 Oil Tank and Tool Box ... 61
    4- 11 Frame ... 61
    4- 12 Handlebars ... 61
    4- 13 Miscellaneous ... 61

CHAPTER 5 ELECTRICAL SYSTEM ... 62
    5- 1 Electrical Equipment ... 62
    5- 2 List of Electrical Components ... 62
    5- 3 Ignition System-Function and Service ... 63
    5- 4 Ignition Timing ... 63
    5- 5 Ignition Coil ... 64
    5- 6 Condenser ... 64
    5- 7 Charging System ... 65
    5- 8 Battery ... 67
    5- 9 Checking the main Switch ... 69
    5- 10 Spark Plug ... 69
    5- 11 Lighting, Signal Systems and Wiring Diagrams ... 70

APPENDICES ... 73
    Parts and Service Bulletins ... 74
    Maintenance and Lubrication Intervals ... 84
    Pre-operation Check List ... 85
    Torque Values for Common Components ... 85
    Cleaning and Storage Hints ... 86
    Metric Inch Conversion Tables ... 87
    Modifications for Increased Performance and Racing ... 89
    Parts Manuals ... 99
    Illustrated Parts Manual JT1 & JT1L ... 105
    Illustrated Parts Manual JT2 & JT2M ... 171

CHAPTER 1 GENERAL

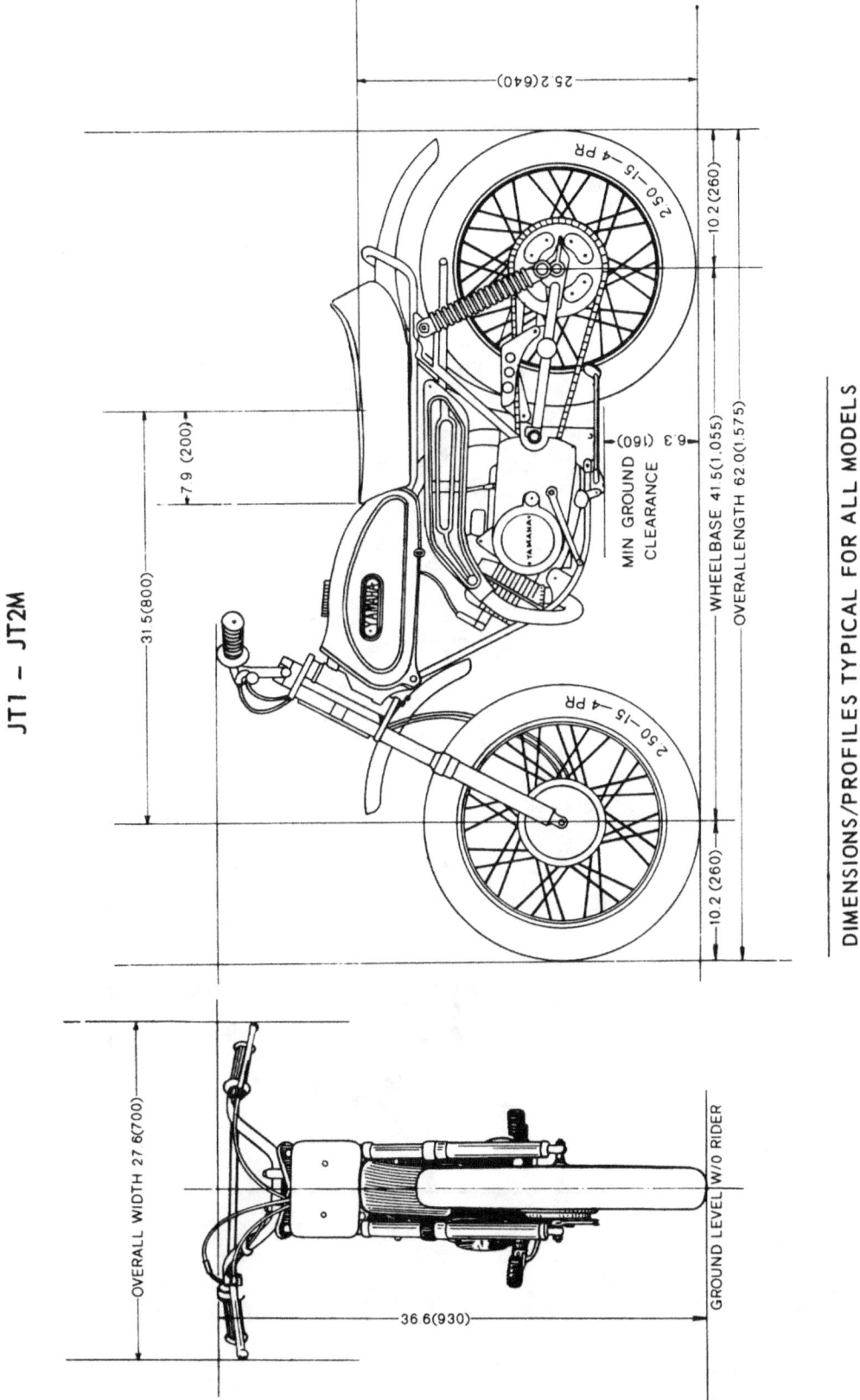

DIMENSIONS/PROFILES TYPICAL FOR ALL MODELS

GENERAL - Profile

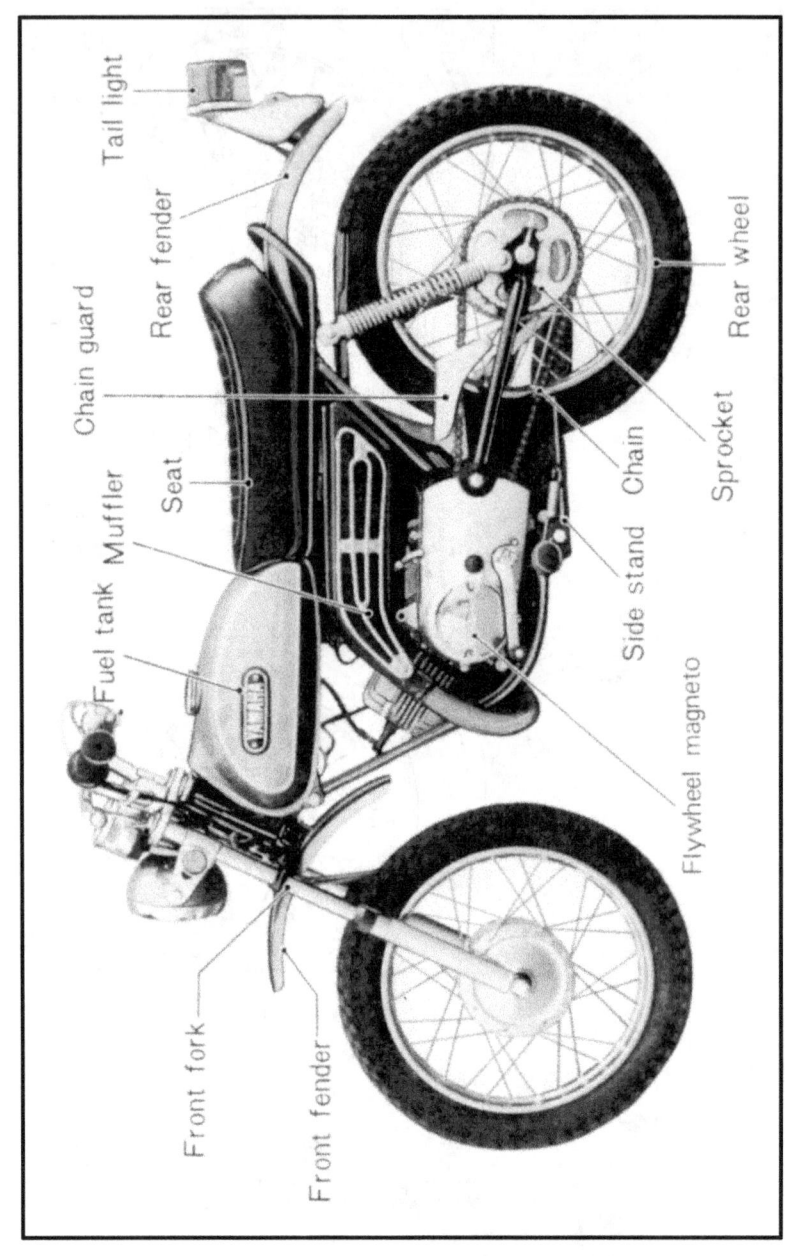

1-3 Specifications & Performance JT2

Model	YAMAHA 60 JT2 <JT1>
Dimensions : 　Overall length 　Overall width 　Overall height 　Wheelbase 　Min. ground clearance	 62.4 in (1580 mm) <62.0> 27.6 in (700 mm.) 36.6 in (930 mm.) 41.5 in (1055 mm.) 6.3 in (160 mm.)
Weight : Gross	60 kg 132 lbs
Performance : 　Fuel consumption 　　(on paved level roads) 　Climbing ability 　Min. turning radius 　Braking distance	 176 mile/gal (19 mph) 22 degrees 59.1 in. (1,500 mm.) 24.6 ft/22 mph (7.5 m/35 km/h)
Engine : 　Model 　Type 　Lubricating system 　Cylinder 　Displacement 　Bore x Stroke 　Compression ratio 　Max. power 　Max. torque 　Starting system 　Ignition system 　Ignition timing	 JT1 2 stroke, gasoline Separate lubrication (YAMAHA Autolube) Single, forward inclined. 3.54 cu. in. (58 cc) 1.654 in x 1.654 in. (42 mm x 42 mm) 6.4 : 1 4.5 hp/7,500 r.p.m. 3.62 ft-lb/5,500 r.p.m (0.5 kg-m/5,500 r.p.m) Kick starter Magneto ignition 1.8 mm. B.T.D.C.
Carburetor : 　Type 　M. J. 　J. N.	 (See 3-19-C) Carb. Specs.
Air cleaner :	Wet , foam rubber
Transmission : 　Clutch 　Primary reduction system 　Primary reduction ratio	 Wet , multiple-disk Gear 3.895 (74/19)

GENERAL - Specifiaations and Performance

Model	YAMAHA 60 JT2 <JT1>

Gear box :
  Type
  Reduction ratio 1st
               2nd
               3rd
               4th
  Secondary reduction system
  Secondary reduction ratio
  Oil capacity
	Constant mesh, 4-speed forward
	3.077 (40/13)
	1.889 (34/18)
	1.304 (30/23)
	1.038 (27/26)
	Chain
	3.153 (41/13)
	0.85 US qts (800–850 cc)

Chassis :
  Frame
  Suspension system, front
  Suspension system, rear
  Cushion system, front
  Cushion system, rear
	
	Tubular-Double loop
	Telescopic fork
	Swinging arm
	Coil spring, oil damper
	Coil spring, oil damper

Steering system :
  Steering angle
  Caster
  Trail
	
	47° both right and left
	63.5°
	2.7 in (68mm)

Braking system :
  Type of brake
  Operation system, front
  Operation system, rear
	
	Internal expansion
	Right hand operation
	Right foot operation

Tire size :
  Front
  Rear
	
	2.50-15-4PR
	2.50-15-4PR

Dynamo :
  Model
  Manufacturer
	
	F11-L46 <F11-L42>
	HITACHI Ltd.

Tanks :
  Gasoline tank capacity
  Oil tank capacity
	
	1.1 U.S. gals (4.3 l)
	1.1 U.S. qts (1.0 l)

1-4 PERFORMANCE CURVES

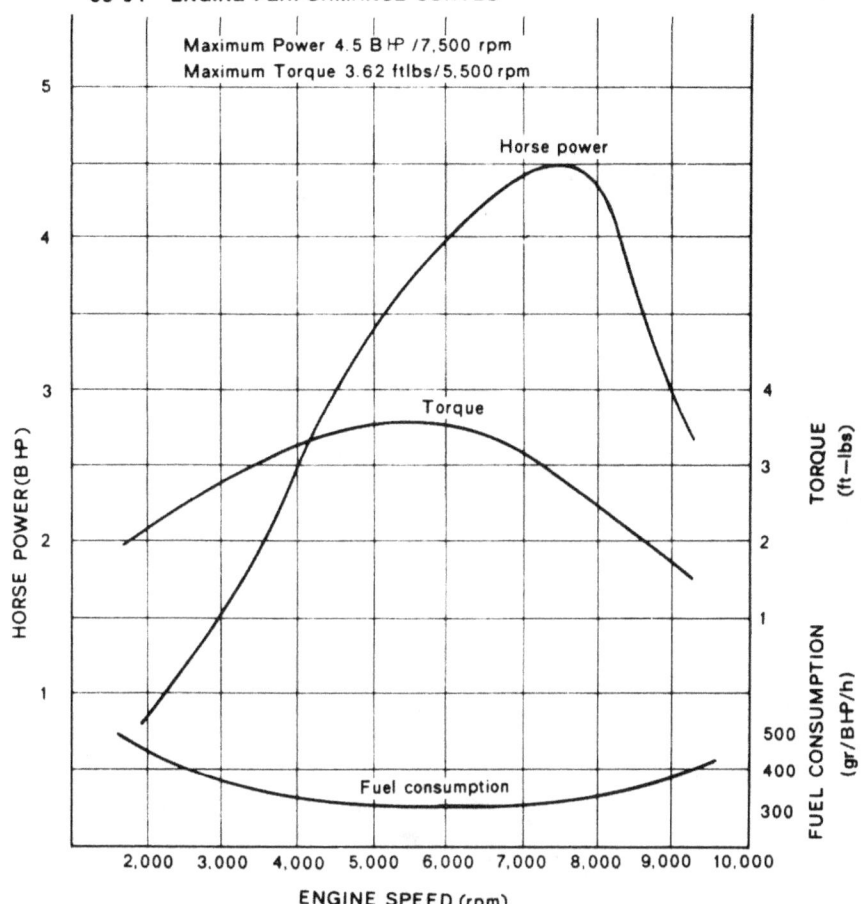

3-port Cylinder Exploded View

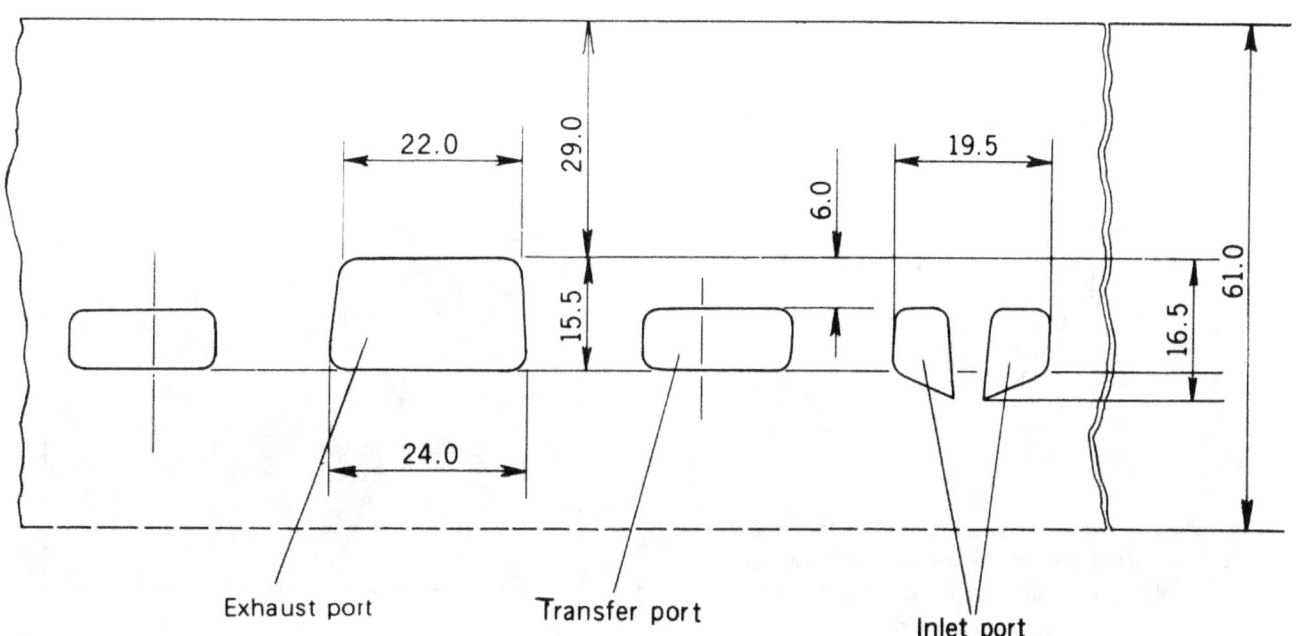

GENERAL - Tools and Instruments for Shop Service

1-6 Tools and Instruments for Shop Service

The following tools and instruments are required to service the JT series

1 General Tools

1) Plug wrench 23x29 mm.
2) A set of wrenches
3) A set of socket wrenches
4) Plastic tip hammer
5) Steel hammer
6) Circlip pliers (ST type)
7) Circlip pliers (RT type)
8) Needle nose pliers
9) Pliers
10) Phillips-head screwdriver
11) Phillips-head screwdriver (L)
12) Phillips-head screwdriver (M)
13) Phillips-head screwdriver (S)
14) Slot-head screwdriver (M)
15) Slot-head screwdriver (S)
16) T-handle socket wrench

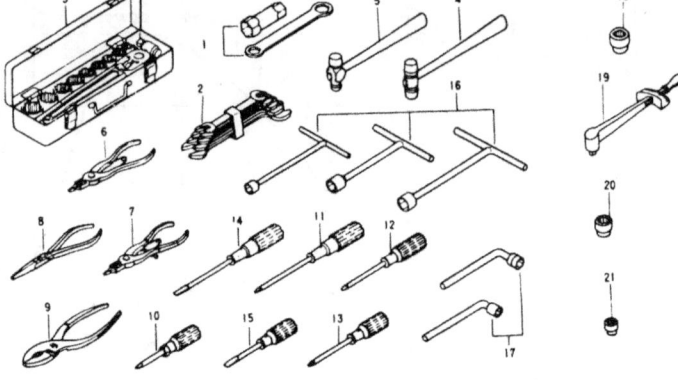

Fig 1-6-1

2 Special Tools and Instruments

1 Clutch holding tool
2 Crankcase disassembling tool
3 Crankshaft assembling tool
4 Flywheel magneto holding tool
5 Flywheel magneto puller

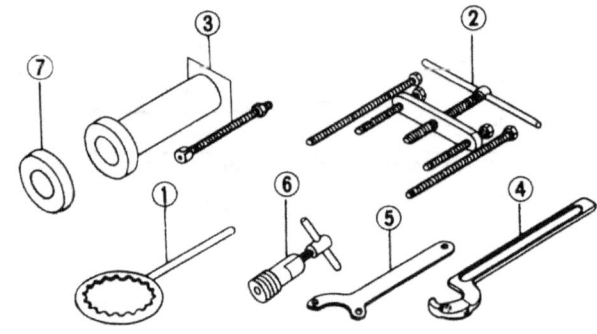

Fig. 1-6-2

In addition an electro-testor, tachometer (engine rpm meter) hydrometer, etc. should and available.

3 Other Material

1) Yamaha Bond (No.5)
2) Gear oil
3) Grease
4) Wiping material
5) Yamaha Bond No.4
6) Wooden box
7) Oiler
8) Oil jug

The use of a wooden box as shown in the above photo will facilitate engine service and overhaul. Consumable parts (such as gaskets) and replacement parts must also be on hand.

Fig. 1-6-3

CHAPTER 2 YAMAHA AUTOLUBE
(Automatic, Separate Lubrication System)

2-1 What is Yamaha Autolube?

Conventional 2-stroke engines are lubricated by oil pre-mixed in gasoline, but YAMAHA's Autolube furnishes an automatic, separate lubrication system. That is, the oil in a separate oil tank is automatically regulated by the oil pump and fed to the engine according to engine speed and load.

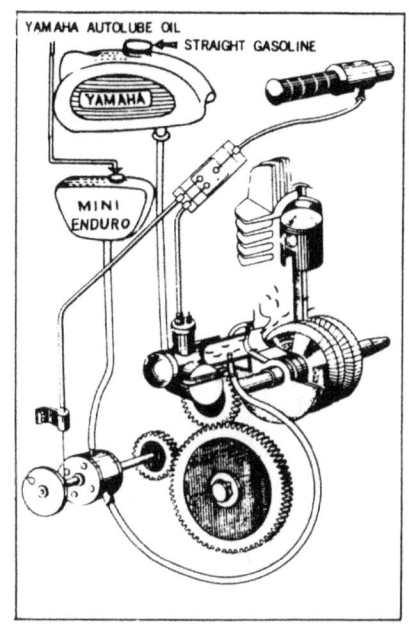

Fig 2-1-1

2-2 Features of Yamaha Autolube

The oil pump is driven by the engine through a reduction gear, and is connected to the carburetor throttle cable, which in turn is controlled by the accellerator grip. The oil pump automatically regulates the volume of lubricating oil according to engine speed and throttle valve opening, thus pumping the optimum amount of oil for engine lubrication under any operating condition.
This "automatic, separate lubrication" does not merely eliminate disadvantages in the conventional pre-mix system, but it further improves the performance and efficiency of 2-stroke designs by eliminating certain oil-starvation conditions which formerly existed.

1. The Autolube feeds an optimum amount of lubricating oil to the engine under any operating condition, thus featuring :
   * Less oil consumption.
   * Less carbon accumulation.
   * Less exhaust smoke.
   * Improved lubricating efficiency.

2. The Autolube simplifies fuel supply, thus featuring:
   * Using straight gasoline directly in the gas tank.
   * Less fuel contamination.

3. The Autolube improves the reliability of lubrication, thus eliminating.
   * Special care concerning oil/fuel mixing ratios.

2-3. Handling the Oil Pump

The oil pump is a precision-machined assembly. Make no attempt to disassemble it. When you remove the oil pump from the engine, protect it from dust, dirt, etc., and after reinstalling it, bleed and adjust the pump correctly. Proper handling will keep the pump free from trouble.

YAMAHA AUTOLUBE - Handling of the Oil Pump

The oil pump is similar in both construction and operation to other Autolube systems. The only difference is the employment of a 4.0 ∅ plunger.

2-3-1 Checking Minimum Pump Stroke

1 Checking

a. Fully close the accelerator grip.
b. Turn the oil pump starter plate in the direction of the arrow marked on the plate. Then measure the gap between the adjustment pulley and the adjustment plate. Keep the gap as wide as possible by observing it with the eye prior to measuring.

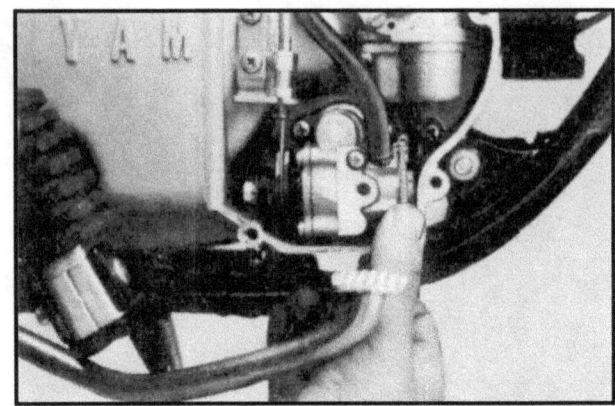

Fig. 2-3-1

c. Insert a feeler gauge (0.15 mm) into the gap.
 If the gap allows it to enter
 ......Stroke is correct.
 If the gap does not allow
 ......Stroke is insufficient.

Fig 2-3-2

2 Adjustment

a. Remove the adjustment plate lock nut, and then remove the adjustment plate.

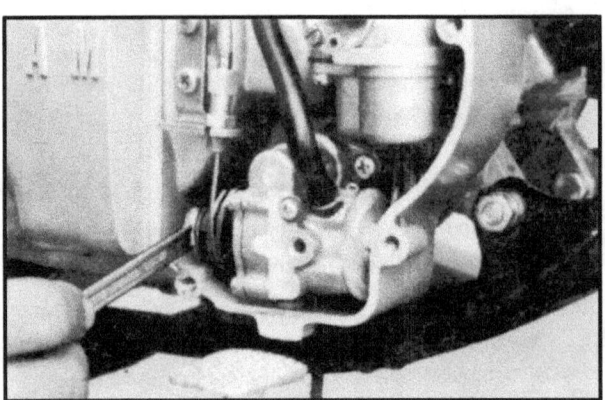

Fig 2-3-3

b Install a 0.1 mm adjustment shim where the adjustment plate was

c Reinstall the adjustment plate lock nut. and measure minimum stroke When the gap allows a 0.20 mm feeler gauge to enter but does not allow a 0.25 mm. the stroke is correctly adjusted
Stroke adjustment tolerance....**0.20 to 0.25 mm.**

Fig 2-3-4

2-3-2 Carburetor and Autolube Cable Adjustment

Follow the preceeding in section 2-3-1 steps to check minimum stroke. and adjust it if incorrect. Then adjust the pump and carburetor as described in the steps below.

1) Throttle Cable Adjustment

a. Adjust the carburetor with the engine at idle. and remove all but 1 mm of slack from cable B
- To bring the play of the throttle cable into correct adjustment. loosen or tighten the throttle cable adjustment screw.
- To check this adjustment. lightly pull throttle cable B. and engine speed should slightly increase from idling r.p.m. after 1mm of travel.

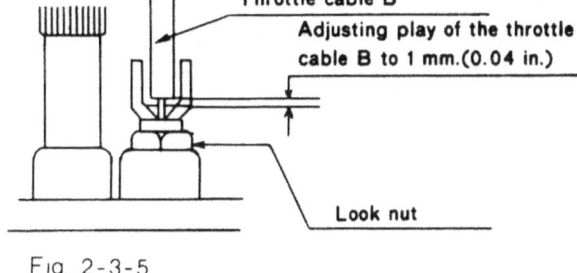

Fig. 2-3-5

b Next, adjust throttle cable (A) so that the gap as shown in Fig.2-3-6 below will be between 0.5 and 1.0 mm (0.02～0.04 in)
- Check the play of the throttle cable (A) by pulling on the outer part of the throttle cable If the play is excessive or insufficent. adjust the play using the adjustor.

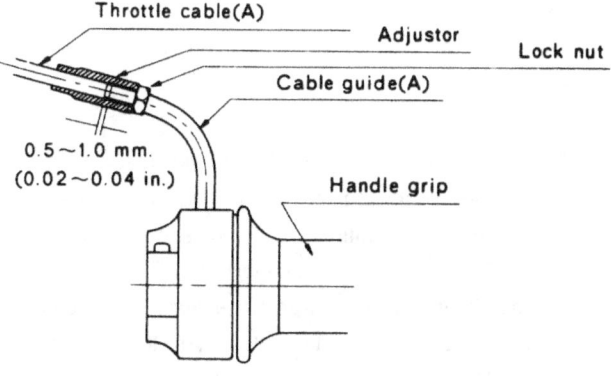

Fig 2-3-6

ENGINE - Handling of the Oil Pump

2) Autolube Cable Adjustment

With the throttle cable properly adjusted, check the pump guide pin location. It should be no closer than 1.5mm (.060") to the raised boss of the pump pulley. If it is too close, loosen the lock nut (see Figure 2-3-7) and turn the adjusting bolt until adjustment is correct. Tighten lock nut.

Next, turn throttle to full open position, the guide pin should not strike the raised boss of the pump pulley in this position, if it does, loosen the adjusting bolt slightly to provide clearance.

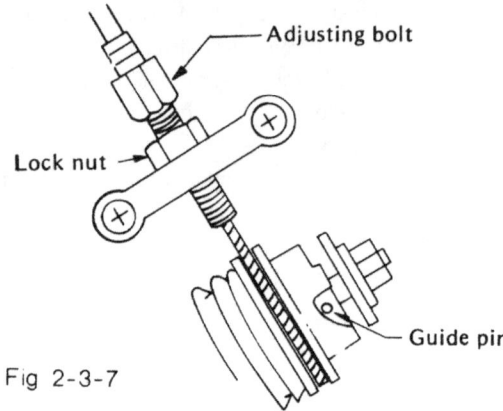

Fig 2-3-7

2-3-3 Bleeding

When the pump has been removed or the Autolube oil has run out, air will enter the pump. The air will cause an irregular flow of oil after the pump is mounted again or the oil tank is refilled. In order to prevent such an irregular flow of oil, bleed the pump in the following manner.

1) Remove the bleeder bolt.

Fig 2-3-8

2) Next, rotate the starter plate in the direction of the arrow marked on the plate. Continue turning the plate until no air comes out with the oil and tighten the bleeder bolt To facilitate this bleeding, fully open the accelerator grip and rotate the starter plate. As the plunger stroke becomes greater, the air can be quickly bled.

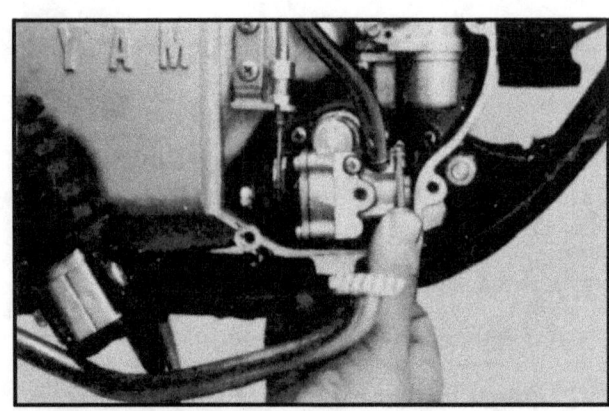

Fig 2-3-9

CHAPTER 3 ENGINE

This chapter describes the disassembly and reassembly of the engine, its removal from the chassis, and the necessary service data. However, except when overhauling the crankshaft assembly, transmission, shifter mechanism or bearings and oil seals in the crankcase, it is suggested that engine be serviced without removing it from the chassis. This will save a lot of time and labor.

Preparation for disassembly of the engine :

1) All dirt, mud, dust, and foreign material should be thoroughly removed from the exterior of the engine assembly before removal and disassembly. This will prevent any harmful foreign material from entering the interior of the engine assembly.
2) Before engine removal and disassembly, be sure you have proper tools and cleaning equipment so you can perform a clean and efficient job.
3) During disassembly of the engine, clean all parts and place them in trays in order of disassembly. This will make assembly time faster and easier, and insure correct installation of all engine parts.

3-1 Engine Removal

1. Start the engine and warm it up for a few minutes, then turn off the engine and drain the transmission oil

(Volume of oil 800-850 cc 10.85 US qt)
YAMALUBE 4-CYCLE or SAE 10W-30 "SE"

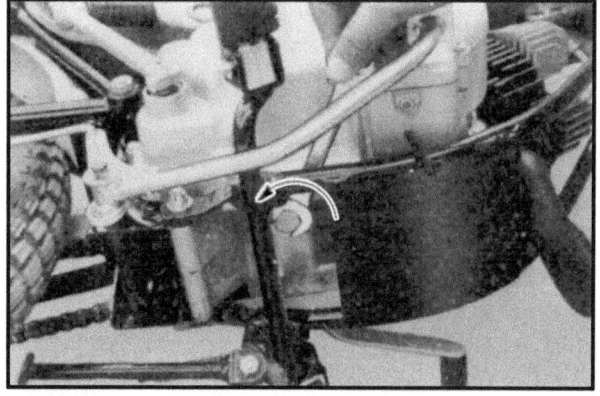

Fig 3-1-1

2. Pull out the seat fitting pin and remove the seat by pulling it backward.

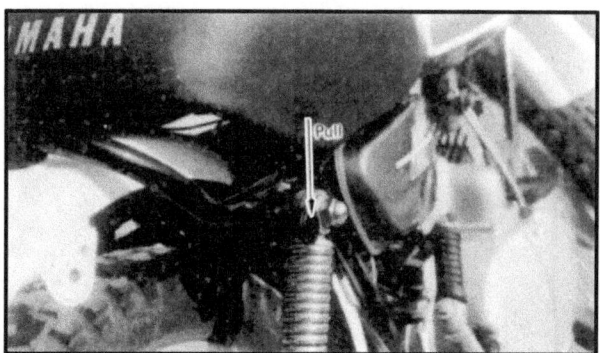

Fig 3-1-2

ENGINE - Engine Removal

3 Disconeect the fuel line at the bottom of the fuel tank. Remove the tank mounting bolt (13) and lift the fuel tank off.

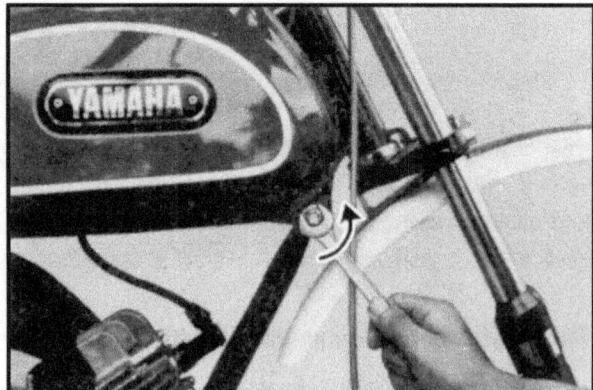
Fig 3-1-3

4 Remove the connector from the magneto lead wire and remove the plug cap.

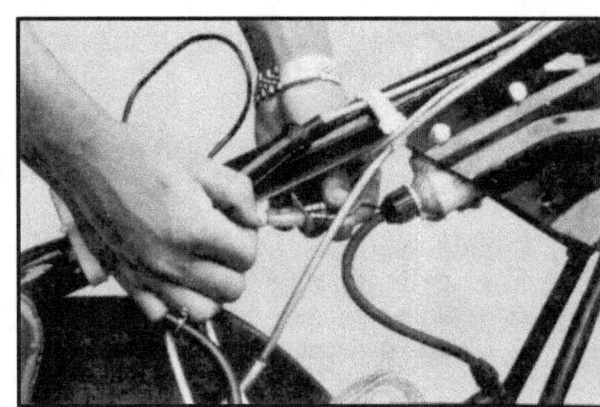
Fig 3-1-4

5 Remove the muffler
   a) Remove the exhaust pipe nut.

   Use the special wrench. Hammering on the nut will only damage it and/or the cylinder.

Fig 3-1-5

   b) Remove the muffler holding bolts (13 mm)

Fig 3-1-6

ENGINE - Engine Removal

6 Remove the change pedal
   (10 mm)

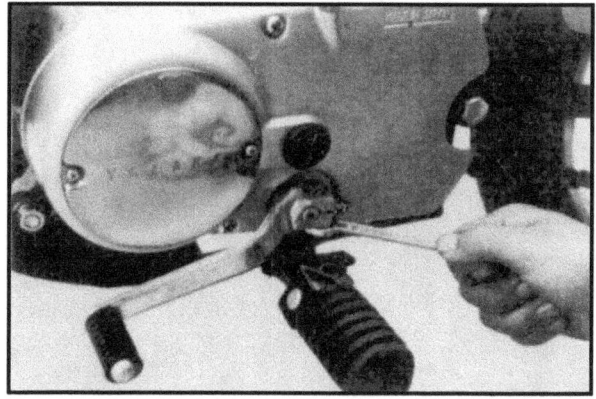
Fig 3-1-7

7 Remove the lefthand crankcase cover
   (⊕ screwdriver)

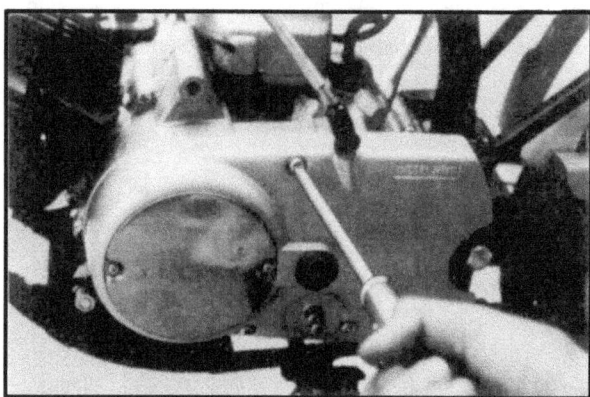
Fig 3-1-8

8 Disconnect the master link and remove the chain.

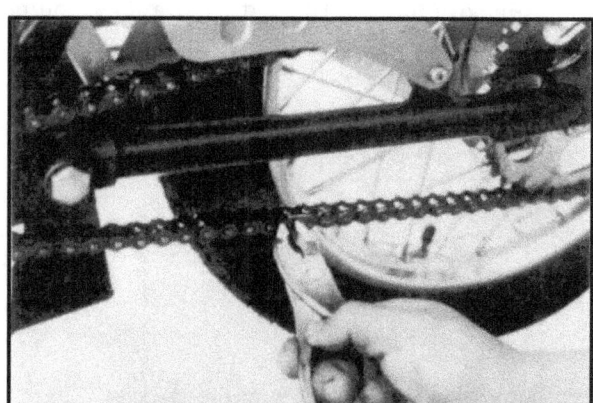
Fig 3-1-9

When reconnecting the chain be sure the master link is facing in the correct direction.

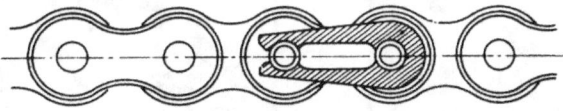

After reconnecting the chain adjust the free play to 25 mm. (1 in.) up and down at the center of the lower section with the rear wheel on the ground.

ENGINE - Engine Removal

9. Remove the pump cover and pump cable
   (⊕ **screwdriver**)

Fig 3-1-10

10. Remove the oil pipe and plug the hole with a bolt to stop the flow of oil from the tank.

Fig 3-1-11

Remove the fuel line and remove the carburetor
(⊖ **screwdriver**)

Fig 3-1-12

12. Remove the four engine mounting bolts
    (13 mm)

Fig 3-1-13

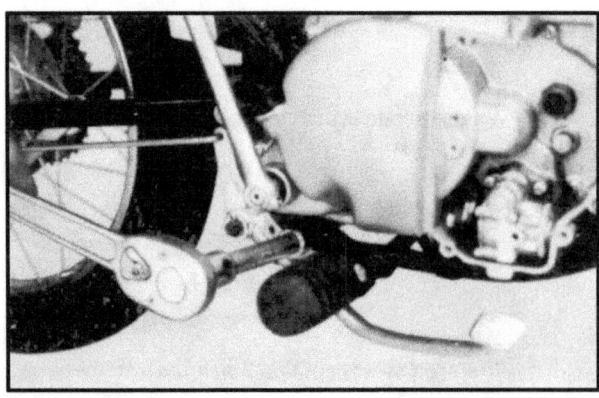

Fig 3-1-14

ENGINE - Cylinder Head

13 Remove the engine from the frame.

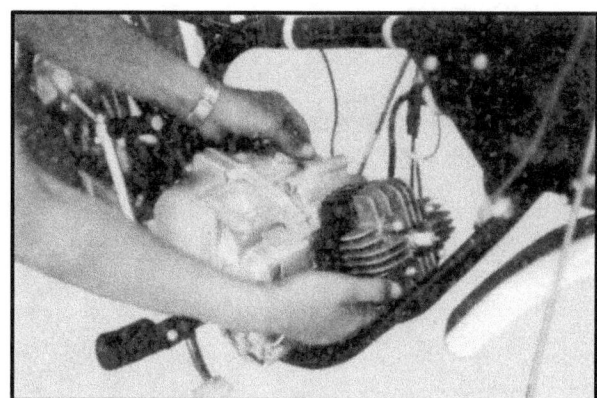
Fig 3-1-15

3-2 Cylinder Head

The cylinder head is bolted on the cylinder with special nuts.

A Removing

Remove the four special nuts from the top of the cylinder head, then the head and head gasket. Reverse the sequence for reinstallation. Replace the gasket, if damaged or in questionable condition.

(10 mm)

Note: During reassembly the head bolts must be torqued to 90 in/lbs in pattern, and in successive stages. Do not torque a hot engine and for most accurate readings place a small amount of light weight oil on the threads first.

Fig 3-2-1

Fig 3-2-2

B Removing Carbon Deposits

Carbon deposits on the cylinder head combustion chamber and top of the piston will result in an increase in the compression ratio, as well as pre-ignition and engine overheating.

Scrape the cylinder head and piston dome clean. **Use a rounded scraper to avoid damaging the aluminum.**

Fig 3-2-3

ENGINE - Cylinder

3-3 Cylinder

A   1) Remove the cylinder by striking it lightly with a soft faced hammer.

Fig 3-3-1

2) Always replace the cylinder base gasket when reassembling.

Fig 3-3-2

B Checking the Cylinder for Wear

1) Measure the amount of wear of the cylinder wall with a cylinder bore measuring micrometer or cylinder gauge. (Measure it at four depths while positioning the instrument parallel, and then at right angles to the crankshaft.) If the difference between the maximum and minimum diameter exceeds 0.05 mm. (0.0019") rebore and hone the cylinder.

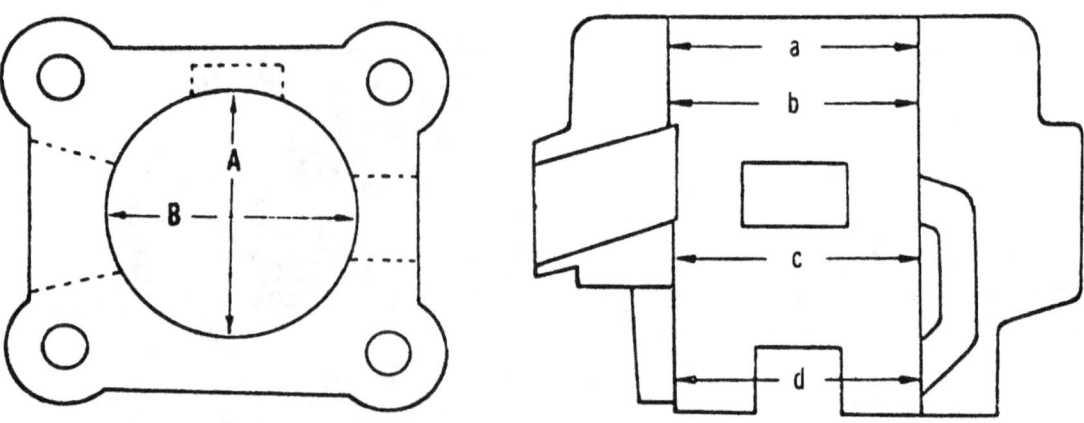

2) The piston clearance between the piston and the cylinder is 0.040-0.045 mm (0.0016"-0.0018")

ENGINE - Cylinder, Piston Pin

C Cylinder Reconditioning

1) Pistons are available in 0.25 and 0.50 mm. (0.010" and 0.020") oversizes.
2) The cylinder should be rebored and honed to the diameter of the oversize piston plus the minimum allowable clearance.
3) The error between the maximum and minimum diameters after honing should be no more than 0.04 mm. (0.0015")
4) If cylinder rebore is necessary, be sure to chamfer all port edges to prevent the rings from catching and breaking on a sharp port edge.

D Removing Carbon Deposits

Scrape off the carbon accumulation in the exhaust port of the cylinder with the dulled end of a hacksaw blade.

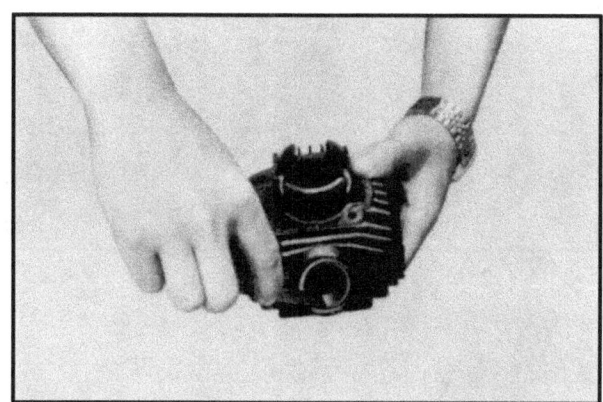

Fig 3-3-3

E Installing the Cylinder

Put your fingers at each end of the piston ring, expand the ring, and slip it onto the piston. Align both ends of the ring with the knock pin in each ring groove. Next, slip the cylinder down over the piston. Compress the rings to prevent ring breakage during installation.

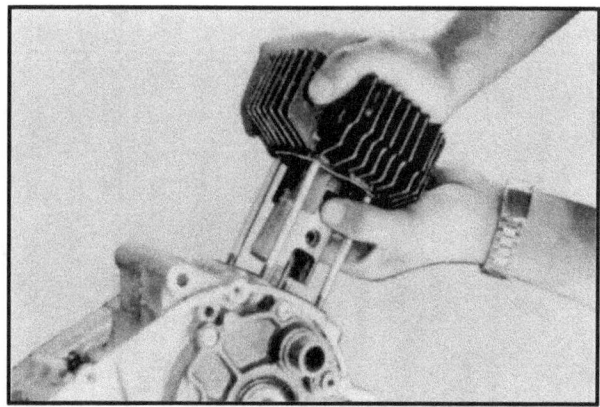

Fig 3-3-4

3-4 Piston Pin

A Pulling out the Piston Pin

Remove the clips at both ends of the piston pin with needle nose pliers, and press out the piston pin with a finger or a slot-head screwdriver.

Note: Before removing the piston pin clips, cover the crankcase with a clean rag, so you will not accidentally drop the clip or other foreign particles into the crankcase.

Fig 3-4-1

ENGINE - Piston Ring

B Piston-to-Piston pin fit

The piston pin should fit snugly in its bore so that it drags a little as you turn it. If the piston pin is loose replace the pin and/or the piston.

If the pin has step-wear in its center, replace the needle bearing as well as the piston pin. Check the small end of the connecting rod for wear by inserting the piston pin and bearing.

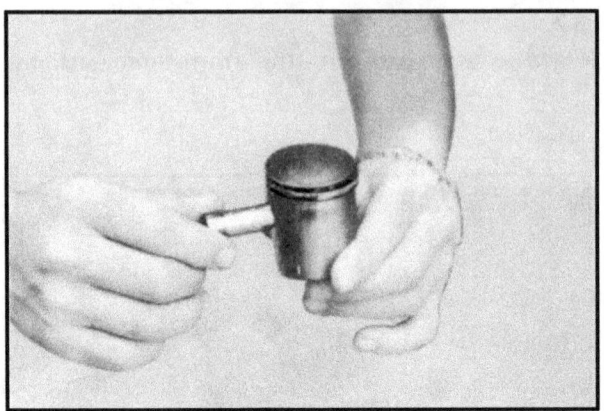
Fig 3-4-2

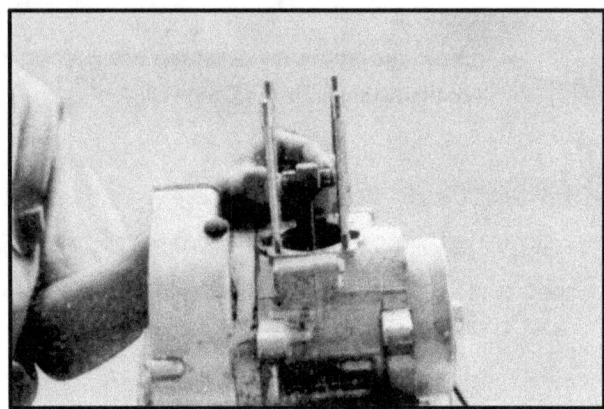
Fig 3-4-3

3-5 Piston Ring

A Removing the Piston Rings

Put your thumbs at each end of the piston ring and pull the piston ring ends apart.
Remove the ring by moving the ring off the piston on the other side of the ring ends and lifting up.

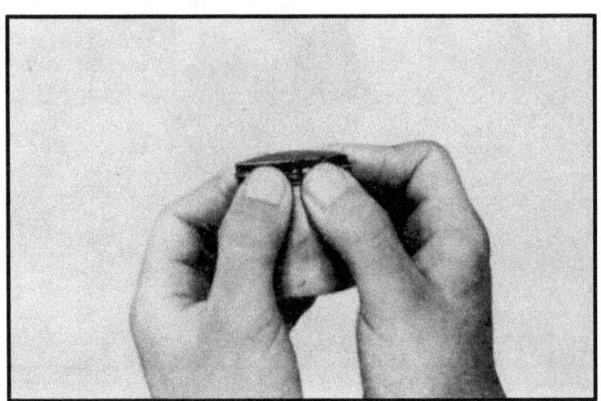
Fig 3-5-1

Fig 3-5-2

B Installing the Piston Rings

First fit No.2 ring over the piston, and then the No.1 ring, and align their end gaps with the locating pin in each ring groove. (Fig. 3-5-3)
The printing on all rings must face up to position the gap properly at the pin.

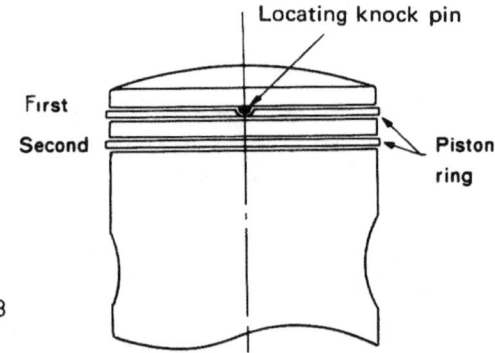
Fig 3-5-3

ENGINE - Piston

C. Checking the Piston Rings

1) Measuring piston ring wear. Put the ring into the cylinder so that the ring is parallel to the cylinder bottom edge, and then measure the end gap with a feeler gauge (Fig. 3-5-4). The end gap should be between 0.15 and 0.35 mm. (0.006"-0.014") for both No.1 and No.2 rings.

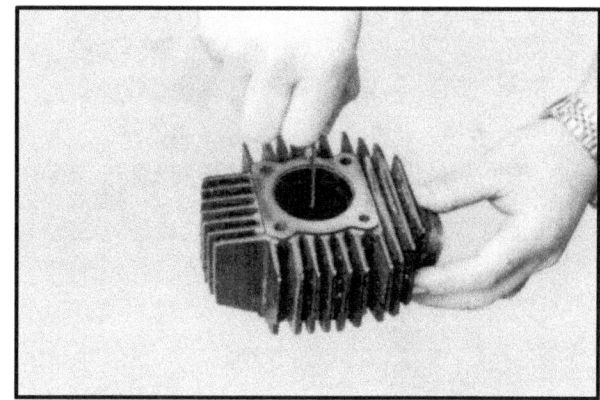

Fig. 3-5-4

2) Removing carbon

Carbon on the piston rings and in the ring grooves will make the rings stick in the piston, thus causing gas blow-by.
Remove the rings from the piston, and clean the carbon from the rings and ring grooves. using the end of an old ring as a scraper.

3-6 Piston

The piston is made of a high-silicon aluminum alloy.

A Checking and Correcting the Piston to Cylinder Wall Clearance

1) Measuring piston clearance

Piston clearance is the difference between the minimum cylinder bore diameter and the maximum outside diameter of the piston. As described in 4-3 Cylinder, piston clearance should be 0.040-0.045mm (0.0016-0.0018") To determine the maximum piston diameter, measure the piston with a micrometer at right angles to the skirt 10 mm. (3/8 in.) from its bottom edge. (Fig. 3-6-1)

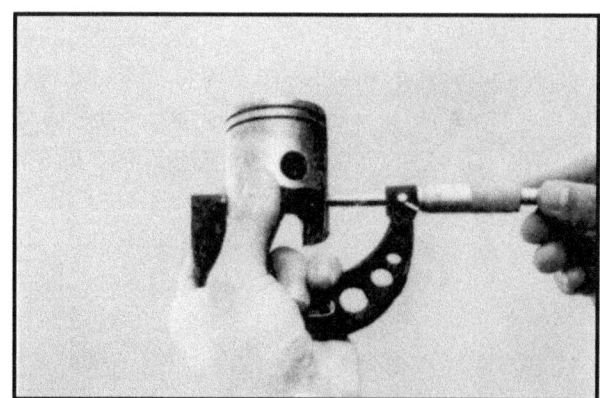

Fig. 3-6-1

2) Checking and correcting scratches on the piston

A piston showing signs of seizure will result in noise and loss of engine power. It will also cause damage to the cylinder wall.
If a piston that has seized is used again without correction, another seizure will develop in the same area. Lightly sand the seizure "high spot" on the piston with wet #400 sand paper until smooth.

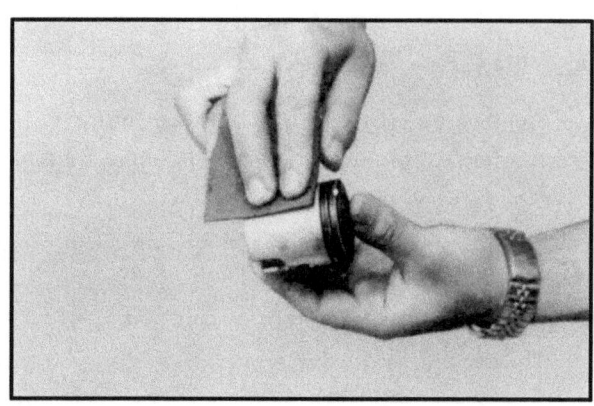

Fig 3-6-2

ENGINE - Piston Flywheel Magnet

3) Removing Carbon
   Remove carbon accumulations on the piston head, using a screwdriver or a saw-blade.

Note   Whenever carbon accumlations are removed, take care that the underlying metal is not scored or otherwise damaged.

Fig 3-6-3

Carbon and gum accumulations in the piston ring grooves will result in piston ring seizure. Remove them from the ring groove.

Fig 3-6-4

B Piston Installation Direction
   Install the piston with the arrow mark on the head pointing forward (toward the exhaust port of the cylinder)

Fig 3-6-5

3-7 Flywheel Magneto

A. Remove the nut using a flywheel magneto holding tool to hold the magneto and a 19 mm socket to loosen it.

Fig 3-7-1

ENGINE - Flywheel Magneto, Crankcase Cover

B Install the flywheel magneto puller.
   Then tighten the bolt. The flywheel magneto will break loose. (left-hand thread)
   (Nut: 17 mm)

Fig 3-7-2

C Remove the two screws holding the flywheel magneto base to the crankcase, and remove the flywheel magneto base.

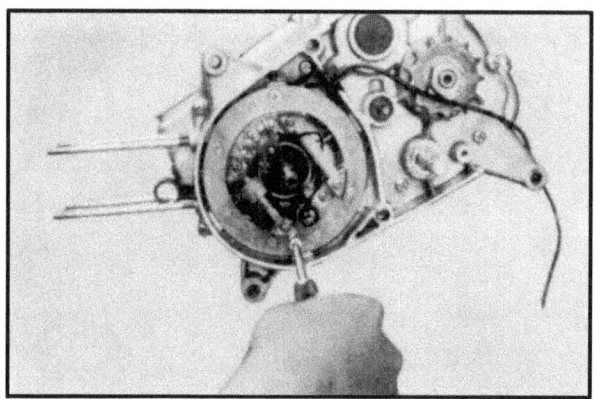
Fig. 3-7-3

D Remove the woodruff key.
   It is advisable to place the woodruff key on the flywheel magnets (using its magnetic force) while the key is removed for engine service. This will keep it from becoming lost.
   (⊖ Screw driver, hammer)

Fig. 3-7-4

3-8 Crankcase Cover (R.H.)

A Removal
  1) Remove the kick crank mounting bolt and the crank.
     (10 mm)

Fig 3-8-1

ENGINE - Crankcase Cover, Clutch

2) Remove the seven pan head screws holding the crankcase cover, and then remove the case cover. (The cover can be removed without taking off the oil pump.)

   Note: In this case, be sure to pull out the Autolube pump banjo bolt before cover removal.

Fig 3-8-2

3) Remove the crankcase cover gasket. Replace it, if damaged.

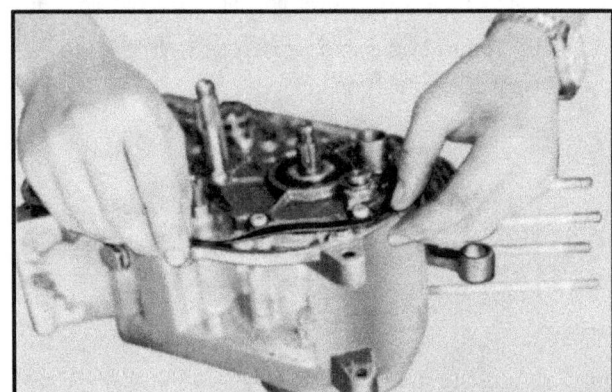

Fig 3-8-3

B Installation

Spread YAMAHA Bond No.5 over the mating surface of the crankcase R. Place the crankcase cover gasket on the crankcase and apply Yamaha Bond No.5 and install the crankcase cover R. Be sure to apply YAMAHA Bond No.5 to the mating surface ; otherwise the crankcase will leak.

Note : When installing the crankcase cover (R) make sure that the pump drive gear (made from synthetic resin) is correctly engaged with the primary drive gear. In addition, make certain that all mating surfaces have been thoroughly cleaned.

Fig 3-8-4

3-9 Clutch

The clutch is of the wet disc type, consisting of two molded cork friction plates and one steel clutch plate.
It is installed on the transmission main shaft.
The clutch housing forms a one piece assembly with the primary driven gear of the primary reduction system. This reduction gear is in mesh with the primary drive gear. The primary reduction ratio is 74/19 (3.894).

ENGINE · Clutch

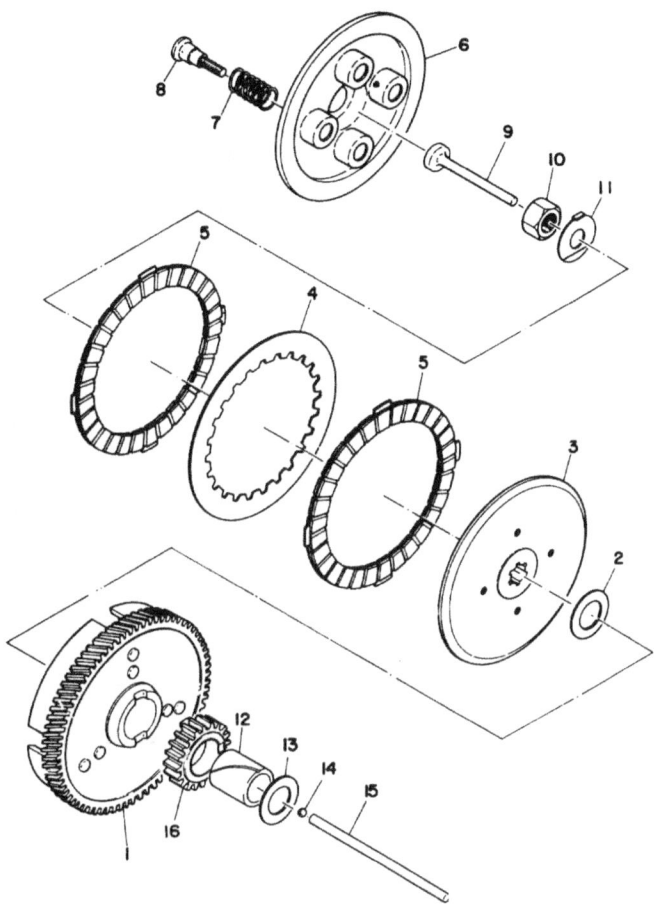

1. Primary driven gear ass'y
2. Thrust plate
3. Clutch boss
4. Clutch plate
5. Friction plate
6. Pressure plate
7. Clutch spring
8. Spring screw
9. Push rod 1
10. Lock nut
11. Lock washer
12. Spacer
13. Thrust plate
14. Ball
15. Push rod 2
16. Kick pinion gear

Fig 3-9-1 Clutch ass'y exploded view

A. Removing the Pressure Plate

Remove the four clutch spring holding screws, and take out the pressure plate and push crown.

(⊖ Screwdriver)

Fig. 3-9-2

Fig. 3-9-3

ENGINE - Clutch

B. Removing the Clutch Boss
Install the clutch holding tool on the clutch boss.
Loosen the lock nut, and then remove the clutch boss.
(19 mm)

Fig. 3-9-4

C. Checking the Clutch Spring
If the free length of the spring is 1 mm. (0.04 in.) or more shorter than the standard free length, replace it.
(Slide calipers)

Free length 34 mm. (1.340 in.)

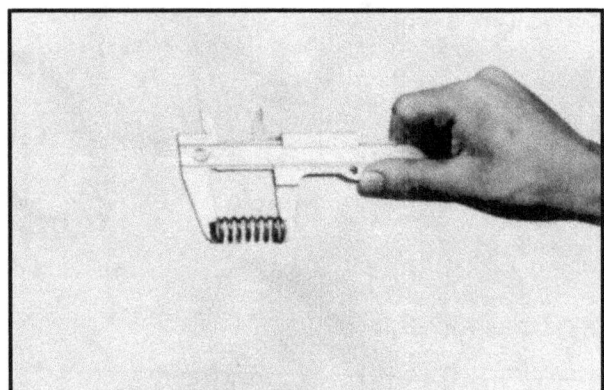
Fig. 3-9-5

D. Checking the Friction Plates
Measure the friction plate at several points for wear. Replace it if it is worn more than 0.35mm.(0.0137in.) or more. Also replace it if uneven contact is quite evident.
(Slide calipers)

Standard thickness = 3.5 mm. (0.137 in.)

Wear limit = 3.15 mm (0.124 in.)

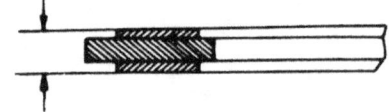
3.5 mm (Standard Thickness)

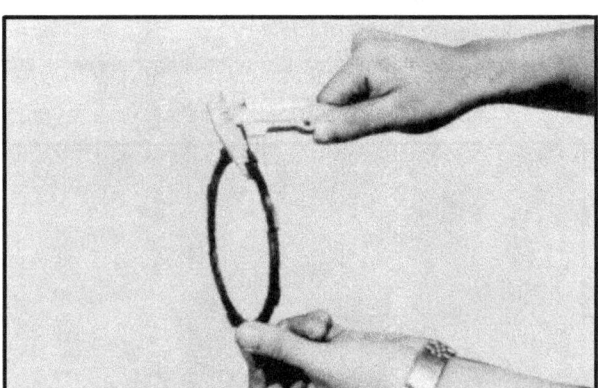
Fig. 3-9-6

ENGINE - Clutch

E. Clutch Housing Assembly
(integrated with the primary driven gear.)

1) Inspection

Insert the primary gear retaining collar (spacer) in the primary driven gear boss and check it for radial play. If the play is excessive (allowable clearance is between 0.009~0.048 mm.) replace the gear retaining collar because it will cause excessive noise. If any scratches are found, replace the spacer to avoid impaired clutch action.

Fig. 3-9-7

F. Checking the Primary Gear Retaining Collar (Spacer)

Place the primary gear retaining collar around the main axle and again check it for radial play. If play exists (allowable clearance is between 0.020~0.062 mm.) replace the gear retaining collar.

Replace any collar with step-wear on its outer surface.

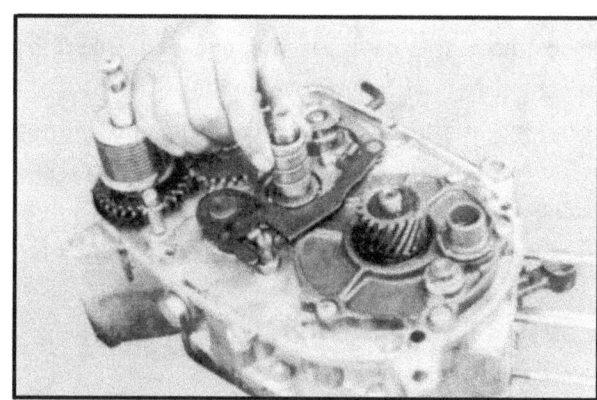

Fig. 3-9-8

G. Checking the Push Rod

Remove the push rod and roll it over a surface plate. If the rod is slightly bent, you could straighten it. Replace it if it is drastically bent or worn.

Fig. 3-9-9

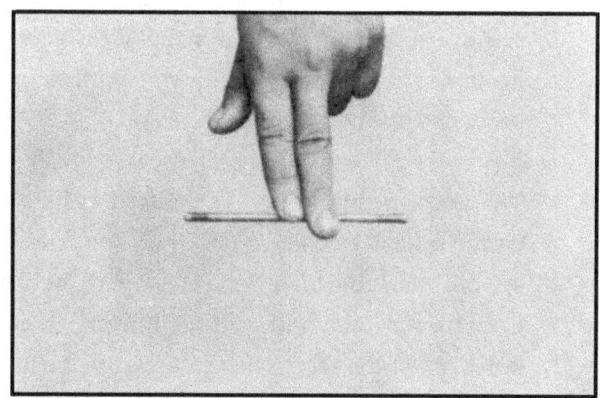

Fig. 3-9-10

ENGINE - Clutch

H. Insepction and Adjustment

This information will also be of value in your daily inspections.

CLUTCH CABLE MAINTENANCE

The clutch cable requires periodic lubrication to prevent the cable strands from rusting or hanging up in the casing. First, disconnect the cable from the clutch lever by screwing the adjuster all the way back to the cable casing. This will provide enough free play in the cable for you to slip the cable out of the lever holder through the slot in the lock nut, adjuster, and holder. Hold the cable upright and allow several drops of liquid graphite to flow down the cable. Hold the cable upright for several minutes to permit complete lubrication.

If the cable needs to be replaced, then perform the steps above and disconnect the cable at the lever. Next, disconnect the cable at the engine. Begin by taking off the cover that houses the clutch activating mechanism (left side of the engine).

Looking at the inside of this cover, you will see the clutch actuating arm. Push the arm up and lift the cable end off. Removing the old cable and hooking up the new one will take but a few moments.

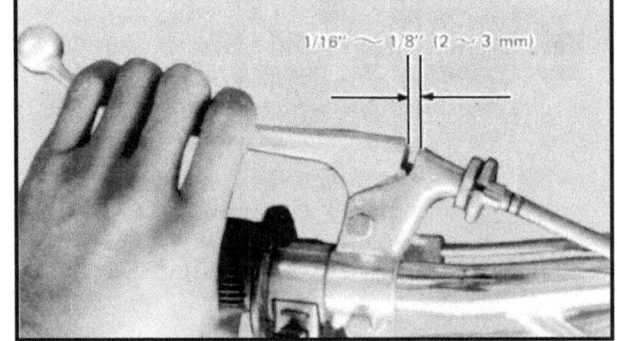

CLUTCH CABLE ADJUSTMENT:

The clutch lever should have .080 to .120 in. (2 to 3mm) free play to maintain full pressure against the clutch facing. If the play is excessive, the clutch will not disengage. If the free play is insufficient, the clutch will slip.

1. First, loosen the lock nut above the left crankcase cover. Then turn the adjuster either in nor out depending on which direction is necessary to arrive at 2-3mm (1/16"-1/8" free play).

2. The second adjustment is located behind the clutch adjuster cover. Removing the cover will expose the adjusting set screw and lock nut. Loosen the lock nut, rotate the set screw in until it lightly seats against a clutch push rod that works with the set screw to operate the clutch. Back the set screw out ¼ turn and tighten the lock nut. This adjustment must be checked because heat and clutch wear will affect this free play, possible enough to cause incomplete clutch operation.

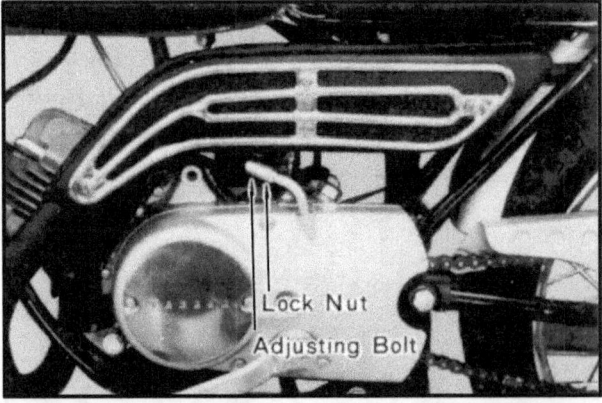

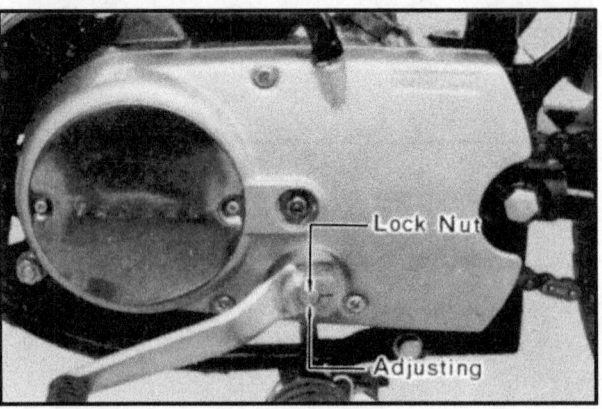

ENGINE - Primary Drive Gear, Kick Starter Mechanism

3-10 Primary Drive Gear

A. Removal

Feed a rolled-up rag between the teeth of the primary drive gear and the primary driven gear to lock them, and loosen the primary drive gear lock nut. The primary gear can then be forced off.

Fig. 3-10-1

ENGINE - Kick Starter Mechanism

3-11 Kick Starter Mechanism

The primary kick-starter system (one-touch kick-starter) is employed. However, a new "non-constant-mesh" mechanism has been introduced into the kick-starter, instead of the constant-mesh kick gear type, such as the ratchet and roller-lock systems.

That is, the kick gear meshes with the idler gear only when the kick starter pedal is kicked. After the engine has started, the kick gear and the idler gear disengage. This mechanism not only eliminates noise resulting from the constant mesh of the kick gear with the idler gear, but also greatly contributes to the durability of the kick starter assembly.

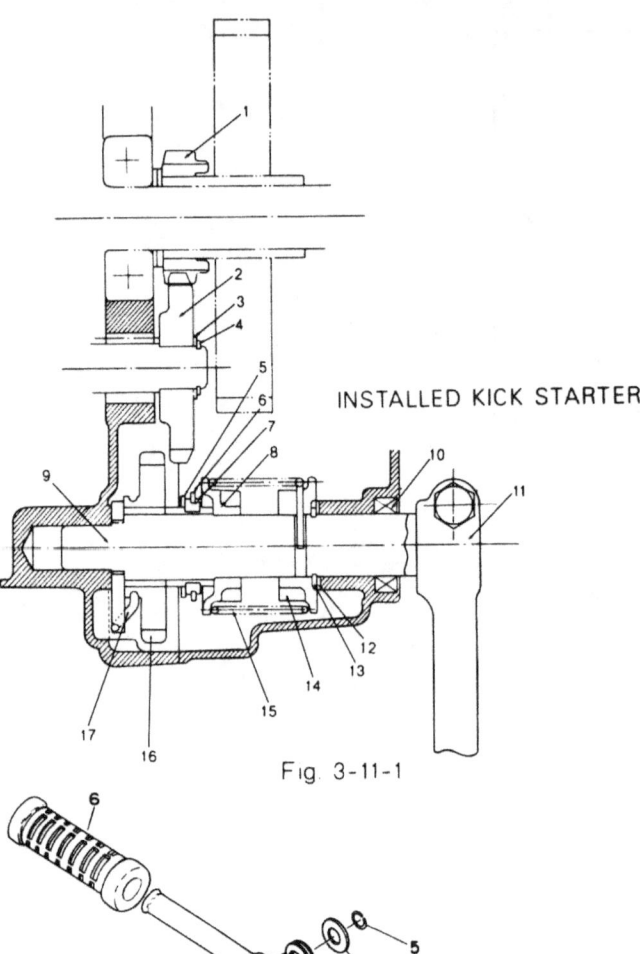

1. Kick pinion gear
2. Kick idle gear
3. Thrust washer
4. Circlip
5. Shim
6. Circlip
7. Kick gear holder
8. Spring guide
9. Kick axle
10. Oil seal (S-20-30-7)
11. Kick crank ass'y
12. Shim
13. Circlip
14. Spring cover
15. Kick spring
16. Kick gear
17. Kick clip

INSTALLED KICK STARTER
Fig. 3-11-1

1. Kick crank
2. Kick lever
3. Spring
4. Washer
5. Clip
6. Kick lever cover
7. Bolt
8. Kick axle
9. Oil seal
10. Cirelip
11. Spring cover
12. Kick spring
13. Spring guide
14. Circlip
15. Shim
16. Kick
17. Kick clip
18. Stopper

KICK STARTER COMPONENTS
Fig. 3-11-2

ENGINE - Kick Starter Mechanism, Shift Mechanism

A. Removing the Kick Idler Gear

Remove the circlip with clip pliers. Then the kick idler gear can be easliy removed.

Note: The location of the shim directly beneath the circlip.

Fig. 3-11-3

b. Removal

1) Remove the kick spring.

Fig. 3-11-4

2) Then remove the kick starter assembly. Disassembly of this assembly is unnecessary unless kickstarter repair is required.

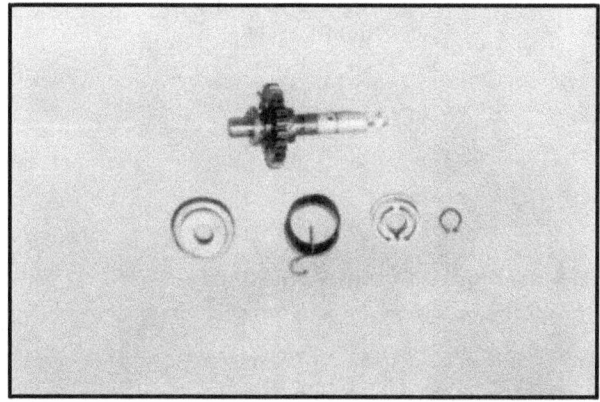

Fig. 3-11-5

3-12 Shift Mechanism

The shift mechanism is designed to select four speeds plus a position neutral position. When the change pedal is moved the gear shift arm A is moved back or forward by the gear shift arm B (see Fig. 3-12-1).
The gear shift drum pin attached to the gear shift drum is pushed by the gear shift arm A, and the gear shift drum begins to rotate.
A total of five gear shift drum pins are attached to the gear shift drum. When the change pedal is moved the unit is designed to shift through five stages. Neutral, Low, Second, Third and Top, throughout one complete turn of the gear shift drum.
The stopper plate holds the gear shift drum pin so that gear shifting can be correctly positioned at each gear position. The gear shiftdrum is provided with grooves on its outer surface, and the shift forks move back and forth along their respective grooves to change gears.

ENGINE - Shift Mechanism

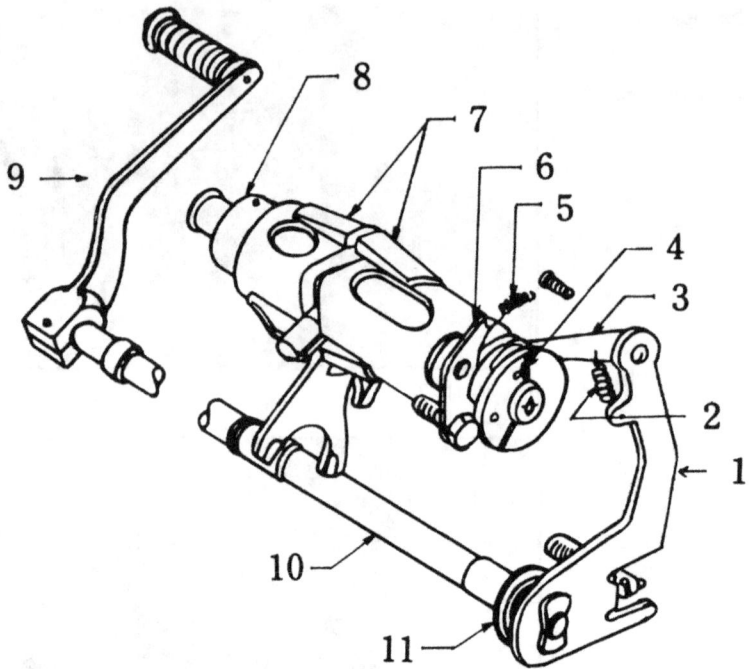

1. Gear shift arm B
2. Gear shift arm spring
3. Gear shift arm A
4. Gear shift drumpin
5. Shift drum stopper spring
6. Shift drum stopper lever
7. Shift fork
8. Gear shift drum
9. Change pedal
10. Change axle Ass'y
11. Gear shift spring

Fig. 3-12-1

A. Gear Shift Pattern

Neutral is at top of the shift pattern. Press down once to select low then remove pressure from the lever. Press down again to select 2nd, and so on for the remainder.

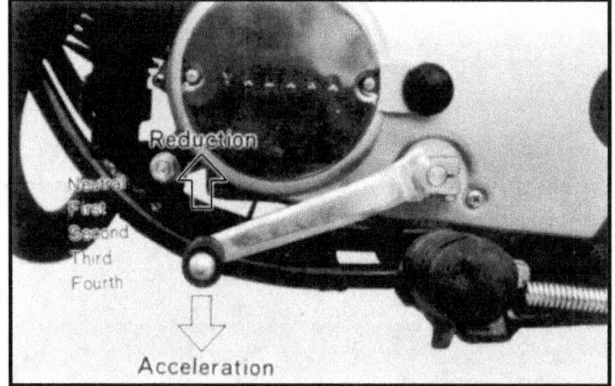

Fig. 3-12-2

A. Removing the Change Axle Assembly

1) Remove the circlip and washer from the change axle (left side crank case).

(⊖ Screw driver)

Fig. 3-12-3

2) Turn the engine over right side up, and pull out the change shaft assembly.

Fig. 3-12-4

B. Checking the gear shift parts (Fig. 3-12-5)
Checking the Gear Shift Return Spring. A broken or fatigued gear shift return spring will impair the return aciton of the shifting mechanism. Also, check for a bent or damaged shaft.

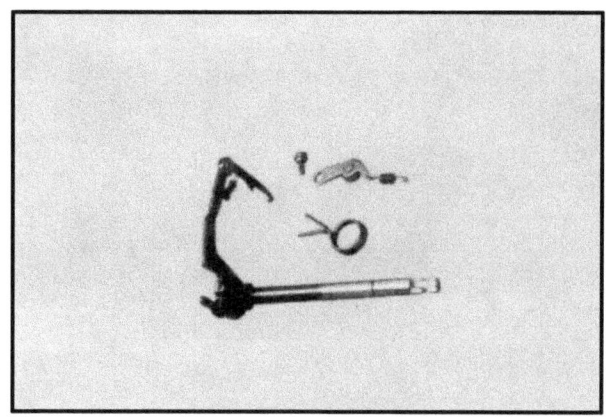
Fig. 3-12-5

C. Adjusting the gear shift arm
Adjusting or correcting the travel of the gear shift arm to prevent improper shifting progression (excess feed or insufficient feed of the gear shift arm) is accomplished by turning the gear shift return spring stop screw (eccentric bolt) in or out.
In second or third gear the measurement A & A' must be equal.

(⊕ **Screwdriver**)

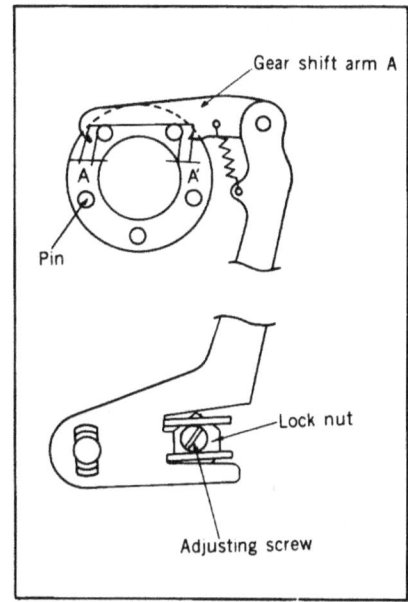
Fig. 3-12-6

3-13 Rotary Valve

A. Removal
1) Remove the six valve cover set bolts and remove the valve cover.

(⊕ **Screwdriver**)

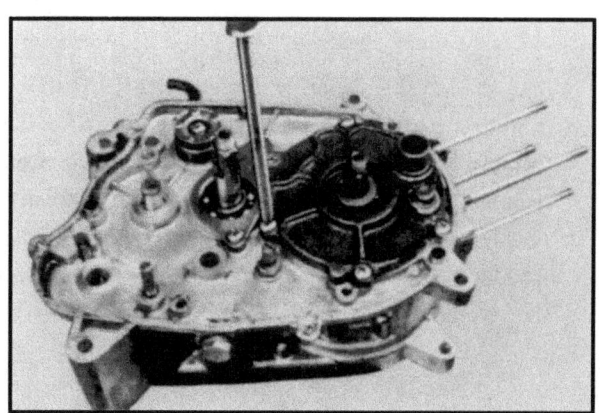
Fig. 3-13-1

ENGINE - Rotary Valve

2) Remove the valve and valve collar.

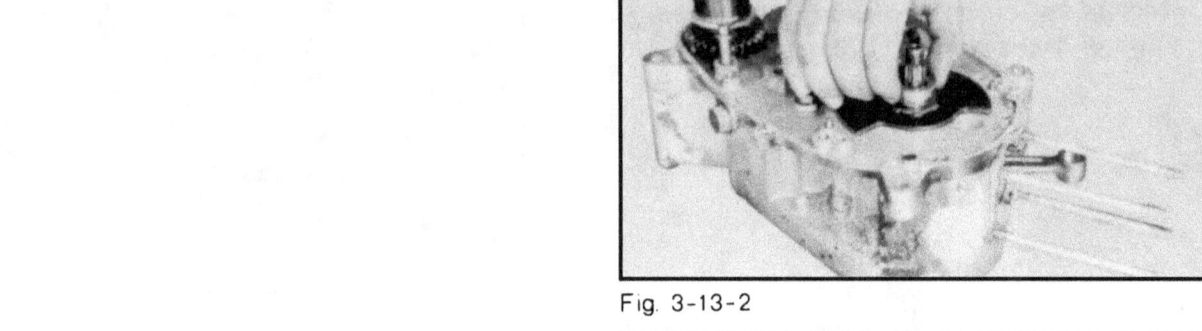

Fig. 3-13-2

3) Remove the valve knock pin. Take care not to damage the surfaces of the crankcase.

See Appendices for proper valve timing during installation.

Fig. 3-13-3

B. Checking the Rotary-valve.

1) Install the valve collar in the valve and check for looseness. If it is found too loose, replace it. If the collar is found to have step wear due to locating pin friction, it should be replaced.

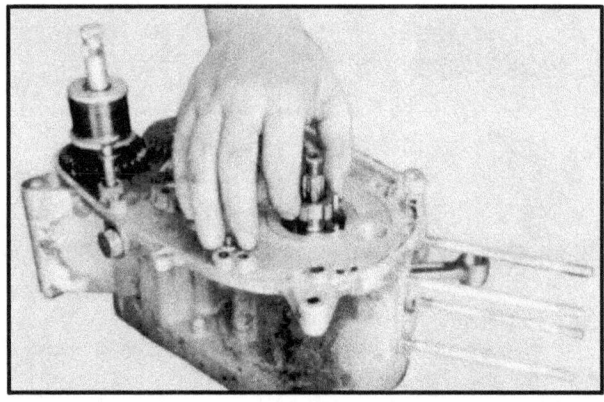

Fig. 3-13-4

2) The O-ring is subject to stretch, flattening or hardening after a long period of use. Any stretched or aged O-ring may fail to snugly fit in the groove. If it is found defective, it should be replaced with a new one. When installing it, grease it.

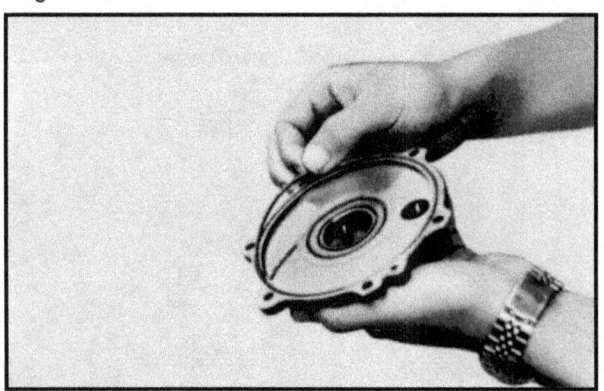

Fig. 3-13-5

3) When the valve collar is installed, care should be taken not to nick the crankshaft O-ring.
   If it is found nicked, replace it. It is advisable to grease the surface of the inner collar and the outer surface of the O-ring.

Fig. 3-13-6

4) When installing the valve cover, apply good quality grease to the lip so it will slip easily over the shaft.

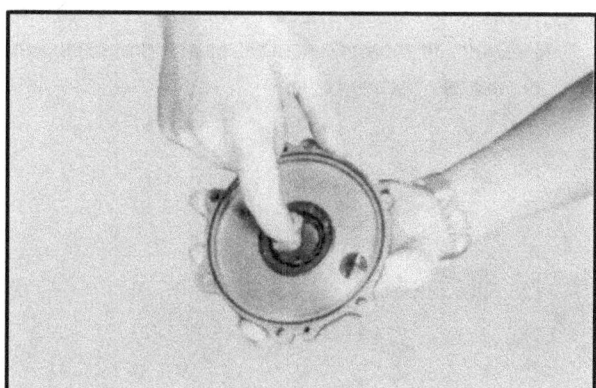

Fig. 3-13-7

3-14 Drive Sprocket

A. Removal

1) Straighten the bent edge of the lock washer with a blunt-ended metal punch.

   (Flat chisel)

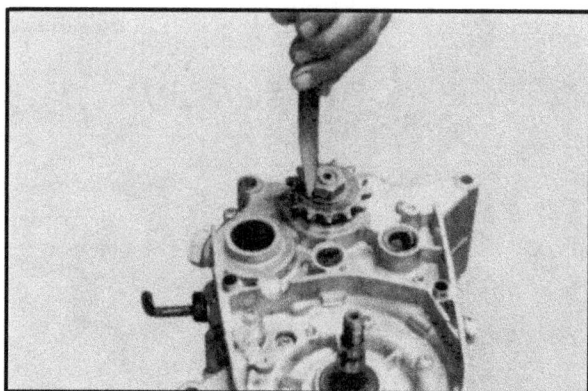

Fig. 3-14-1

ENGINE - Drive Sprocket

2) Hold the drive sprocket with the flywheel magneto holding tool, and remove the sprocket nut. If the flywheel magneto holding tool is not available, shift the transmission to low gear, and fit a monkey wrench on the sprocket nut. Then tap the handle of the wrench with a hammer and the shock will loosen the nut. The best method of removal is an air impact wrench. (21 mm)

Fig. 3-14-2

3) Remove the distance collar with pliers. (When re-installing the distance collar, apply grease to the oil seal lip groove.)

Fig. 3-14-3

B. Inspection

A worn drive sprocket will result in excessive chain noise and shorten the life of the chain. Check the sprocket for worn teeth, and replace if they are worn to the extent shown.

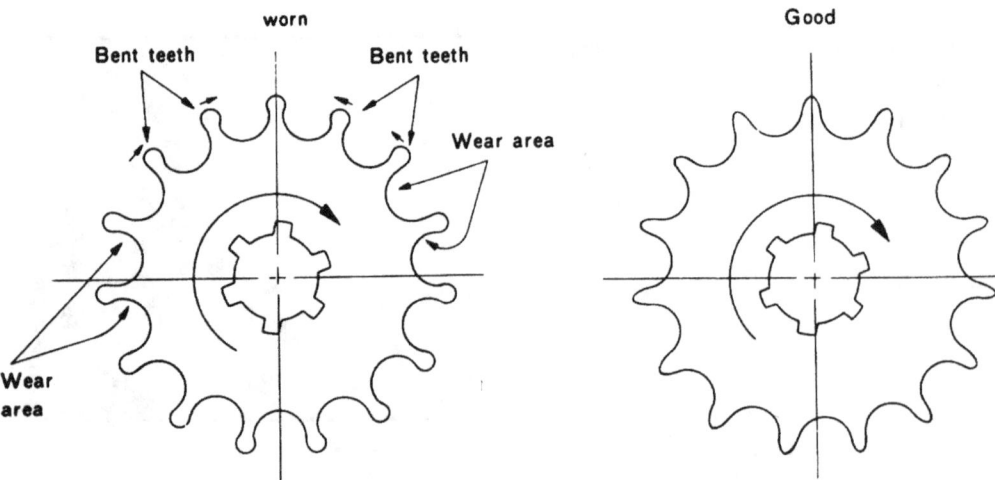

Fig. 3-14-4

ENGINE · Crankcase

3-15 Crankcase

A. Separating

1) Remove the neutral stopper.

   (21 mm)

Fig. 3-15-1

2) Remove the shift drum stopper lever and stopper spring.

   (10 mm)

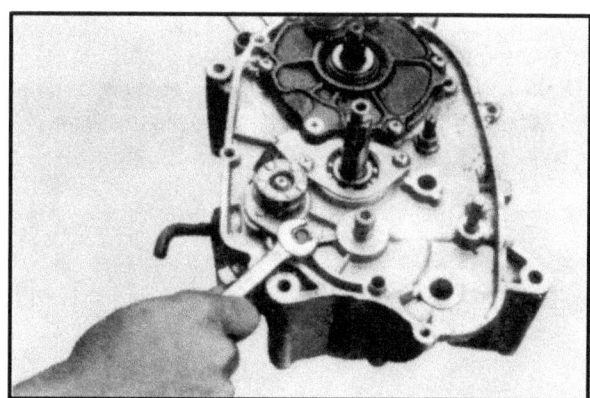

Fig. 3-15-2

3) Remove the twelve pan head screws from the left crankcase.

   (⊕ Screw driver)

Fig. 3-15-3

4) Install the crankcase separating tool on the right crankcase. Divide the crankcase while alternately tapping the main axle and the crankcase with a soft-faced-hammer.

ENGINE - Crankcase, Transmission Assembly

Fig. 3-15-5

Fig. 3-15-6

Note: Fully tighten the bolts of the crankcase dividing tool, keeping the tool in a horizontal position.

The crankcase is designed to split into two halves, right and left. Only one drain plug is provided for both the transmission and clutch housings. Both housings can be drained at the same time by removing the drain plug.

B. Reassembling

a) When reassembling the crankcase, be sure to apply YAMAHA BOND **No. 5** to the mating surfaces of both halves after cleaning them thoroughly.

Fig. 3-15-7

3-16 Transmission Assembly

The constant mesh, wide ratio, 4-speed transmission makes it possible to fully utilize the steady performance of the engine throughout the entire speed range from low to high speed.

For layout of the transmission and related parts, refer to Fig. 3-16-1 and 2. The primary reduction ratio is 74/19 = 3.894. Therefore the total reduction ratios will be: Primary reduction ratio × Transmission gear reduction × Secondary reduction ratio = Total reduction radio.

	Primary Reduction Ratio............74/19 = 3.894	
	Secondary Reduction Ratio............41/13 = 3.153	
	Transmission Gear Reduction Ratio	Total Reduction Ratio
1st	40/13 = 3.077	37.773
2nd	34/18 = 1.889	23.193
3rd	30/23 = 1.304	16.010
4th	27/26 = 1.038	12.188

ENGINE - Transmission Assembly

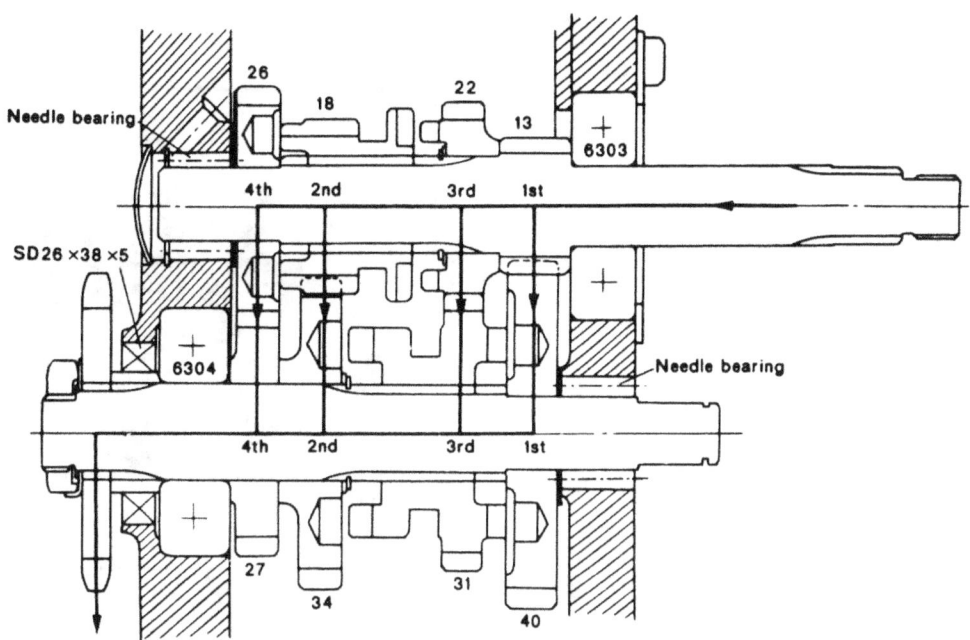

Fig. 3-16-1

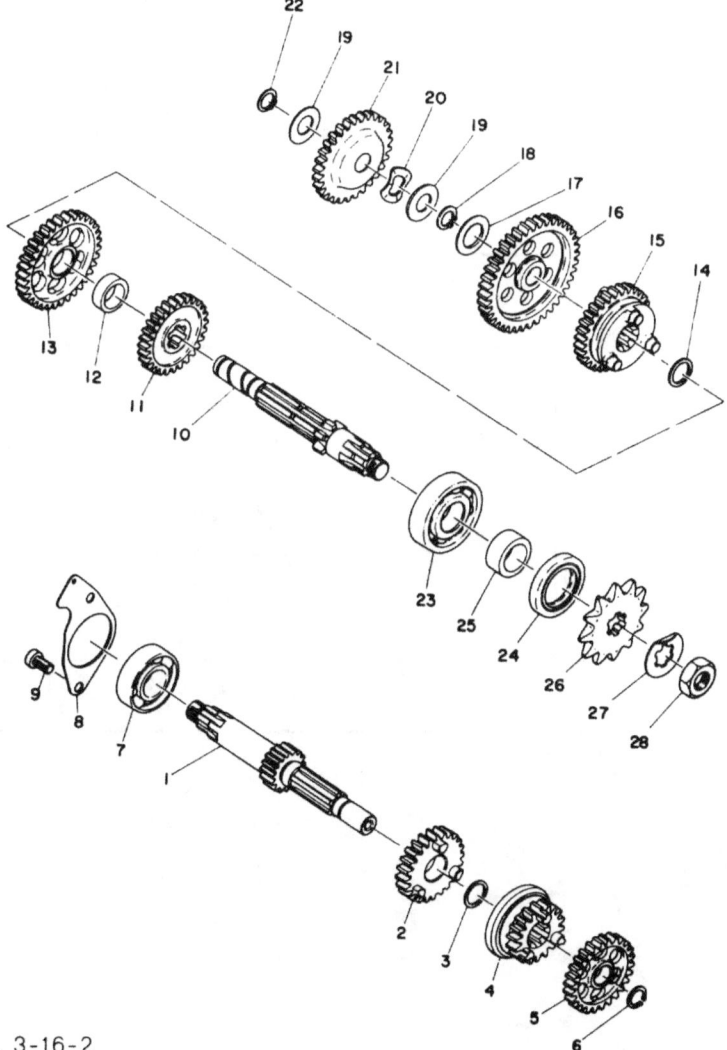

1. Main axle
2. 3rd pinion gear
3. Circlip
4. 2nd pinion gear
5. 1st pinion gear
6. Circlip
7. Bearing
8. Bearing cover plate
9. Bolt
10. Drive axle
11. 4th wheel gear
12. Distance collar
13. 2nd wheel gear
14. Circlip
15. 3rd wheel gear
16. 1st wheel gear
17. Shim
18. Circlip
19. Thrust washer
20. Wave washer
21. Kick idle gear
22. Circlip
23. Bearing
24. Oil seal
25. Distance collar
26. Drive sprocket
27. Lock washer
28. Nut

Fig. 3-16-2

ENGINE - Transmission Assembly.

A. Removal

1) Pull out the two shift fork guide bars.

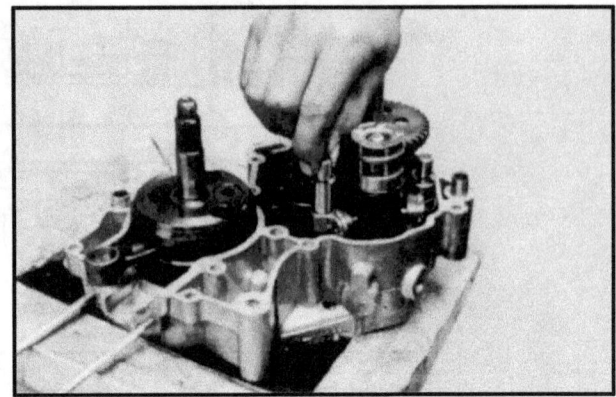
Fig. 3-16-3

2) Remove both the transmission assembly and the shift assembly from the crankcase, while tapping the drive shaft end with a soft-faced-hammer.

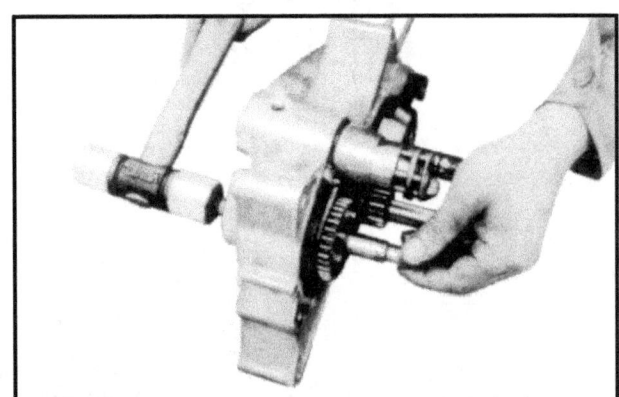
Fig. 3-16-4

B. Reinstallation

Reinstall the transmission and shifter as a unit in the left crankcase half after they are sub-assembled. They cannot be installed separately. The transmission unit must be in neutral during installation.

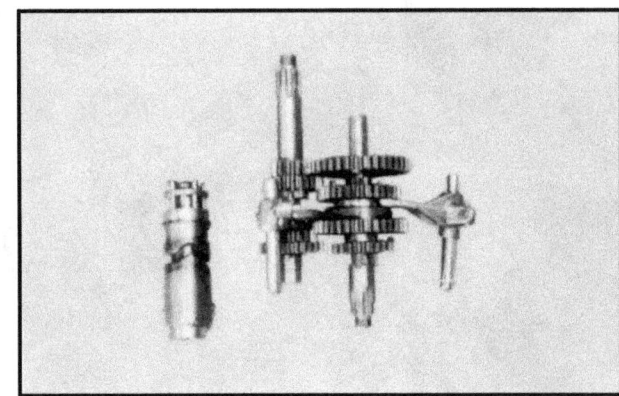
Fig. 3-16-5

3-17 Crankshaft

The crankshaft is a precision piece of work and is subjected to extreme stresses. It should be handled and inspected with special care.

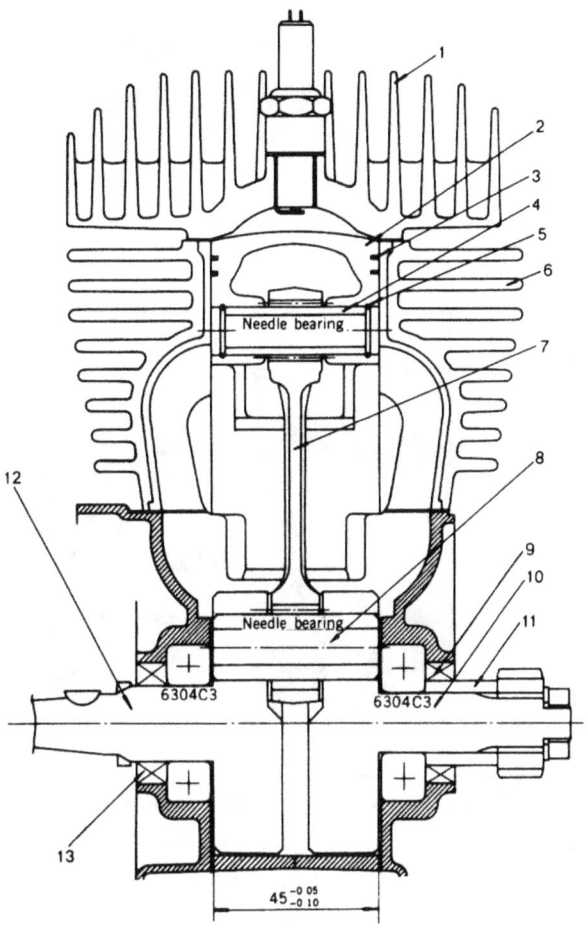

1. Cylinder head
2. Piston
3. Piston ring
4. Piston pin
5. Piston pin clip
6. Cylinder body
7. Connecting rod
8. Crank pin
9. SW28-47-8
10. Crank (R H)
11. Distance collar
12. Crank
13. SD20-40-8

Fig. 3-17-1

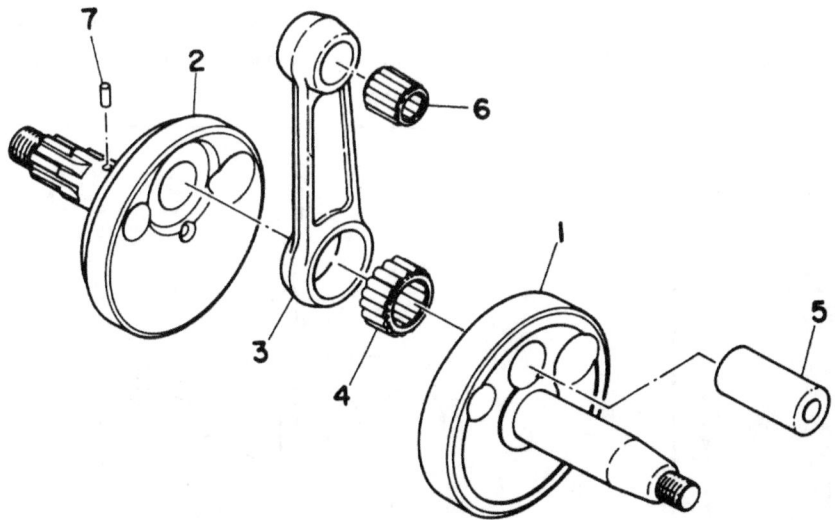

1. Crank left
2. Crank right
3. Rod connecting
4. Bearing con-rod big end
5. Pin crank
6. Bearing con-rod small end
7. Pin dowel

Fig. 3-17-2 Crankshaft component parts

ENGINE - Crankshaft

A. Removing the Crankshaft Assembly

Remove the crankshaft assembly with the crankcase separating tool.

Note: Fully tighten the bolts of the crankcase dividing tool, and keep the tool parallel with the crankcase surface.

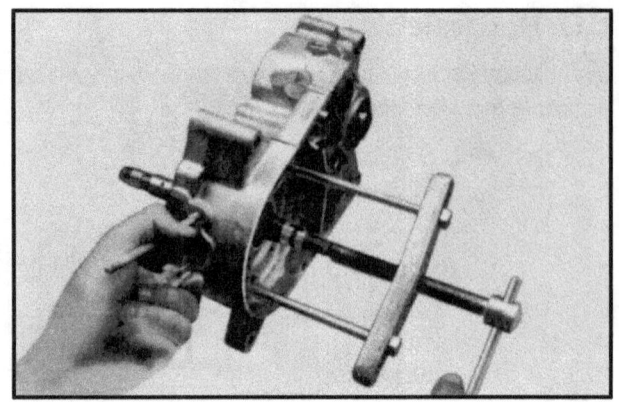

Fig. 3-17-3

B. Installing the Crankshaft Assembly

Install the crankshaft by using the crankshaft fitting tool. Take care not to allow the connecting rod to contact the crankcase. For this, hold the piston at top-dead-center and turn the handle, then tighten the bolt of the special tool.

Fig. 3-17-4

C. Inspection and Servicing

1) Checking the crankshaft components

Check connecting rod axial play at the small end (to determine the amount of wear of crank pin and bearing at large end) (Fig. 3-17-5)	Small end play should not exceed 2 mm. (0.078 in.)	If small end play exceeds 2 mm, disassemble the crankshaft, check connecting rod crank pin and large end bearing. Replace defective parts. Small end play after reassembly should be within 0.8~1.0 mm. (0.031~0.04 in.)
Check accuracy of the crankshaft assy runout. (Misalignment of parts of the crankshaft) (Fig. 3-17-6)	Dial gauge readings should be within 0.03 mm. (0.0012 in.)	Correct any misalignment by tapping the flywheel with a brass hammer and by using a wedge.

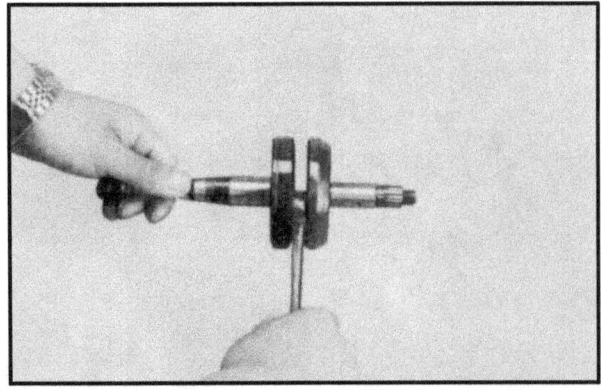

Fig. 3-17-5

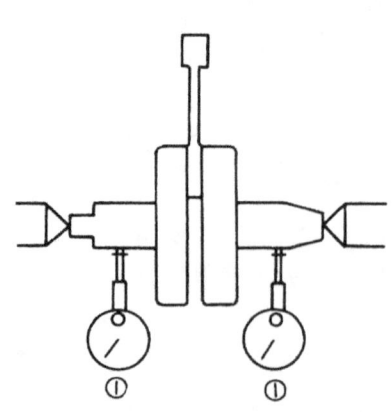

Fig. 3-17-6

3-18 Bearings and Oil Seals

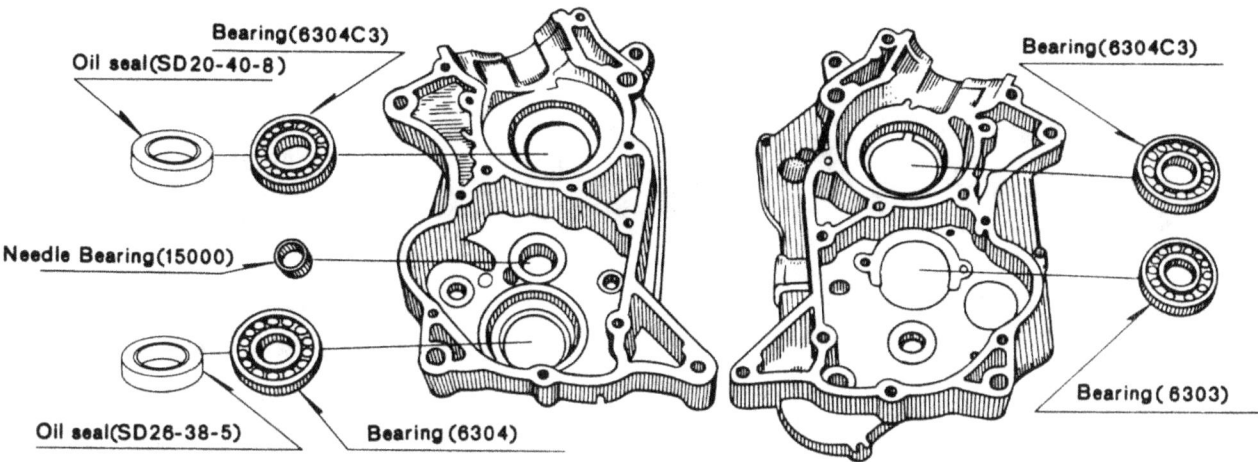

Fig. 3-18-1

1. Removal and Installation
   1) Removal
   a. Pry the oil seals out of place with a slot head screwdriver. Always replace the oil seals when overhauling the engine.

   (⊖ Screw driver)

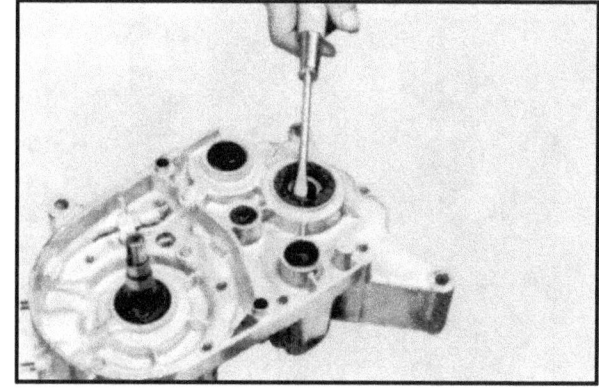

Fig. 3-18-2

   b. Drive out the bearing with a bearing tool.
   (It is preferable to heat the case to approximately 120°C (250°F) to remove bearings).

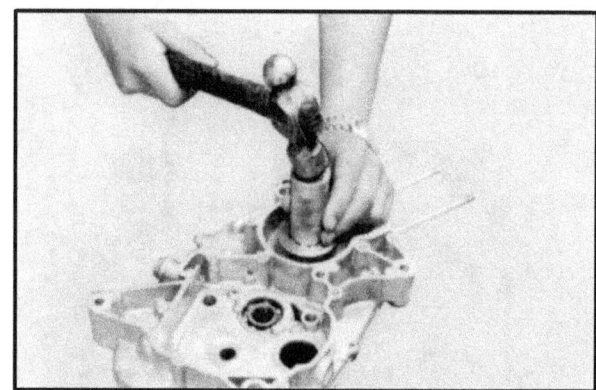

Fig. 3-18-3

   2) Installation
   Install bearings and oil seals with their stamped manufacturer's marks or numerals facing outward (In other words, the stamped letters must be on the exposed view side.)
   When installing bearings, pack them with grease.

ENGINE - Carburetor

3-19 Carburetor

The JT is equipped with a Y16P 16mm Venturi carburetor that is equipped with a built-in starter jet.

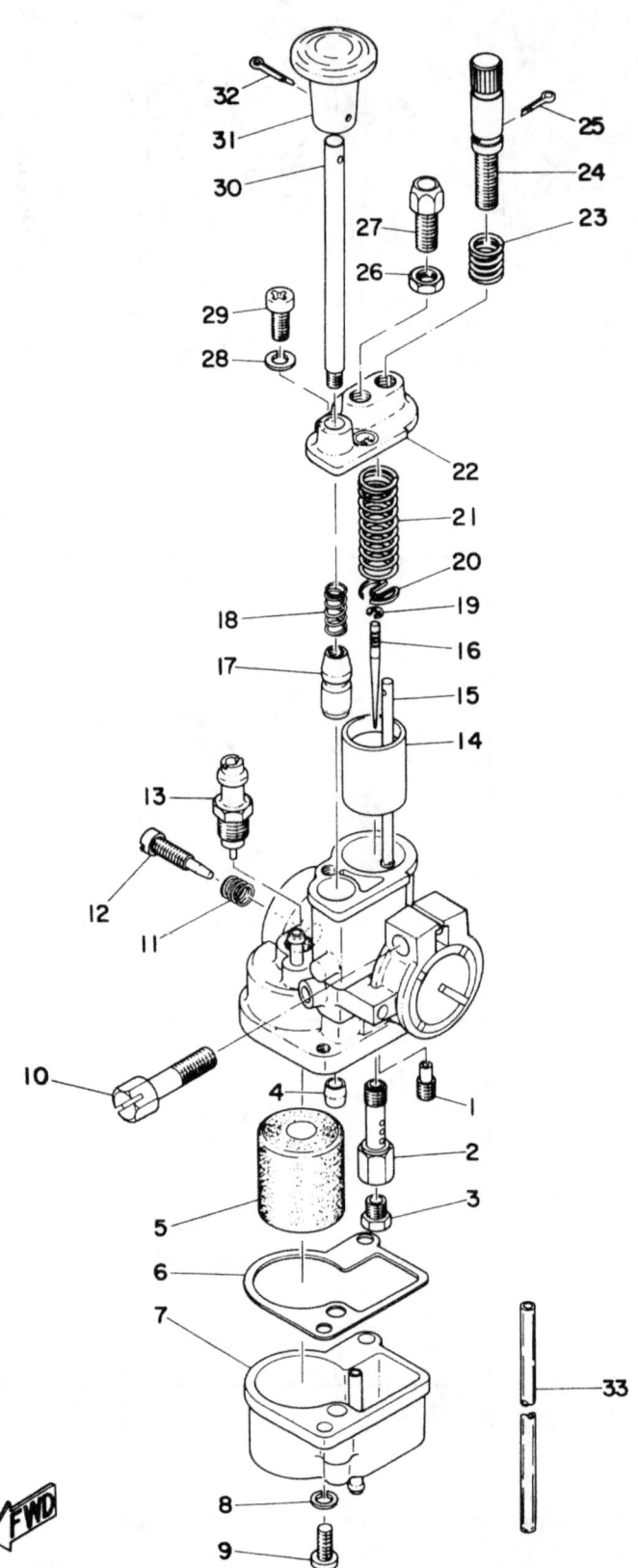

1. Pilot jet
2. Main nozzle
3. Main jet
4. Starter jet
5. Float
6. Gasket
7. Float chamber body
8. Spring washer
9. Pan head screw
10. Body fitting screw
11. Air adjusting spring
12. Air adjusting screw
13. Valve seat assembly
14. Throttle valve
15. Throttle bar
16. Needle
17. Plunger starter assembly
18. Plunger spring
19. Clip
20. Spring seat
21. Throttle valve spring
22. Mixing chamber top
23. Throttle stop spring
24. Throttle screw
25. Cotter pin
26. Wire adjusting nut
27. Wire adjusting screw
28. Spring washer
29. Pan head screw
30. Starter rod
31. Starter knob
32. Cotter pin
33. Air vent pipe

Fig. 3-19-1 Explosion diagram of carburetor

ENGINE - Carburetor

A. Checking the Carburetor

1) Float

   Remove the float and shake it to check if gasoline is inside. If fuel leaks into the float while the engine is running, the float chamber fuel level will rise and make the fuel mixture too rich. Replace the float if it is deformed or leaking. Do not try to solder a leaking float.

2) Float valve

   Replace the float valve if its seating end is worn with a step or if it is scratched. Check the float valve spring for fatigue. Depress the float valve with your finger, and make sure that it properly seats against the valve seat. If the float valve spring is weakened, fuel will overflow, flooding the float chamber while the gas is on.

3) Overflowing

   If fuel overflows, check the carburetor as described in 1) and 2) above. If neither 1) nor 2) cures the overflowing, it may be caused by dirt or dust in the fuel preventing the float valve from seating properly. If any dirt or dust is found, clean the carburetor, petcock and gas tank.

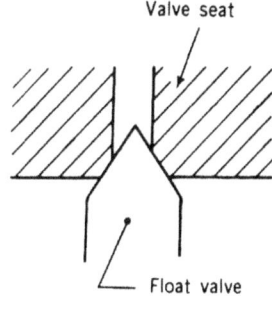

Fig. 3-19-2

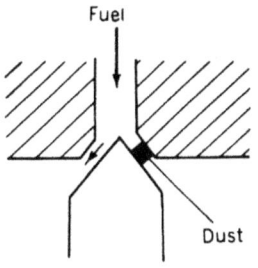

Fig. 3-19-3

4) Cleaning the carburetor

   Disassemble the carburetor, and wash all its parts in a suitable solvent.
   Then blow all the parts off with compressed air. All jets and other delicate parts should be cleaned by blowing compressed air through them after the float bowl has been removed.

B. Idle Mixture-Idle Speed Adjustments

The idle Mixture adjustment should be set exactly to factory specifications. First, turn the air screw in until it lightly seats then back it out 1 ½ turns. Next, adjust the throttle stop so that the engine idles at 1250~1350 rpm.

ENGINE - Air Cleaner

C. CARBURETOR SETTING TABLE

	JT1	JT1	JT1L	JT2	JT2	JT2M
Type/Mfr.	Y16P Teikei	←	←	←	←	←
Identification	288E1	←	←	288E2	288E3	288E3
Main Jet	No. 86	←	No. 84	No. 80	No. 84	←
Needle Jet	2.085	←	←	2.080	←	←
Jet Needle	032-2	←	←	035-3	←	←
Cut Away	1.5	←	←	←	←	←
Pilot Jet	No. 38	←	←	←	←	←
Air Screw (turns out)	1½	←	←	1¾	1¼	←
Starter Jet (G.S.)	No. 50	←	←	←	←	←
Engine Number	000101 ~	016139 ~	200101 ~	050101 ~	053801 ~	300101 ~
Identification Mark	None	"Y" on Float Bowl*	←	None	None	None

*Vent diameter changed.
NOTE: Best performance = E3 settings — Do not use Main Jets smaller than No. 82!

Float Level

With the float bowl removed note the location and condition of the inlet needle seat on the top of the float. If it is in good condition, float level will be correct. This is due to the fact that as fuel level increases the float is raised until it touches and then shuts off the inlet needle. There is no float arm or shut-off tang as found on other Yamaha models.

3-20 Air Cleaner

This model is equipped with a reuseable, oil impregnated, foam air filter. It must be removed and cleaned at least once a month, and more often if the motorcycle is ridden mainly in the dirt-preferably each time after you spend the entire day in the dirt (8- 10 hours operation).

1) Remove the air cleaner mounting bolt and loosen the air cleaner. (JT2-JT2M)

Fig. 3-20-1

2) Remove the air cleaner case cap. (JT2-JT2M)

Fig. 3-20-2

ENGINE - Air Cleaner

3) The cleaner element can be pulled out.
(JT2-JT2M)

Fig. 3-20-3

B. Cleaning

The element is of the wet type made of foam rubber and is oiled so that its dust removal efficiency and service life are greatly improved compared with a conventional paper element. Accordingly it is advisable that the element be washed in solvent mixed with oil (10.1) it. After washing, shake off the excess solvent and install the element in the case. Never allow the element to dry out as its efficiency will be greatly reduced.

AIR CLEANER JT2

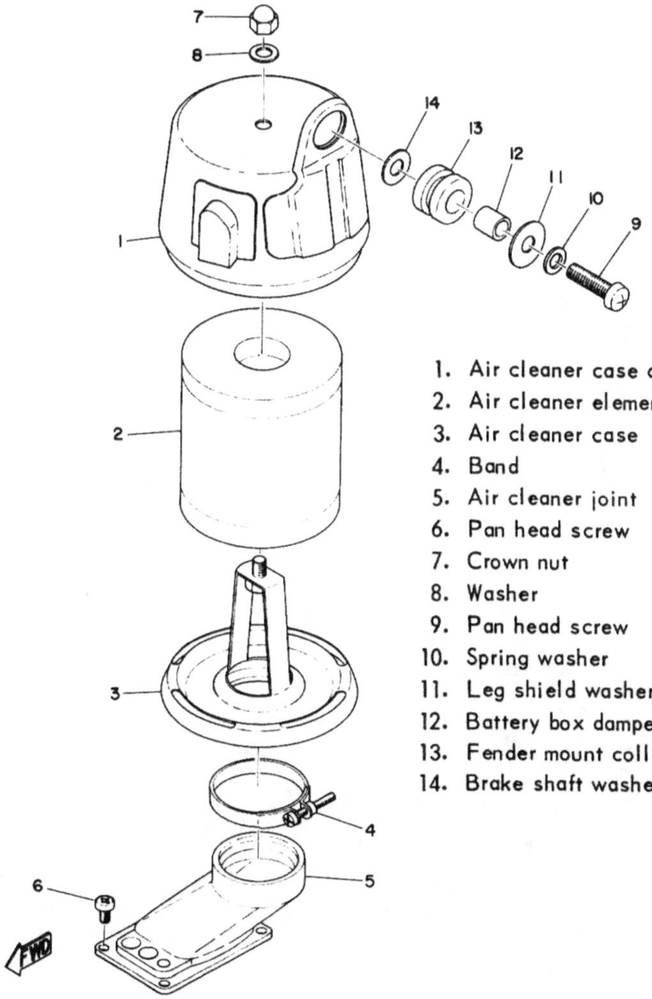

1. Air cleaner case cap
2. Air cleaner element
3. Air cleaner case
4. Band
5. Air cleaner joint
6. Pan head screw
7. Crown nut
8. Washer
9. Pan head screw
10. Spring washer
11. Leg shield washer #2
12. Battery box damper
13. Fender mount collar
14. Brake shaft washer

AIR CLEANER JT1

1. Air cleaner case
2. Air cleaner case cap
3. Air cleaner element
4. Air cleaner joint
5. Pan head screw

AIR CLEANER

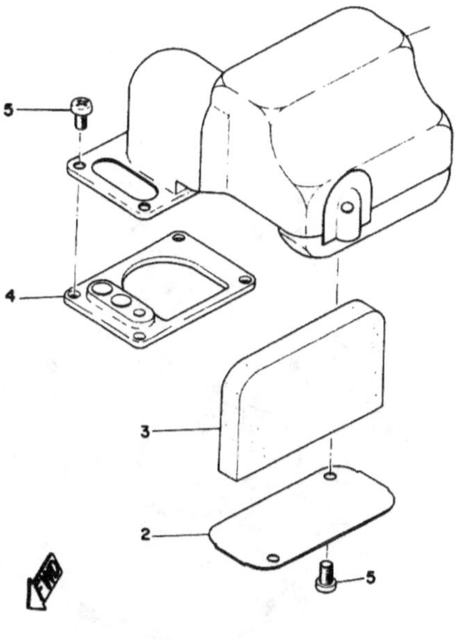

Chapter 4 Chassis

The Yamaha JT has been designed for versatility and a combination of uses. This machine has been engineered to have a minimum weight factor. Yet with the reduction in weight; rigidity, strength, and safety have been incorporated in the design of the frame to provide an unexcelled machine.

4-1 Front Wheel

The 15" front wheel is equipped standard with a 2.50-15" Trials Universal tire. This tire gives the rider assurance of maximum performance and safety for both road riding and trail riding. The front wheel brake size is 110 mm. x 25 mm (4.33 x 0.98 in.) A labyrinth seal is installed between the wheel hub and brake plate to provide a seal against dust and water.

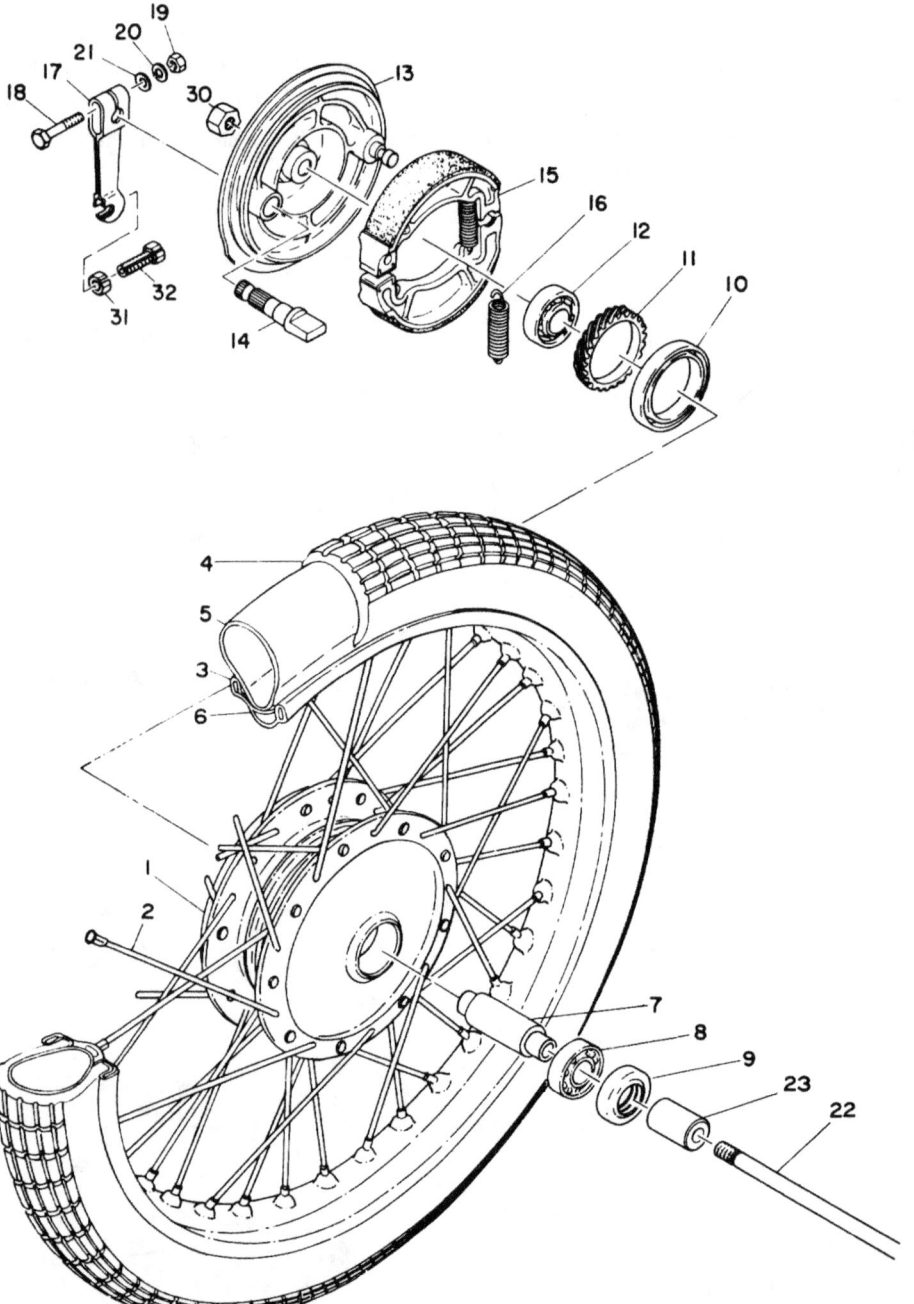

1. Hub
2. Spoke set
3. Rim
4. Front tire
5. Tube
6. Rim band
7. Spacer
8. Bearing
9. Oil seal
10. Oil seal
11. Drive gear
12. Bearing
13. Brake shoe plate
14. Cam shaft
15. Brake shoe comp
16. Return spring
17. Cam shaft lever
18. Bolt
19. Nut
20. Spring washer
21. Plain washer
22. Wheel shaft
23. Wheel shaft collar

Fig. 4-1-1

CHASSIS - Front Wheel

A. Removal

1) Disconnect the brake cable from the front wheel hub plate.

Fig. 4-1-2

2) Remove the front wheel nut.
   (17 mm)

Fig. 4-1-3

3) Pull out the front wheel shaft. Take care not to lose the distance collar, as it will come loose when the shaft is removed.

Fig. 4-1-4

4) Raise the front of the machine and set it on a box. Then remove the wheel assembly.

Fig. 4-1-5

CHASSIS - Front Wheel

B. Checking

1) Run out of the rim

   As shown if Fig. 4-1-6, measure the runout of the rim with a dial gauge. Run out limits: 2 mm. (0.07 in.) or less.

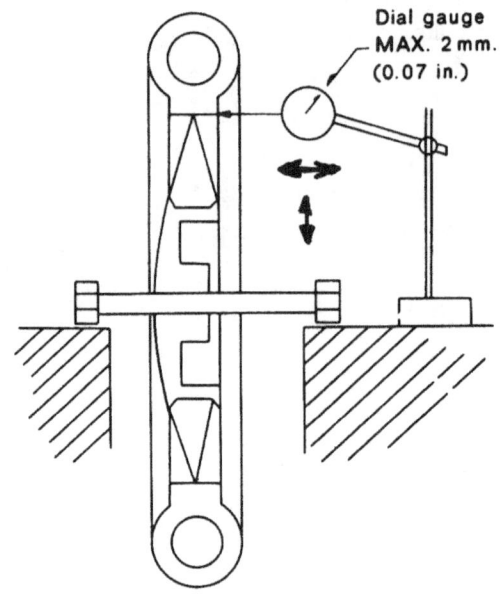

Fig. 4-1-6

2) Brake shoe

   Measure the outside diameter at the brake shoe with slide calipers. If it measures less than 104 mm. (4.09 in.) replace it.

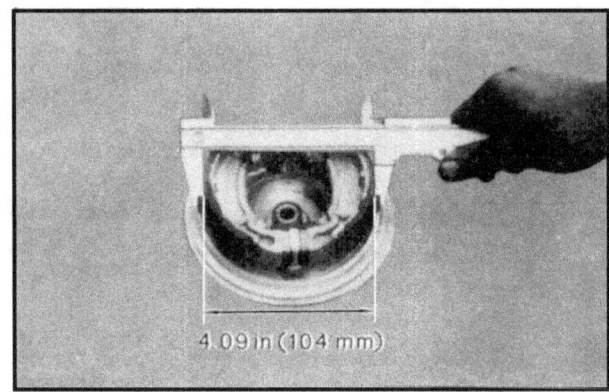

Fig. 4-1-7

3) Brake drum

   Oil or scratches on the inner surface of the brake drum will impair braking performance or result in abnormal noises. Clean or smooth out the surface with a rag soaked in lacquer thinner or with sandpaper.

Fig. 4-1-8

4) Check the spokes. If they are loose or bent, replace or tighten them. If the machine is ridden in rough country often, or raced, the spokes should be checked regularly.

CHASSIS - Front Wheel, Rear Wheel

5) Repairing the brake shoe

   If the brake shoe has uneven contact with the brake drum or scratches, smooth out the surface with sandpaper or hand file. If the surface is glazed use the file to remove the hard smooth finish.

6) If the tire is excessively worn, replace it.

7) Regularly check the tires for damage.

8) If the bearings allow excessive play in the wheel or if it does not turn smoothly, replace the bearing.

9) Replace a bent or damaged front wheel axle.

10) Check the lips of the seals for damage or warpage. Replace if necessary.

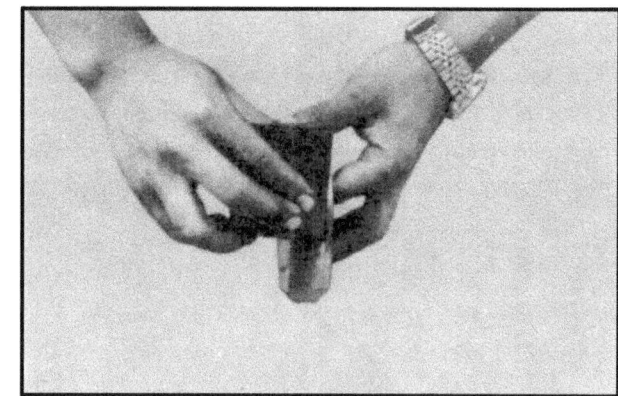

Fig. 4-1-9

Replacing the Wheel Bearing

a. First clean the outside of the wheel hub.

b. Insert the bent end of the special tool (as shown in Fig. 4-1-11) into the hole located in the center of the bearing spacer, and drive the spacer out from the hub by tapping the other end of the special tool with a hammer. (Both bearing spacer and spacer flange can easily be removed.)

c. Then push out the bearing on the other side.

d. To install the wheel bearing, reverse the above sequence. Be sure to grease the bearing before installation and use the bearing fitting tool (available from Yamaha.)

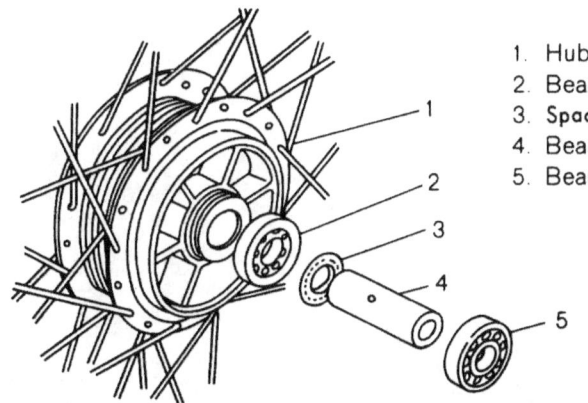

1. Hub
2. Bearing (6202RS)
3. Spacer flange
4. Bearing spacer
5. Bearing (6202RS)

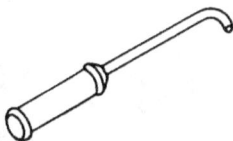

Insert the bent end of the special tool into the hole located in the center of the bearing spacer.

Fig. 4-1-10

Fig. 4-1-11

CHASSIS - Rear Wheel

4-2 Rear Wheel

The rear wheel is 15-in. size, and the rear tire is the 2.50-15 Trials Universal. The single leading shoe type brake is 130 mm. × 28 mm. (5.12 × 1.10 in.) in size. A labyrinth seal between the wheel hub and the brake plate is provided to prevent water and dust leakage. The brake tension bar is of link design to minimize the shifting of the brake cam lever position when the rear swing arm is moving up and down.

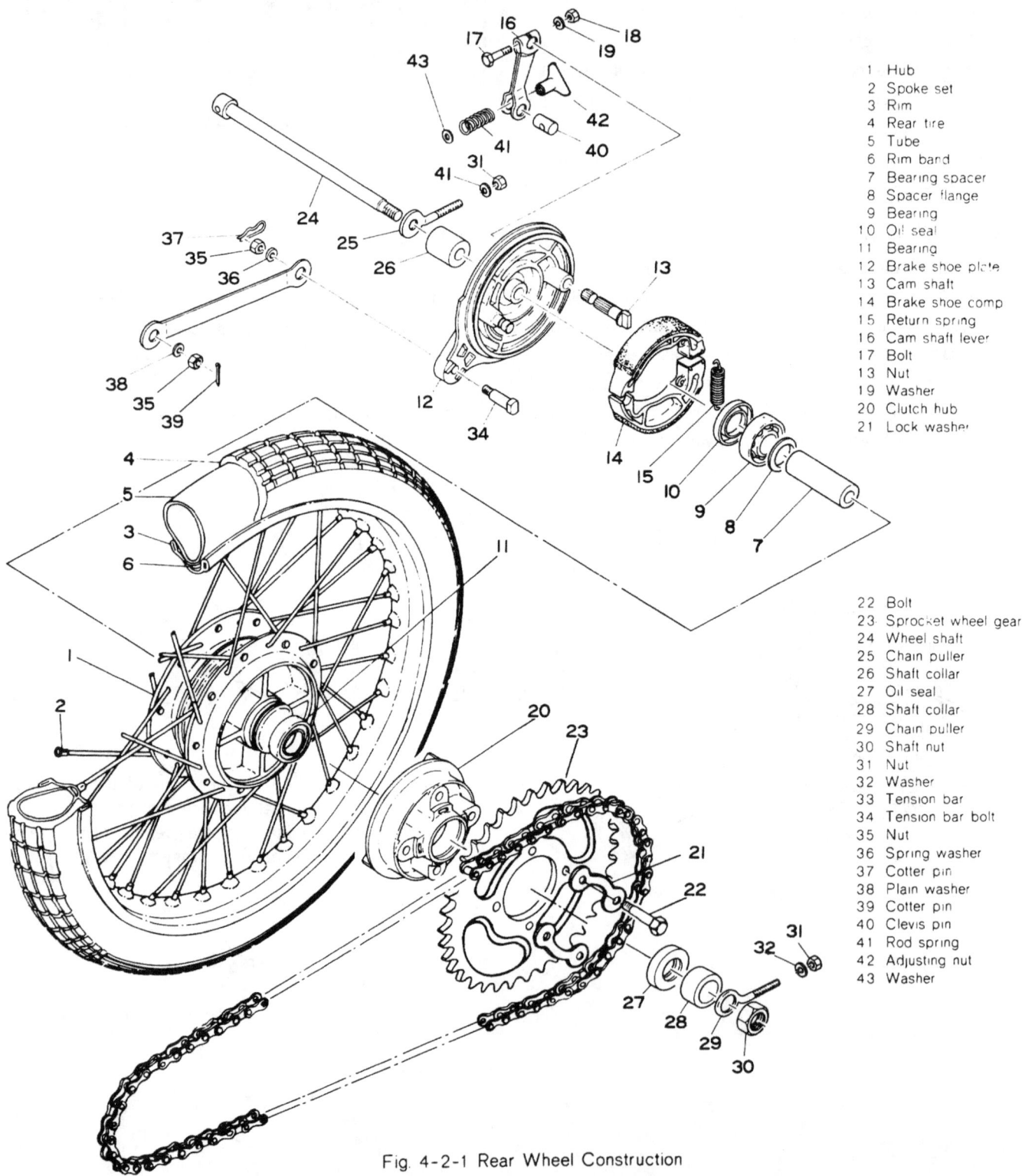

1. Hub
2. Spoke set
3. Rim
4. Rear tire
5. Tube
6. Rim band
7. Bearing spacer
8. Spacer flange
9. Bearing
10. Oil seal
11. Bearing
12. Brake shoe plate
13. Cam shaft
14. Brake shoe comp
15. Return spring
16. Cam shaft lever
17. Bolt
18. Nut
19. Washer
20. Clutch hub
21. Lock washer
22. Bolt
23. Sprocket wheel gear
24. Wheel shaft
25. Chain puller
26. Shaft collar
27. Oil seal
28. Shaft collar
29. Chain puller
30. Shaft nut
31. Nut
32. Washer
33. Tension bar
34. Tension bar bolt
35. Nut
36. Spring washer
37. Cotter pin
38. Plain washer
39. Cotter pin
40. Clevis pin
41. Rod spring
42. Adjusting nut
43. Washer

Fig. 4-2-1 Rear Wheel Construction

CHASSIS · Rear Wheel

A. Removal

1) Remove the tension bar and brake rod from the rear shoe plate.

Fig. 4-2-2

Fig. 4-2-3

2) Loosen the chain tension adjusting nut and bolt on both right and left sides.

(10 mm)

Fig. 4-2-4

3) Remove the rear wheel shaft nut.

(19 mm)

Fig. 4-2-5

4) Pull out the rear wheel shaft by striking it with a soft-faced-hammer.

Fig. 4-2-6

CHASSIS - Rear Wheel

5) Remove the right-hand chain adjuster and distance collar.

   Remove the axle.

Fig. 4-2-7

6) Remove the rear brake plate.

Fig. 4-2-8

7) Lean the machine to the left and remove the rear wheel assembly.

Fig. 4-2-9

Replacing the Wheel Bearing

Replace the rear wheel bearing in the same way as the front wheel bearing.

1) Tire and Tube Removal and Installation
   a) Whether it is the front tire or the rear tire to be changed, the procedure of tire and tube removal is identical. The explanation that follows is the proper method for both wheels.
   b) Remove the valve cap, valve stem, and valve stem lock nut. Use two tire irons (with rounded edges) and begin to work the tire bead over the edge of the rim, starting opposite the tube stem. Take care to avoid pinching the tube. After one bead of the tire has been completely worked off the rim, slip the tube out.
      Be very careful not to damage the stem as it is pushed back out of the rim hole.

CHASSIS - Rear Wheel Sprocket

c) If the tire is to be completely removed, then work the tire off the same rim edge.

d) Installing the tire can be accomplished by reversing the disassembly procedure. The only difference in procedure would be to inflate the tube momentarily before both tire edges have been compeltely slipped onto the rim. This removes any creases that might exist. After the tire has been completely slipped onto the rim, check to make sure that the stem is squarely in the center of the hole in the rim. Then inflate the tube to 40 + psi several times. Check for leaks, and set at prescribed pressure.

B. Inspection

1) Run out of the rim

Check the rim for run out in the same way as the front wheel. Maximum limit of runout......2 mm.(0.07 in.) or less.

2) Brake shoe

Check the brake shoe in the same way as the front wheel. Wear limit......124mm. (4.9 in.)

3) Brake drum

Check the brake drum in the same way as the front wheel.

4) The spokes are measured in the same way as the front wheel. A loose spoke should be tightened.

5) If the bearing has excessive play or it does not turn smoothly, replace it.

6) If the tire or the pattern is worn out, replace the tire.

7) If the lip of the oil seal is damaged or warped, replace it.

4-3 Rear Wheel Sprocket

A. Checking and Adjustment

The rear wheel sprocket is installed on the clutch hub. To replace the sprocket, take the following steps.

1) Removing the sprocket

a. Bend the lock washer ears flat.

(flat chisel)

Fig. 4-3-1

b. Remove the sprocket mounting bolts.

(14 mm)

Fig. 4-3-2

CHASSIS - Tires and Tubes, Front Forks

2) Checking

Check the lock washer and hexagonal bolt for breakage and damage. If the lock washer is not bent, over the hexagon bolt head, or is broken, or if the bolt is loose, the sprocket can come loose. Make sure that both lock washers and the mounting bolts are tight

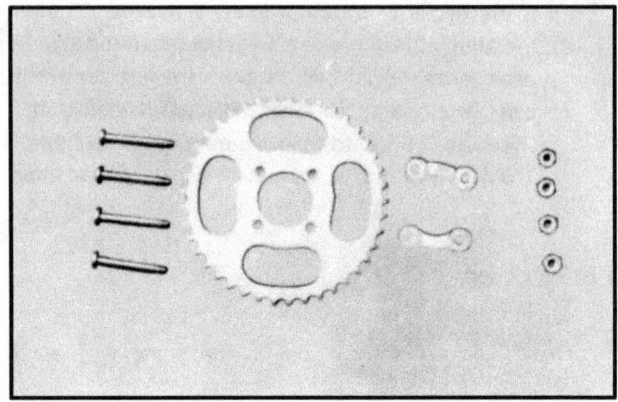

Fig. 4-3-3

Drive Chain Adjustment

To adjust drive chain, proceed as follows:

1. Loosen rear axle securing nut.

2. With rider in position on machine, both wheels on ground, set axle adjusters until there is 3/4 to 1 inch slack in the drive chain at the bottom of the chain at a point midway between the drive and driven axles.

3. Turn adjusting nuts in or out to obtain correct free play, and at the same time insure that both ends of axle are positioned evenly. This can be checked by utilizing the marks on end of swing arms and notch cut into top of adjusting bolt.

Tighten the rear axle securing nut.

Axle Nut Torque: 4.5 – 5.0 kg-m (400 – 440 in.-lbs.)

4-4 Tires and Tubes

1) Normal tire pressure

Though tire pressure is the rider's choice, the standard tire pressure is as follows:

Front . . . . 22.4 lbs./in^2 (1.6 kg./cm^2)
Rear . . . . 28.0 lbs./in^2 (2.0 kg./cm^2)

When the tire pressure is reduced below the specified amount because of some reason, the tire may slip around the rim and destroy the valve stem (unless rim locks are installed).

4-5 Front Fork Removal

1) Remove the inner tube cap bolt.

(17 mm)

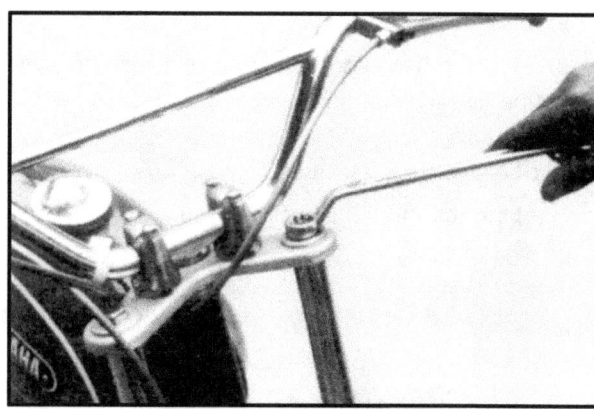
Fig. 4-5-2

3) Loosen the inner tube pinch bolt on the under-bracket.

(14 mm)

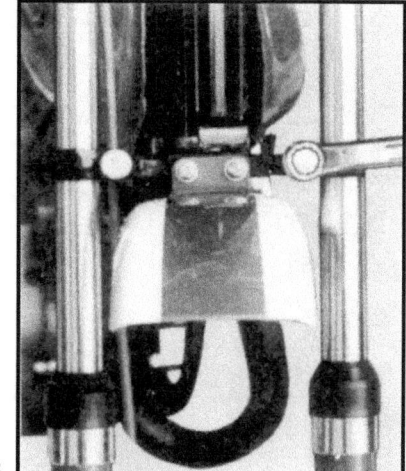
Fig. 4-5-3

4) Pull the outer tube downward.

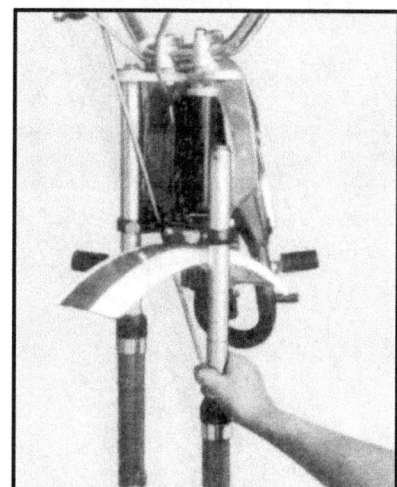
Fig. 4-5-4

B. Disassembling the Inner and Outer Tubes

1) Drain the oil from the fork

Fig. 4-5-5

CHASSIS - Front Forks

2) Place a rubber sheet or tire tube around the outer tube nut, install a strap wrench, and turn it counter clockwise.
   The inner tube can be separated from the outer tube once this tube nut is threaded off.

Fig. 4-5-6

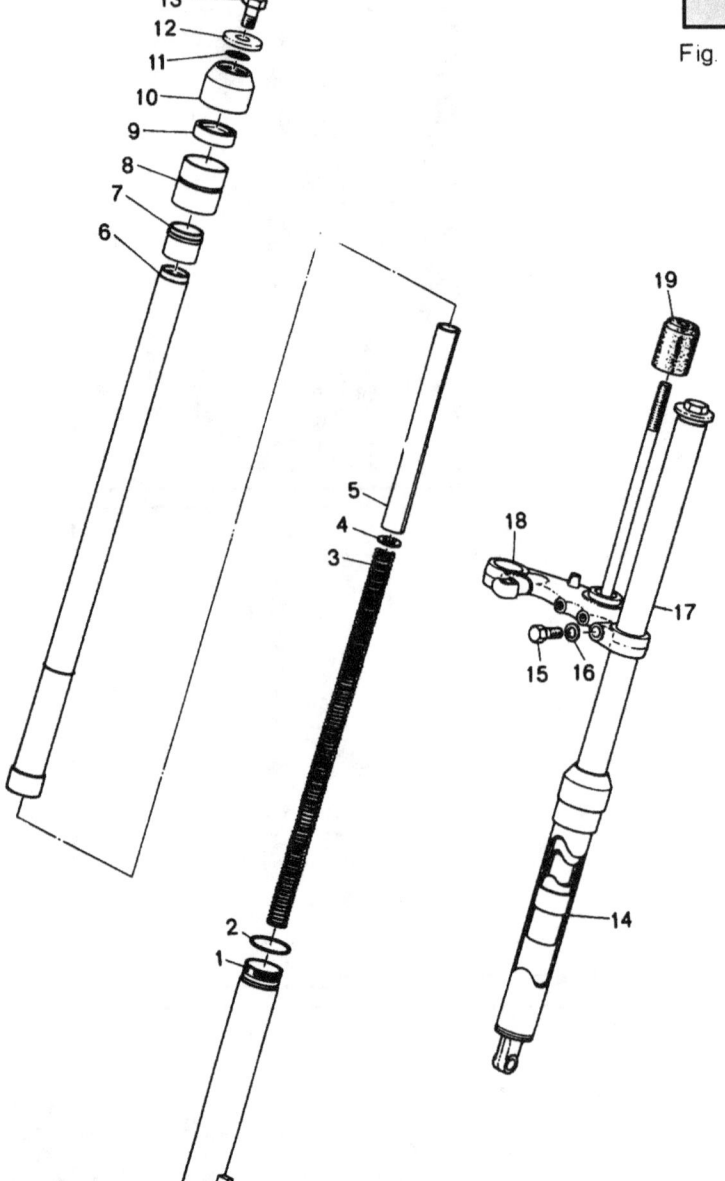

1. Outer right tube
2. O-ring
3. Fork spring
4. Spring upper washer
5. Spacer
6. Inner right tube
7. Slide metal
8. Outer nut comp
9. Oil seal
10. Dust seal
11. Packing
12. Cap washer
13. Cap bolt
14. Outer left tube
15. Underbracket bolt
16. Spring washer
17. Inner left tube
18. Underbracket comp
19. Front fork guide

Fig. 4-5-7 Front Fork Exploded View

CHASSIS - Front Forks, Rear Shocks

C. Checking

1) Inner tube

   Check the inner tube for bends or scratches. If the bend is slight, it can be corrected with a press. It is recommended, however, to replace the tube if possible.

2) Oil seal

   When disassembling the front fork, replace the oil seal in the outer tube nut.

D. Assembling

1) When assembling the front fork, reverse the order of disassembly. Check if the inner tube slides in and out smoothly.

2) Installing the front fork on the frame

a. Bring up the front fork to the correct position and tighten the underbracket pinch bolt slightly. Fill the fork tube with oil (see below) and tighten the cap bolt thoroughly. Then tighten teh pinch bolts completely.

Fig. 4-5-8

b. Pour oil into the inner tube through the upper end opening:

   Front fork oil: **Yamaha shock fluid** Right 97 cc (3.3 fl. oz)

   Left 120 cc (4.1 fl. oz)

c. Install the cap bolt.

4-6 Rear Snocks

The rear shocks have a maximum stroke of 55 mm. (2.16 m.)

A. Checking the Condition of the Damping Units.

1) Remove the rear shock assembly.

   (17 mm)

Fig. 4-6-1

CHASSIS · Gas Tank, Rear Swing Arm

2) Make sure that the rear cushion moves up and down completely from bottom to top.

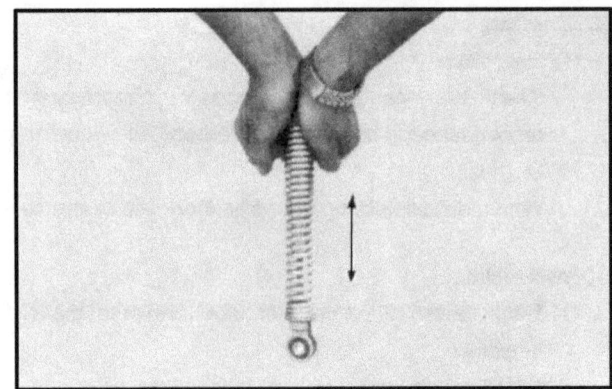
Fig. 4-6-2

4-7 Gas Tank

A. Removing

1) Pull out the seat fitting pin and remove the seat by pulling it backward.

Fig. 4-7-1

2) Set the petcock lever at the "Stop" position and disconnect the fuel line at the petcock.

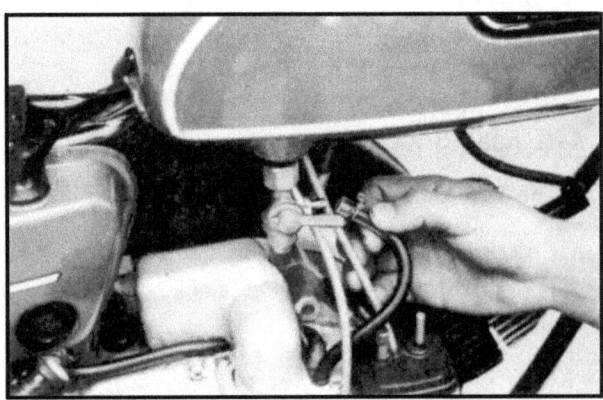
Fig. 4-7-2

3) Next, remove the tank holding bolt and remove the tank by pulling it backward.
(13 mm)

4-8 Rear Swing Arm

The rear swing arm is made of steel tubing that improves the strength and torsional rigidity. The pivot employs permanently lubricated bearings.

CHASSIS - Rear Swing Arm

A. Removing

1) Remove the two chain case mounting bolts.
   (⊕ Screw driver)

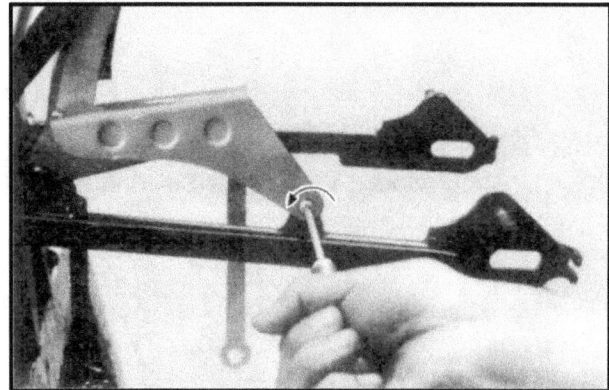

Fig. 4-8-1

2) Remove the rear swing arm shaft nut, pull out the shaft, and remove the rear swing arm.
   (17 mm)

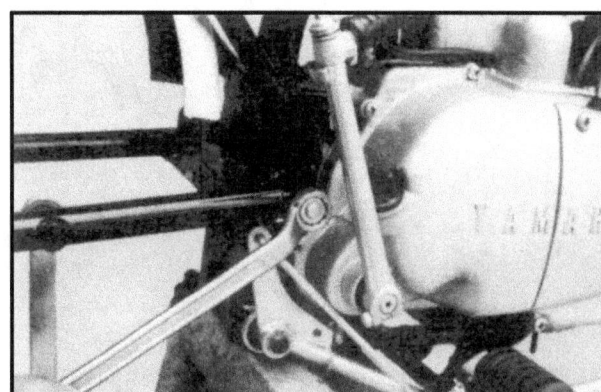

Fig. 4-8-2

B. Checking

1) Check the play of the rear swing arm by shaking it as show in Fig. 4-8-3, with the rear swing arm installed. If the play is excessive, replace the rear swing arm bushing or the rear swing arm shaft.
2) Insert the bushing as indicated in Fig. 4-8-4, and check it for play It the play is excessive, replace the bushing.

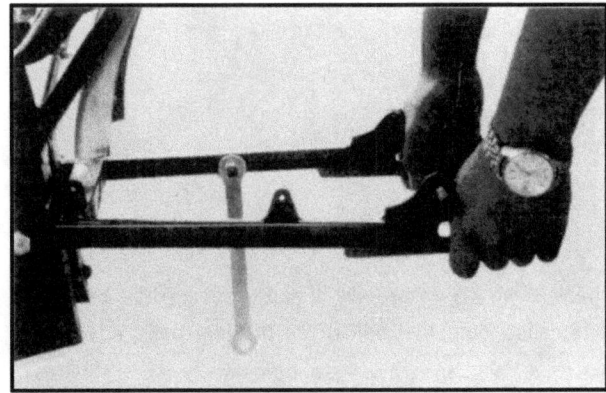

Fig. 4-8-3

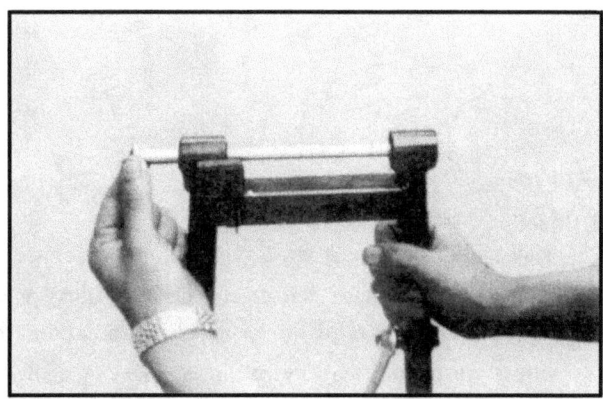

Fig. 4-8-4

3) Grease the rear arm shaft periodically.

CHASSIS - Steering Head

Replacing Rear Swing Arm Bushings

Replacement should be made according to machine condition such as excessive play of the rear swing arm, or hard steering (wander, shimmy or rear wheel hop.) or upon requiest of the customer.

EXPLODED VIEW

4-9 Steering Head

A. Exploded View of the Steering Head

STEERING

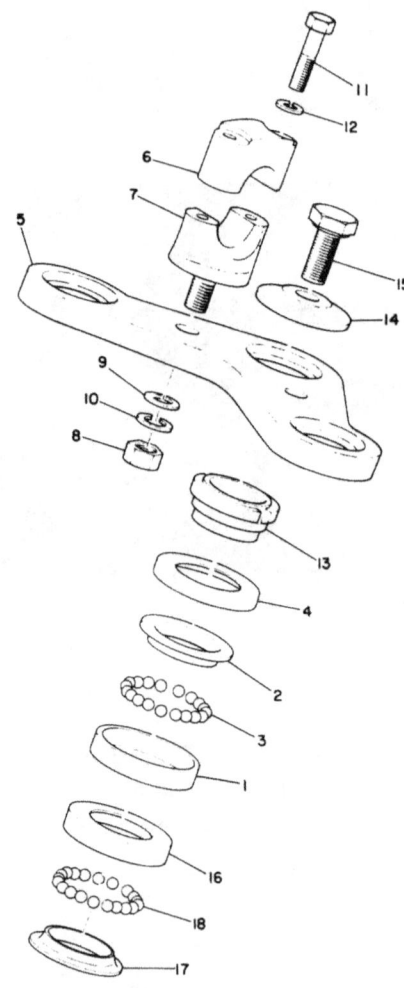

1. Ball race #2
2. Ball race #1
3. Ball (3/16 inch)
4. Ball race cover
5. Handle crown
6. Handle upper holder
7. Handle under holder
8. Nut
9. Plain washer
10. Spring washer
11. Bolt
12. Spring washer
13. Fitting nut
14. Crown washer
15. Fitting bolt
16. Ball race #2
17. Ball race #1
18. Ball (¼ inch)

Fig. 4-9-1

B. Checking

1) Ball Races and Steel Balls

Check the ball races and steel balls for pitting or wear. Check them very carefully if the machine has been in long use If any are worn or cracked, replace all of them, because defective ball races or steel balls adversely affect the maneuverability of the machine. Clean and grease the balls and races periodically.

Note: Do not use a combination of new balls and used races or vice versa. If any of these are found defective, replace the whole ball and race assembly.

4-10 Oil Tank, and Tool Box

The oil tank is located on the right side under the seat. It is designed to be as narrow as possible so that it will not contact the rider's lower limbs when he stands upright on the footrests. To fill the autolube oil tank, lift the seat and the tank cap will be exposed Oil tank capacity.........1.0 litres.(1.1 u. s qts)

4-11 Frame

The double cradle-type frame is made of high tension steel tubes that provide strength, rigidity and light weight. Other dimensional features include high ground clearance, narrow width, and long wheelbase. The engine is bolted to the frame at three positions. The caster is measured at 63.50°

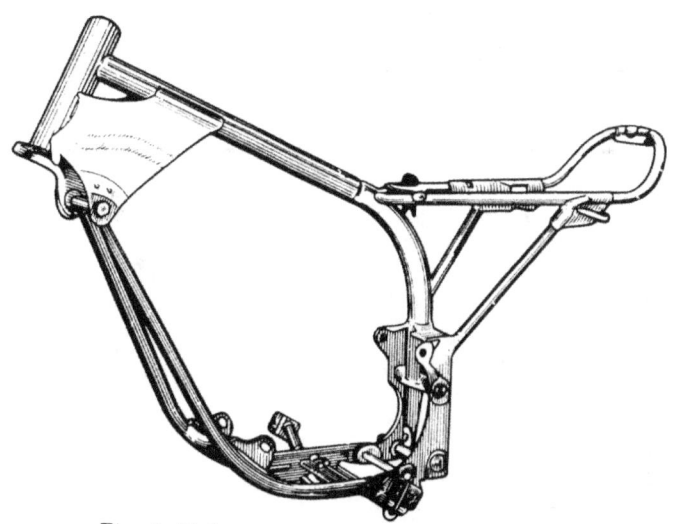

Fig. 4-11-1

4-12 Handlebars

The upswept type longer handlebars are ideal for leverage on rough terrain and are provided with deep-cut pattern grips to prevent hand slippage.

4-13 Miscellaneous

The footrest is made of a single steel tube extending under the lower part of the frame, and bolted to the frame. The engine guard is bolted to the frame to protect the entire crankcase......covering from the exhaust system to the drain plug.

ELECTRICAL – Electrical Equipment, List of Electrical Components

CHAPTER 5. ELECTRICAL

5-1 Electrical Equipment

Equipment

The Yamaha JT2 is equipped with a flywheel, silicon rectifier and 6-volt, 2 amp/h battery. The JT1 has no lighting equipment. The JT1L has lights only.

5-2 List of Electrical Components

JT1

Parts	Manufacturer	Model & Type
Flywheel magneto	Hitachi Ltd.	F11-L42
Spark plug	NGK	B-7HS

JT2

Parts	Manufacturer	Model & Type
Engine:		
Flywheel magneto	Hitachi	F11-L46
		Sparking
		7mm or more/500 rpm
		8mm or more/5,000 rpm
		Charging
		0.4 A or more/2,500 rpm
		4 A or less/8,000 rpm
		Lighting (load = 21.8W)
		5.6 V or more/2,500 rpm
		7.8 V or less/8,000 rpm
Spark plug	NGK	B-8HS
Neutral switch	Asahi Elec.	YNS type
Frame:		
Battery	GS	6N2-2A-3 6V 2AH
Main switch	Asahi Elec.	
Silicon rectifier	Fuji Elec.	
Horn	Nikko	GF-6
Ignition coil	Hitachi Elec.	CM61-50
Fuse holder	Mitsuba Elec.	10A, 2 pcs.
Front End:		
Headlight	Koito Elec.	6V 15W/D
Speedometer	Nippon Seiki	Neutral light 6V 3W
		Meter light 6V 1.5W
Rear End:		
Taillight (stop light)	Imasen Elec.	6V 5.3W/17W
Stop switch	Asahi Elec	

NOTE: See Appendices for JT1L components.

ELECTRICAL SYSTEM—Ignition System, Ignition Timing

5-3 Ignition System—Function and Service

1. Function

The ignition system consists of the components as shown in Fig. 5-3-1. As the flywheel rotates, the contact breaker points begin to open and close, alternately. This make-and-break operation develops an electromotive force in the ignition power source coil, and produces a voltage in the ignition coil primary windings. The ignition coil is a kind of transformer, with a 1:50 turn ratio of the primary to the secondary winding. The voltage (150-300 V) which is produced in the primary coil, is stepped up to 12,000-14,000 V by mutual-induction, and the electric spark jumps across the spark plug electrodes.

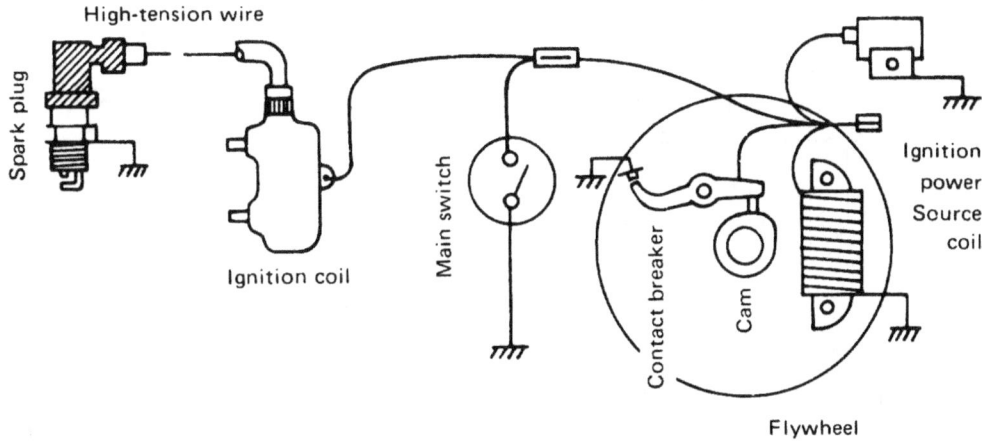

Fig. 5-3-1

5-4 Ignition Timing

Remove the spark plug and screw the dial indicator holder into the plug hole. Next, insert the dial indicator into the holder. Bring the piston up to T.D.C. and set the zero on the dial face to line up exactly with the dial indicator needle. The crankshaft should then be turned backwards, so that the piston travels down past 1.8 mm B.T.D.C. and slowly brought back up to precisely 1.8 mm B.T.D.C. (This removes any posible backlash). Adjust the points so that they are just beginning to open with the piston in this position. A low resistance point checker (100 Ohms or less) should be used to determine the opening and closing of the ignition points.

Ignition Timing, 1.8 mm. B.T.D.C.
Maximum ignition point gap 0.3 to 0.4 mm. (0.012"-0.015")

ELECTRICAL SYSTEM - Ignition Coil, Condenser

5-5 Ignition Coil

Primary coil resistance value . . . . 4.9 Ω ±10% (20°C or 68°F)
Secondary coil resistance value . . . . 11 KΩ ±10% (20°C or 68°F)
(For measuring methods, refer to Fig. 5-5-1)

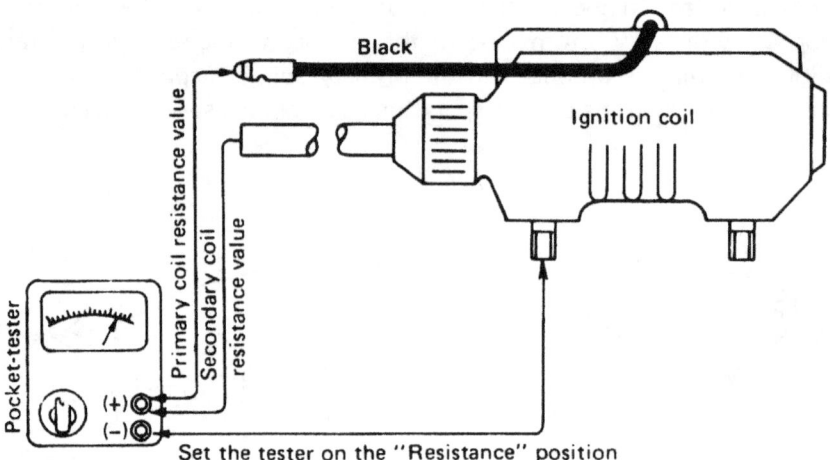

Fig. 5-5-1

Note: When measuring the secondary coil resistance value, disconnect the plug cap. Otherwise, the resistance of the 5KΩ noise suppressor incorporated in the plug will be added to the tester reading.

Spark Test:

Remove spark plug from cylinder head and reconnect the high voltage lead. Then hold the spark plug approximately 7 mm away from the head and see if it sparks as you crank the kickstarter.
If it sparks at 7 mm. or so, and has blue white color, the ignition coil should be considered to be in good condition.

5-6 Condenser

The condenser instantly stores a static electric charge as the contact breaker points separate, and the energy stored in the condenser discharges instantly when the points are closed. If it were not for the condenser, an electric arc would jump across the separating contact points, causing them to burn.
Burned contact points greatly affect the flow of current in the primary winding of the ignition coil.
If the contact points show excessive wear, or the spark is weak (the ignition coil is in good condition), check the condenser.

ELECTRICAL SYSTEM-Condenser, Charging System

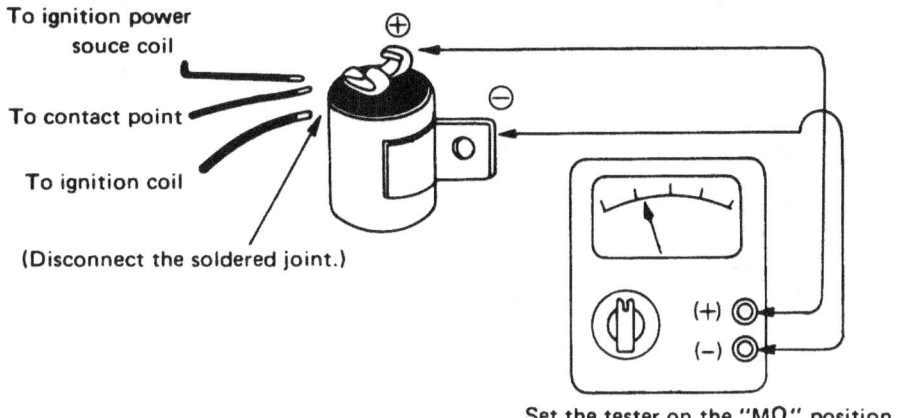

Set the tester on the "MΩ" position.

Fig. 5-6-1

Insulation resistance tests should be conducted by connecting the tester as shown in Fig. 5-6-1; If the pointer swings fully and the reading is more than 3MΩ, the insulation is in good condition. If the insulation is faulty, the pointer will stay pointing at the uppermost reading, indicating very little resistance.

Note: After this measurement, the condenser should be discharged by connecting the positive and negative sides with a thick wire.

Capacity tests can be performed by simply setting the tester to the condenser capacity. The tester should be connected with the condenser in the same way as in the case of the insulation resistance test. Before this measurement, be sure to set the tester correctly.

If the reading is within 0.22 μF±10%, the condenser capacity is correct

5-7 Charging System (JT2 – See Appendices for JT1L information.)

The charging system consists of the flywheel magneto (charging and lighting coils), rectifier, and battery.

1. Flywheel Magneto

As the flywheel rotates, an alternating current is generated in the charging and lighting coils and converted to a half-wave current by means of a silicon rectifier. This half-wave current is charges battery.

Charging Capacity (Daytime)
Green lead: Charging begins at 2,500 r.p.m.　⎫
　　　　　　0.4 A or more at 2,500 r.p.m.　　⎬ JT2
　　　　　　4.0 A or less at 8,000 r.p.m.　　⎭

ELECTRICAL SYSTEM-Charging System

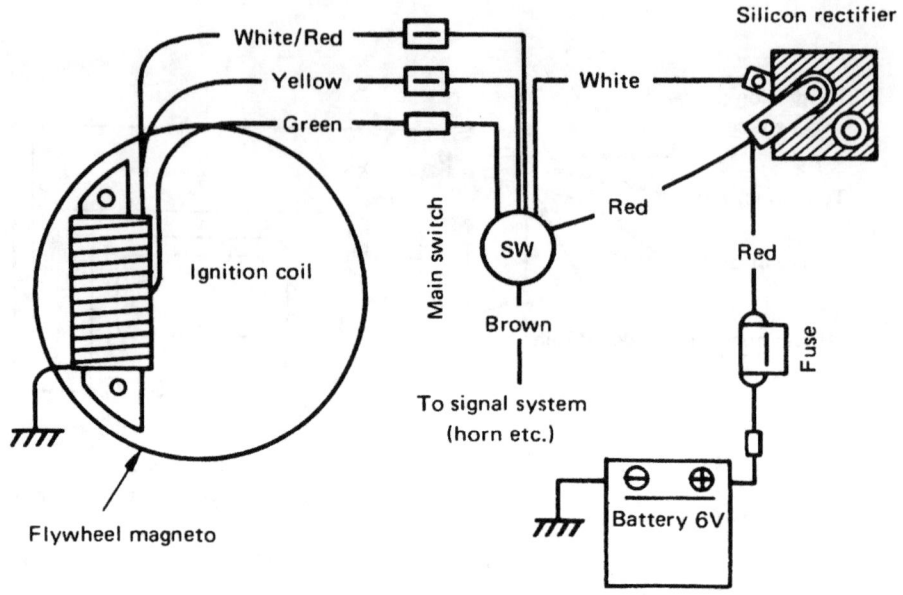

Fig. 5-7-1

Lighting Capacity (Night time)
(With normal loads and normal wiring.)

$\left. \begin{array}{l} 5.6\text{V or more at } 2,500 \text{ r.p.m.} \\ 7.8\text{V or less at } 8,000 \text{ r.p.m.} \end{array} \right\}$ (JT2)

* The charging and lighting capacity is obtained when the battery is fully charged. If the battery is in a low state of charge and low in voltage, the charging rate will be not exactly the same as above. However, it is desirable that the figures are as close as possible.

2. Silicon Rectifier

The alternating current, which is generated by the flywheel magneto, is rectified and charged to the battery. For this rectification, a single-phase halfwave silicon rectifier is employed.

Characteristics: $\left. \begin{array}{l} \text{Rated output } -4\text{A.} \\ \text{Rate peak inverse withstand voltage } 400 \text{ V.} \end{array} \right\}$ (JT2)

Polarity:

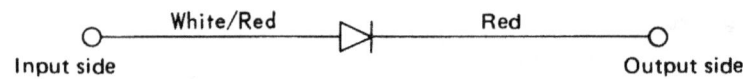

ELECTRICAL SYSTEM-Spark Plug, Lighting and Signal Systems

a. Checking the Silicon Rectifier

For measurements, as ohmmeter can be used.

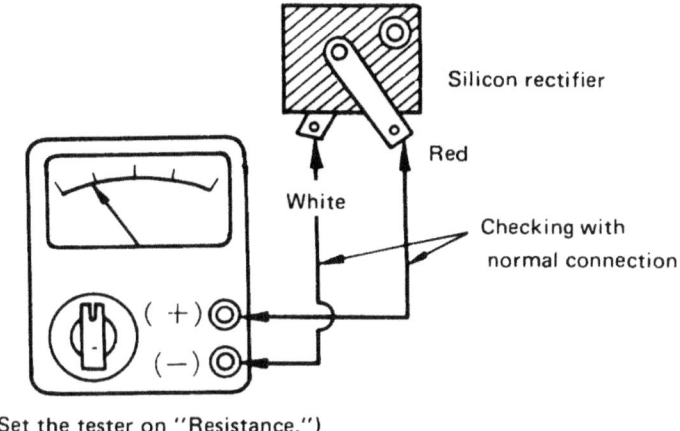

(Set the tester on "Resistance.")

Fig. 5-7-2

Checking with Normal Connection

Connect the tester's red lead (+) to the silicon rectifier's red terminal, and connect the tester's black lead (−) to the rectifier's white terminal.

Standard value: 9–10 Ω

If the tester's pointer will not swing back from the over scale, the rectifier is defective.

Checking with Reversal Connection

Connect the tester the other way round.

Standard value: If the pointer will not swing, the rectifier is in good condition. If the pointer swings, the rectifier is faulty.

3. Operational Note

The silicon rectifier can be damaged if subjected to overcharging. Special care should be taken to avoid a short circuit and or incorrect connection of the positive and negative leads at the battery. Never connect the rectifier directly to the battery to make a continuity check.

5-8 Battery – JT2

The battery is a 6 volt–2 AH unit that is the power source for the horn and stoplight. Because of the fluctuating charging rate due to the differences in engine R.P.M.s, the battery will lose its charge if the horn and stoplight are excessively used. The charging of the battery begins at about 2,500 R.P.M. Therefore, it is recommended to sustain engine R.P.M.s at about 2,500 to 3,500 R.P.M. to keep the battery charged properly.

ELECTRICAL SYSTEM-Battery

1. Checking

1) If sulfation occurs on plates due to lack of the battery electrolyte, showing white accumulations, the battery should be replaced.
2) If the bottoms of the cells are filled with corrosive material falling off plates, the battery should be replaced.
3) If the battery shows the following defects, it should be replaced.
   * The voltage will not rise to a specific value even after long hours charging.
   * No gassing occurs in any cell.
   * The 6V battery requires a charging current of more than 8.4 volts in order to supply a current at a rate of 1 amp. per hour for 10 hours.

2. Service Life

The service life of a battery is usually 2 to 3 years, but lack of care as described below will shorten the life of the battery.

1) Negligence in re-filling the battery with electrolyte.
2) Battery being left discharged.
3) Over-charging by rushing charge.
4) Freezing.
5) Feeding of water or sulfuric acid containing impurities when re-filling the battery.

3. Storage

If any motorcycle is not used for a long time, remove the battery and have it stored by a battery service shop. The following instructions should be observed by shops equipped with chargers.

1) Recharge the battery.
2) Store the battery in a cool, dry place, and avoid temperatures below 0°C. (32°F)
3) Recharge the battery before mounting it on the motorcycle.

4. Service Standards

Battery: 6N2-2A-3   (Nippon Battery)

Battery Spec.	6V-2AH	
Electrolyte-Specific gravity and quantity	1.25-1.27, 10 cc (1 cell)	At full charge
Initial charging current	0.2 A for 25 hours	Brand new motorcycle
Charging current	0.2 A for 13 hours (Charge until specific gravity reached 1.25-1.27)	When discharged
Refilling of electrolyte	Distilled water up to the max. level line.	Once a month

ELECTRICAL SYSTEM-Battery, checking the main switch, Spark plug

5-9 Checking the Main Switch (removed from the chassis) – JT2

Key "O" position
B—B/W

Key "I" Position
R—Br
G—W

Key "II" Position
R—Br
Br—L/W
R—L/W
W—G/R
Y—L

	B	B/W	R	Br	L/W	G	W	G/R	Y	L
OFF	O—O									
I			O—O			O—O				
II			O—O—O			O—O	O—O			

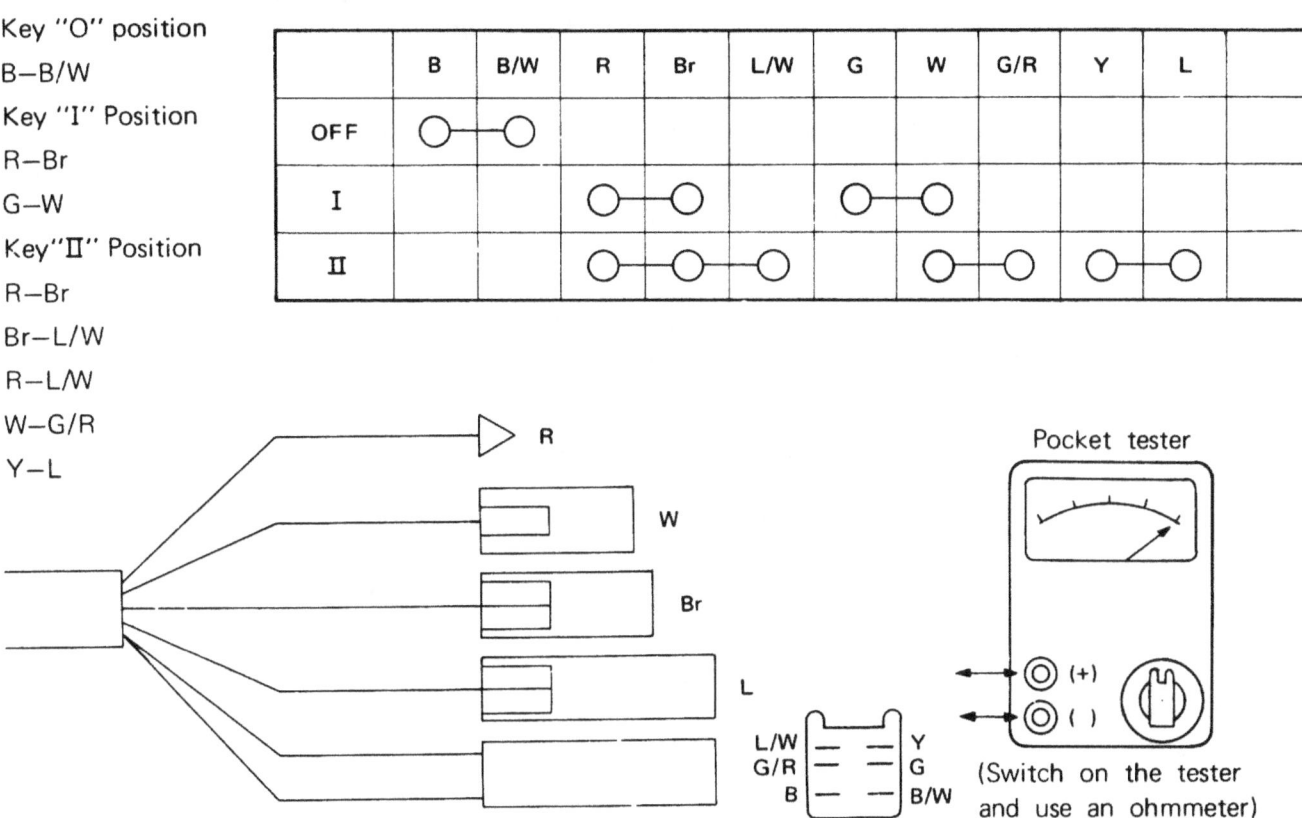

NOTE – Models JT1, JT2M equipped with "Kill Button" only.
Model JT1L equipped with handlebar light switch.

If the readings or the above eight measurements are nearly 0Ω, and no short-circuit is noticed between the terminals, as well as between the lead terminal and the switch body, the main switch is in good condition.

5-10 Spark Plug

The life of a plug and its discoloring vary, according to the habits of the rider. At each periodic inspection, replace burned or fouled plugs with suitable ones determined by the color and condition of the bad plugs. One machine may be ridden only in urban areas at low speeds, whereas another may be ridden for hours at high speeds, so confirm what the present plugs indicate by asking the rider how long and how fast he rides, and recommend a hot, standard, or cold plug accordingly. It is actually economical to install new plugs every 3,000 km (2,000 miles) since it will tend to keep the engine in good condition and prevent excessive fuel consumption.

ELECTRICAL SYSTEM - Charging System, Battery

1. How to "read" spark plug (condition)

a. Best . . . . . . When the porcelain around the center electrode is a light tan color.
b. If the electrodes and porcelain are black and some what oily, replace the plug with a hotter-type for low speed riding.
c. If the porcelain is burned white and/or the electrodes are partially burned away, replace the plug with a colder-type for high speed riding.

2. Inspection

Instruct the rider to:
Inspect and clean the spark plug at least once a month or every 1,000 km. (600 miles). Clean the electrodes of carbon and adjust the electrode gap to 0.5-0.6 mm. (0.023 in.) Be sure to use standard B-7HS plug as replacements to avoid any error in reach or heat range.

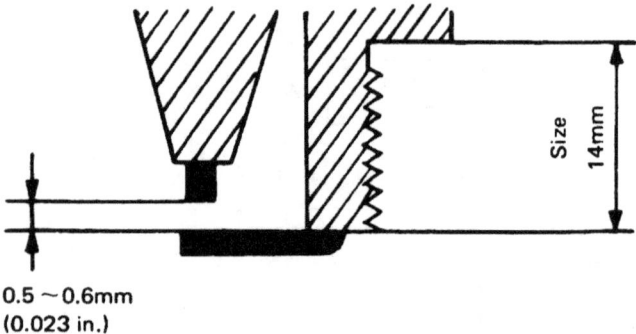

Fig. 5-10-1

5-11 Lighting and Signal Systems – JT2

The lighting and signal systems consist of the horn and stop light (power source-battery) and the head light, tail light and meter lamps. (Power source-flywheel magneto.)

1. Head light

The head light has two 6V, 1.5W bulbs, and a 6V, 1.5W neutral pilot light on its top. A beam directing adjusting screw is fitted on the right side of the light rim so that the horizontal direction of the beam can be adjusted (not vertically).

2. Tail Light and Stop Light

A 6V. 5.8W tail light and a 6V, 17W stop light are mounted. The lens of the tail light is provided with reflectors on its three sides—rear, right and left.

3. Horn

The horn is a 6V, flat type, and has a tone-volume adjusting nut on its back.

ELECTRICAL SYSTEM - Lighting and Signal System

After adjustment is made, apply paint or lacquer to the nut for water proofing purposes.

4. Speedometer

A circular type speedometer is mounted on the bracket. For illumination, a 6 V, 3 W bulb is provided.

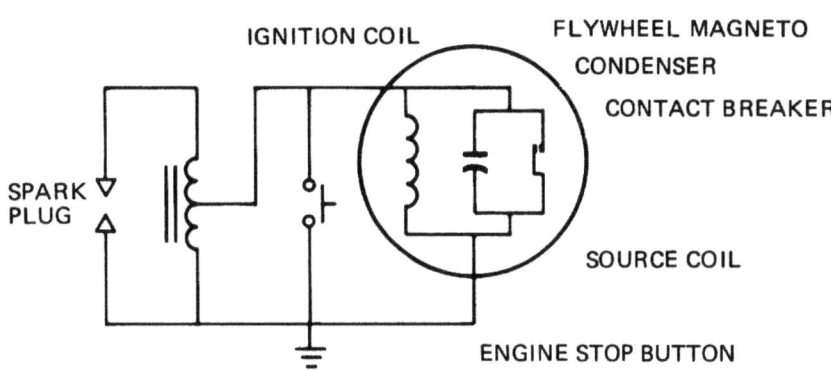

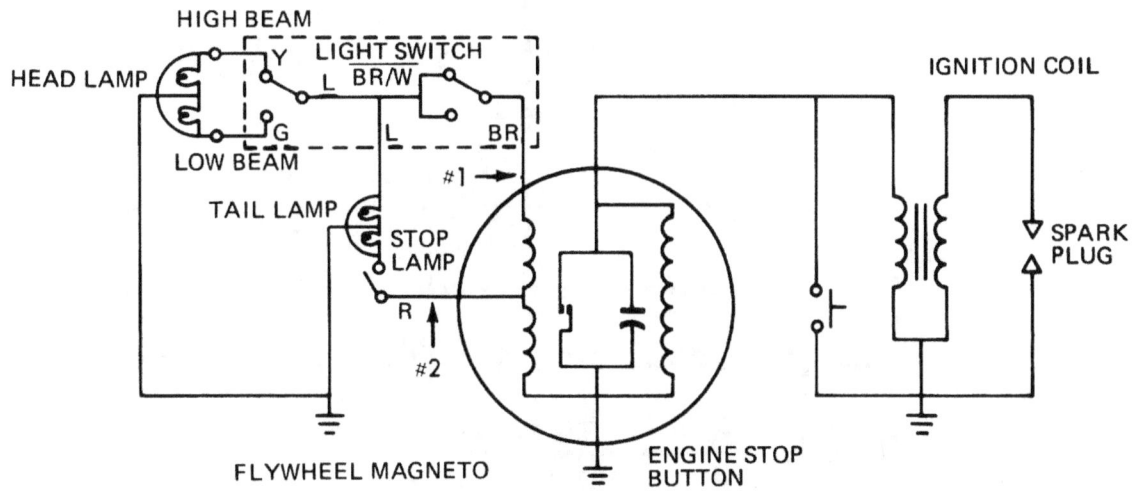

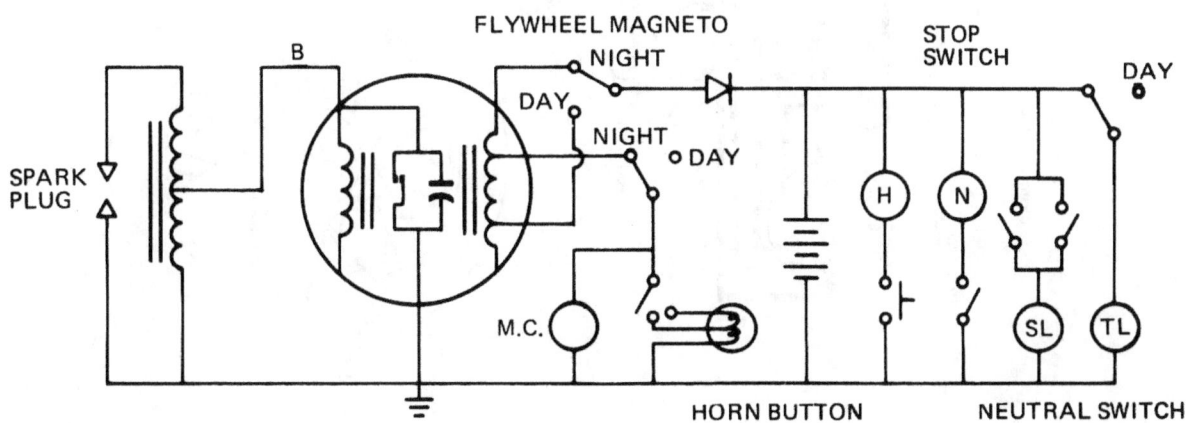

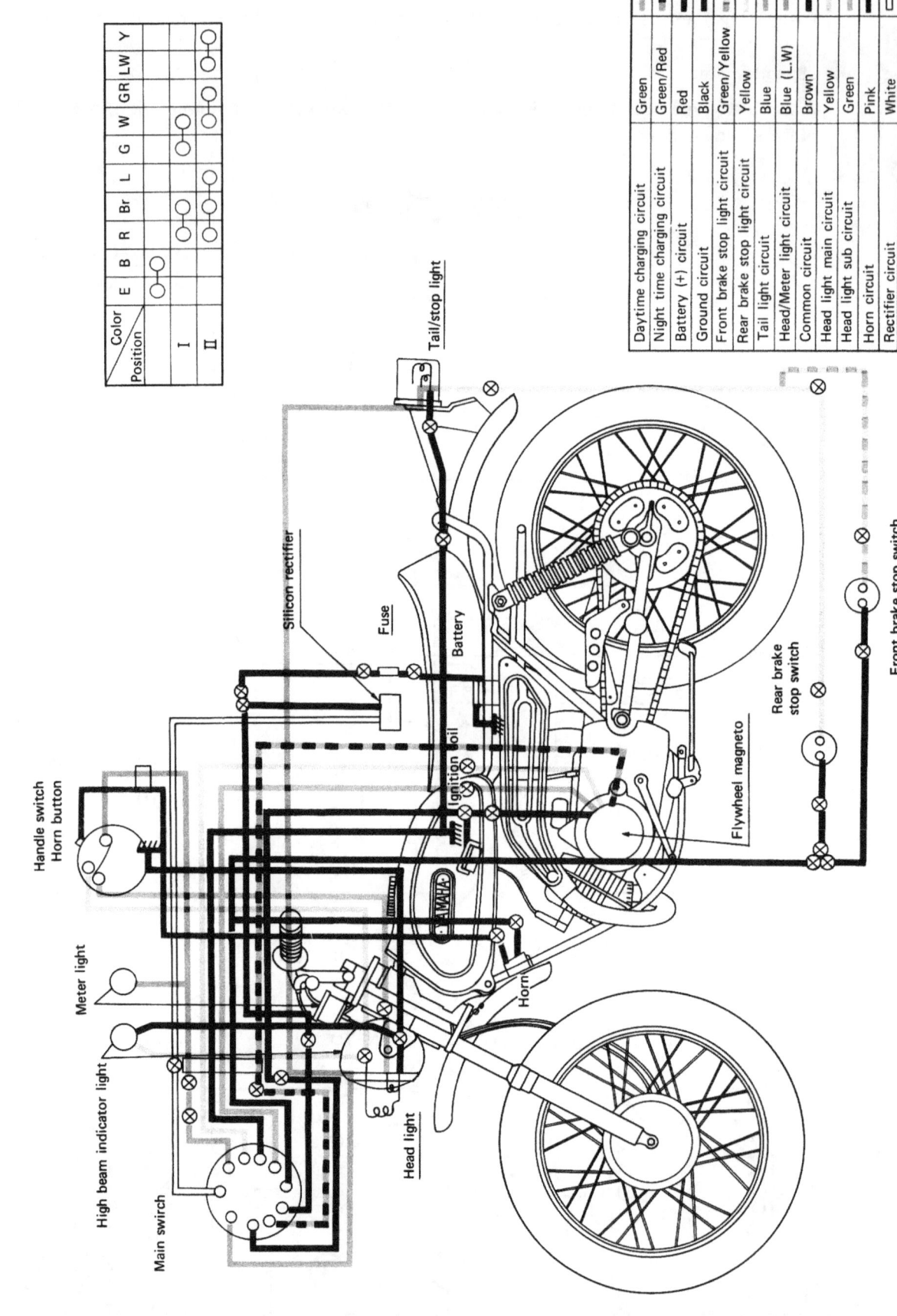

APPENDIX

PERTINENT

PARTS and SERVICE

BULLETINS

Note

THE FOLLOWING INFORMATION MUST BE USED AS A GUIDE ONLY TO INDICATE THE DIRECTION TAKEN BY VARIOUS MODIFICATIONS. IT IS INCLUDED ONLY AS AN AID TO SERVICING THE JT SERIES AND, SHOULD A QUESTION ARISE REGARDING A CERTAIN PART, THE MECHANIC SHOULD REFER TO AN UP-TO-DATE MODEL PARTS BOOK, SERVICE OR PARTS NEWS BULLETIN, OR THE MANUFACTURER.

MOTORCYCLE SERVICE NEWS

YAMAHA INTERNATIONAL CORPORATION
MONTEBELLO, CALIFORNIA
DATE 12/2/70

NUMBER **256**

JT1   ROTARY VALVE INSTALLATION (TIMING)

The JT1 rotary valve mounts to the crankshaft in a slightly different manner than previous Yamaha rotary valve models. This requires special valve installation instructions which are given below.

A collar fits over the crankshaft (notch in collar fits over pin in shaft), then the valve fits over the collar. To install the valve in proper relation to the crankshaft, the two indentations in the outer valve surface must line up with the pin in the crankshaft.

Rotary valve timing can also be checked by rotating the piston to top dead center (indicated with dial indicator) and checking that the valve closing edge just lines up with the left edge of the intake port (see drawing).

PIN LOCATION NOTE: The locating pin in the shaft is removable. Although the pin hole is drilled thru the shaft, permitting the pin to protrude from either end of the hole, follow factory installation recommendations. Position the pin to protrude out of the hole end 180° from the crank pin. However, no matter which end the pin extends from, the rotary valve can be correctly timed by lining up the valve closing edge with the intake port.

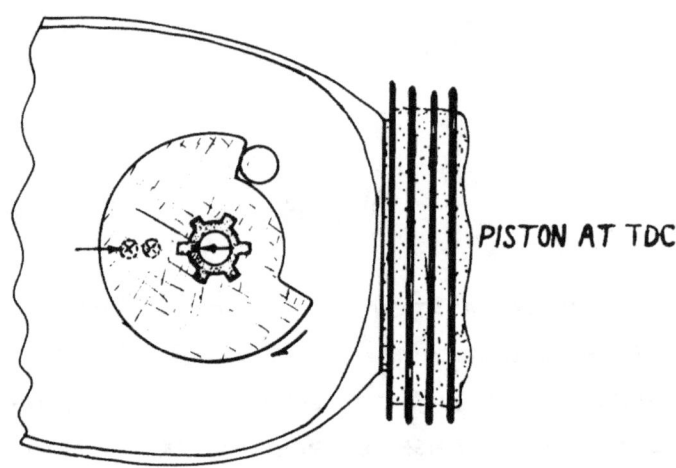
PISTON AT TDC

MOTORCYCLE SERVICE NEWS

NUMBER 258 A

YAMAHA INTERNATIONAL CORPORATION
BUENA PARK, CALIFORNIA 90620
DATE 12/10/71

<u>1969 thru 1972 Models</u>　　　　　　　　AUTOLUBE OUTPUT & COLOR CODE

NOTICE: THIS BULLETIN TAKES THE PLACE OF SNB #258 - PLEASE DESTROY SNB #258

OUTPUT

The charts on pages two and three, used in conjunction with the test procedure below, can be used to check the pump's actual output against factory nominal specifications.

HOWEVER, pump output variations from nominal specifications very rarely occur. More often than not, the problem is in minimum stroke and/or cable length adjustments....or a mechanical problem such as a loose delivery line fitting, leaky engine seal or gasket, or, occasionally, failure to reinstall the check ball(s) and/or spring(s) in the delivery line.

COLOR CODES

Color codes have been included so that a mechanic can identify a pump installed on a machine or lying loose on a shelf. Note: See Motorcycle Service News Bulletin #198A for color code identification on earlier models.

A. MATERIALS REQUIRED TO CHECK OUTPUT

Purchase a tube graduated in cubic centimeters (purchase from any laboratory equipment & supply house; check local listing in telephone yellow pages) and attach an Autolube delivery line to one end of the tube. Leave the banjo fitting on the other end of the delivery line to provide a universal adaptor for all models.

B. PROCEDURE

Whether checking the pump on the machine or bench, the procedure is identical.

1. Disconnect original oil delivery line and attach graduated tube/delivery line unit to outlet hole.
2. Make sure oil tank has a sufficient oil supply to complete this procedure.
3. Determine if output check is to be done at minimum or maximum stroke, and set pump pulley in appropriate position. IMPORTANT! When checking at maximum stroke, rotate pump pulley so ramp follows guide pin to maximum stroke position. DO NOT push pulley straight in by hand as this will cause the pump stroke to be greater than determined by factory.
4. Rotate plastic pump starter wheel 200 revolutions and compare measured output with specifications listed on page 2.
5. Pump output can be checked within 10-15 minutes. This is much more beneficial than just guessing that pump might be bad, replacing the pump, and running the engine again. It will prevent repeated engine damage (when machine is damaged again after replacing pump) and unnecessary time invested by customer and mechanic.

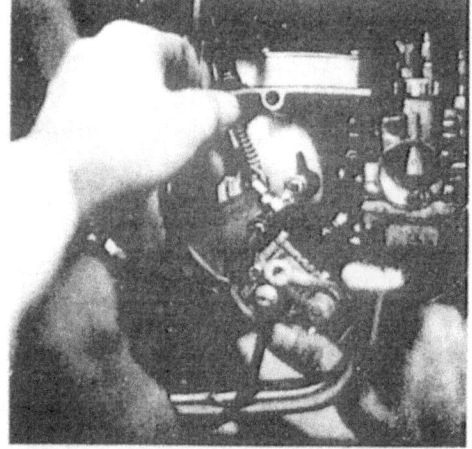

MOTORCYCLE SERVICE NEWS

YAMAHA INTERNATIONAL CORPORATION
BUENA PARK, CALIFORNIA 90620

DATE 12/10/71

NUMBER 258A

1969 thru 1972 Models AUTOLUBE OUTPUT & COLOR CODE (cont'd.)

C. WHAT IF OUTPUT IS CORRECT, AND PROBLEM CONTINUES?

Troubleshooting is a process of considering all possibilities, and eliminating them until the problem(s) is found. Such items and systems to be checked include type of oil, rider habits, timing, piston clearance, and compression (not particularly in this order, nor only those items listed).

<u>1969 thru 1971 Models</u>

	MINIMUM STROKE; cc @ 200 STROKES*	MAXIMUM STROKE; cc @ 200 STROKES*	PUMP COLOR CODE	**REDUCTION RATIOS
JT1	.50 - .63	4.65 - 5.15	White	30/19 x 62/1
G5S	.50 - .63	4.65 - 5.15	Light Blue	28/19 x 55/1
G6S	.50 - .63	4.65 - 5.15	Light Blue	28/19 x 55/1
G6SB	.50 - .63	4.65 - 5.15	Light Blue	28/19 x 55/1
HT1	.50 - .63	4.65 - 5.15	Red	28/19 x 55/1
HT1B	.50 - .63	4.65 - 5.15	Red	28/19 x 55/1
HS1	.50 - .63	4.20 - 4.80	Blue	34/19 x 62/1
HS1B	.50 - .63	4.20 - 4.80	Blue	34/19 x 62/1
YL1 (E)	.50 - .63	4.20 - 4.80	Yellow	34/19 x 62/1
L5T	.50 - .63	4.65 - 5.15	Green	34/19 x 36/1
L5TA	.50 - .63	4.65 - 5.15	Green	34/19 x 36/1
AT1	.95 - 1.19	8.80 - 9.76	Yellow	28/19 x 55/1
AT1B (MX)	.95 - 1.19	8.80 - 9.76	Yellow	28/19 x 55/1
AT1C	.95 - 1.19	8.80 - 9.76	Yellow	28/19 x 55/1
AS2C	.50 - .63	4.17 - 4.80	White	34/19 x 55/1
CT1	.95 - 1.19	8.80 - 9.76	Yellow	28/19 x 55/1
CT1B	.95 - 1.19	8.80 - 9.76	Yellow	28/19 x 55/1
CT1C	.95 - 1.19	8.80 - 9.76	Yellow	28/19 x 55/1
CS1C	.50 - .63	5.15 - 5.70	Dark Blue	20/16 x 55/1
CS3B	.50 - .63	5.15 - 5.70	Dark Blue	20/16 x 55/1
CS3C	.50 - .63	5.15 - 5.70	Dark Blue	20/16 x 55/1
DT1B	.95 - 1.19	8.80 - 9.76	Black	20/21 x 55/1
DT1C	.95 - 1.19	8.80 - 9.76	Black	20/21 x 55/1
DT1E	.95 - 1.19	8.80 - 9.76	Black	20/21 x 55/1
DS6B	.50 - .63	5.15 - 5.70	Pink	20/20 x 40/1
DS6C	.50 - .63	5.15 - 5.70	Pink	20/20 x 40/1
R2/R2C	.50 - .63	5.15 - 5.70	Green	19/23 x 32/1
R3	.50 - .63	5.15 - 5.70	Green	19/23 x 32/1
R5	.50 - .63	5.15 - 5.70	Red	21/23 x 32/1
R5B	.50 - .63	5.15 - 5.70	Red	21/23 x 32/1
RT1 (Old)	1.19 - 1.44	9.10 - 10.05	Green	20/21 x 55/1
RT1 (New)	.95 - 1.19	8.80 - 9.70	Green	20/21 x 55/1
RT1B	.95 - 1.19	8.80 - 9.70	Green	20/21 x 55/1

MOTORCYCLE SERVICE NEWS

YAMAHA INTERNATIONAL CORPORATION
BUENA PARK, CALIFORNIA 90620
DATE 12/10/71

NUMBER **258A**

1969 thru 1972 Models AUTOLUBE OUTPUT & COLOR CODE (cont'd.)

1971-1/2 & 1972 Models

	MINIMUM STROKE; cc @ 200 STROKES*	MAXIMUM STROKE; cc @ 200 STROKES*	PUMP COLOR CODE	**REDUCTION RATIOS
U7E	.63 - .73	2.76 - 3.37	Red	68/19 x 56/1
G7S	.50 - .63	4.27 - 4.90	Blue	28/19 x 55/1
LS2	.50 - .63	4.17 - 4.80	Sky Blue	34/19 x 62/1
LT2	.50 - .63	4.65 - 5.15	Blue	28/19 x 40/1
LT2-M	.50 - .63	4.65 - 5.15	Blue	28/19 x 40/1
CS5	.50 - .63	5.15 - 5.65	Brown	20/16 x 55/1
DS7	.50 - .63	5.15 - 5.70	Green	22/21 x 40/1
R5C	.50 - .63	5.15 - 5.70	Red	21/23 x 32/1
JT1L	.75 - .88	3.64 - 4.27	White	30/19 x 62/1
JT2	.75 - .88	3.64 - 4.27	White	30/19 x 62/1
JT2-MX	.75 - .88	3.64 - 4.27	White	30/19 x 62/1
HT1B-MX	.50 - .63	4.65 - 5.15	Red	28/19 x 55/1
AT2	.95 - 1.19	8.80 - 9.76	Yellow	28/19 x 55/1
AT2-M	.95 - 1.19	8.80 - 9.76	Yellow	28/19 x 55/1
CT2	.95 - 1.19	8.80 - 9.76	Yellow	28/19 x 55/1
DT2	.95 - 1.19	8.80 - 9.76	Black	20/21 x 55/1
DT2-MX	.95 - 1.19	8.80 - 9.76	Black	20/21 x 55/1
RT2	.95 - 1.19	8.80 - 9.76	Green	20/21 x 32/1
RT2-MX	.95 - 1.19	8.80 - 9.76	Green	20/21 x 32/1
TD3				
TR3				

*STROKES: 1 pumping stroke occurs for each pump revolution. This is true even for twin cylinder models, as there is only 1 pump stroke for <u>each</u> cylinder per revolution. The quantity is <u>measured only out of one oil delivery line at a time.</u>

**Pump drive gear/primary driven gear x worm wheel/worm shaft.

MOTORCYCLE SERVICE NEWS

YAMAHA INTERNATIONAL CORPORATION
MONTEBELLO, CALIFORNIA
DATE 1/18/71

NUMBER 261

JT1   LIGHTING KIT

In order to make the JT1 Mini-Enduro more useable we are now offering a lighting kit for the machine. THE KIT IS <u>NOT</u> STREET LEGAL. It is quite adequate for use in providing off-the-road illumination but has not been approved, at this time, by the various government regulating agencies.

A. Lighting source coil
1. Remove magneto cover.
2. Remove flywheel.
3. Remove stator plate.
4. Remove empty source shoe.
5. Install coil in place of (4.).
6. Install new grommet (bigger hole for loom, see sketch #3).
7. Re-install stator.
8. Route new wires with ignition wire.

B. Main harness
1. Remove tank.
2. Route alongside frame tube (see sketches 1 and 2).

C. Handle switch
1. Remove left grip.
2. Install switch.
3. Re-install grip.
NOTE: The handle switch is a combined type similar to the DS3 switch. Check the schematic (page 4) carefully in order to wire correctly.

D. Headlamp stay
1. Remove triple clamp.
2. Slide stays over fork tubes.
3. Tighten 6mm bolts.
4. Re-install triple clamp.

E. Headlamp
1. Install.
2. Remove lens.
3. Insert main harness through left hand hole.
4. Insert handle switch harness through right hand hole.
5. Hook up wires.

F. Taillight
1. Use as template to drill three 6.5mm holes in fender; top hole approximately 3" from fender tip.

MOTORCYCLE SERVICE NEWS

YAMAHA INTERNATIONAL CORPORATION
MONTEBELLO, CALIFORNIA
DATE 1/18/71

NUMBER 261

JT1   LIGHTING KIT (Continued)

      2. Install light.
      3. Route wiring through fender brace hole and under seat.

  G. Brake light switch
      1. Bolt stay to upper rear engine mount, right hand side.
      2. Insert switch rod in brake lever hole.
      3. Adjust as necessary.

  H. Connections
      1. Main harness, taillight leads, and source wires terminate under seat.
      2. Use nylon clip to secure to righthand frame tube next to (and over) oil tank (do not allow wires to touch muffler).
      3. Caution: See sketches as otherwise shorts may occur.
      4. Hook up according to schematic, page 4.
      5. Re-install seat, tank, etc.
      6. Check output per voltage curve, Page 3.

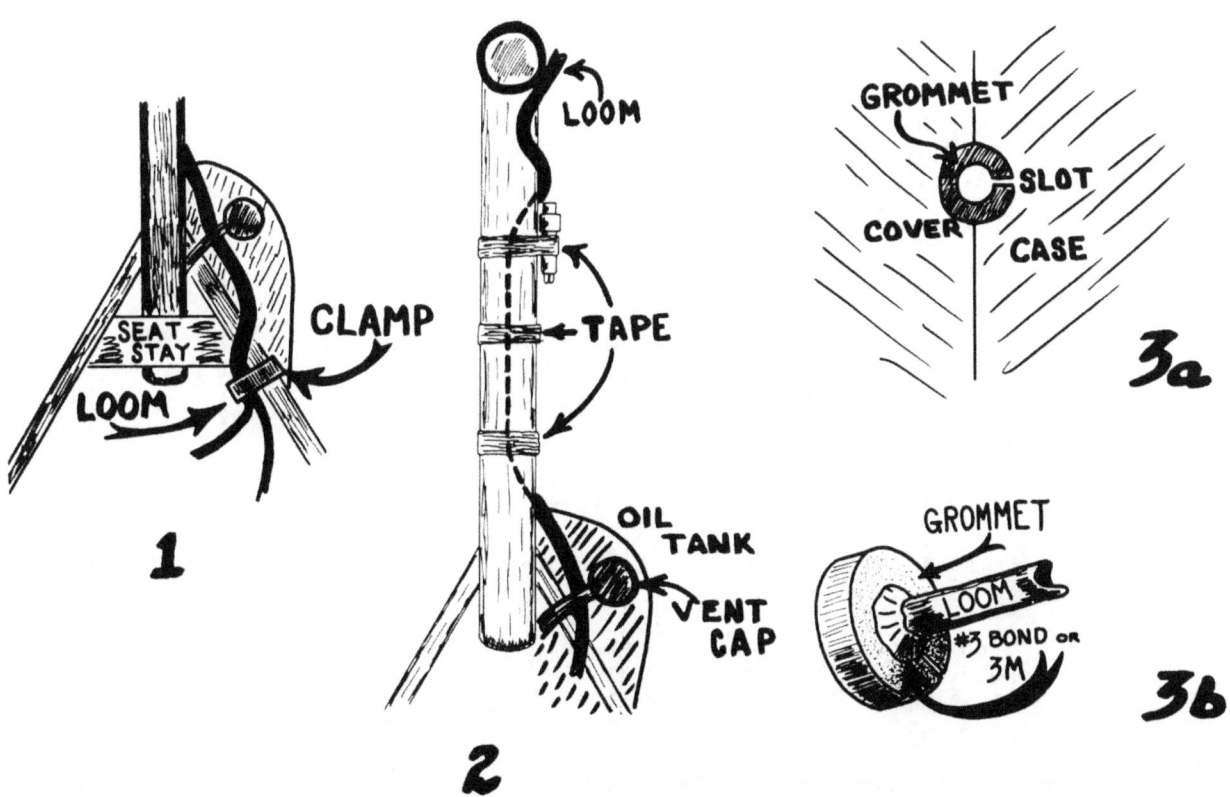

# MOTORCYCLE SERVICE NEWS

NUMBER 261

YAMAHA INTERNATIONAL CORPORATION
MONTEBELLO, CALIFORNIA
DATE 1/18/71

JT1   LIGHTING KIT (Continued)

Motorcycle Parts News Bulletin #304 (next page) gives complete ordering information on the above kit. However, for your convenience, we are adding a parts list only.

PART NUMBER	DESCRIPTION	QUANTITY
ACC-01100-04-00	JT1 Lighting Kit (comp)	1
288-84110-60-00	·HEADLAMP UNIT ASSY	1
241-84330-00-74	·BODY	1
473-84313-00-00	·WIRE, Earth	1
195-84325-00-00	·SCREW	1
290-84118-00-00	·STAY, Headlamp	1
290-84119-00-00	·STAY, Headlamp	1
91201-06015-00	·BOLT	2
92901-06200-00	·WASHER	2
97204-08020-00	·BOLT	2
92903-08200-00	·WASHER	2
92901-08100-00	·WASHER	2
98801-08100-00	·NUT	2
288-84510-60-00	·TAILLAMP UNIT ASSY	1
288-34551-09-00	·BRACKET	1
152-84518-00-00	·GROMMET	2
91201-06012-00	·BOLT	3
98801-06100-00	·NUT	3
92201-06100-00	·WASHER	3
290-82530-00-00	·STOP SWITCH	1
290-82539-99-00	·STAY, Switch	1
288-83973-00-00	·SWITCH, Handle	1
214-83974-00-00	·HOLDER, Switch	1
98503-05018-00	·SCREW	1
288-81313-10-00	·COIL LITE	1
288-82590-20-00	·WIRE, Harness	1
803-82591-00-00	·CLAMP, Wiring	1

VOLTAGE CHECK: After installation, start the machine and check the lighting coil output. (Voltage will be ± 10%)

		3,000 rpm	8,000 rpm
Stop Lamp only	#2	8.9V	8.5V
Head lamp/tail lamp	#1	4.5V	8.0V
ALL lamps burning	#1	4.0V	7.5V
	#2	1.7V	3.5V

NOTE: See JT1L schematic in ELECTRICAL SYSTEM for measurement points #1 and #2.

MOTORCYCLE PARTS NEWS

YAMAHA INTERNATIONAL CORPORATION
MONTEBELLO, CALIFORNIA

DATE 1/27/71

NUMBER **304**

JT1 LIGHTING KIT (P/N ACC-01100-04-00)

As mentioned in Service News Bulletin #261 the following lighting kit is available for the JT1.

THE KIT DOES NOT MAKE THE JT1 LEGAL FOR STREET USE AND IS OFFERED AS AN ACCESSORY ONLY TO MAKE THE MACHINE MORE USEABLE FOR THE DIRT RIDER.

PART NUMBER	DESCRIPTION	Q'TY	PRICE	DISCOUNT
ACC-01100-04-00	JT1 Lighting Kit (comp)	1	$17.50	N/D
288-84110-60-00	.Headlamp Unit Assy	1		
241-84330-00-74	.Body	1		
173-84313-00-00	.Wire, earth	1		
195-84325-00-00	.Screw	1		
290-84118-00-00	.Stay, headlamp	1		
290-84119-00-00	.Stay, headlamp	1		
912-01060-15-00	.Bolt	2		
929-01062-00-00	.Washer	2		
972-04080-20-00	.Bolt	2		
929-03082-00-00	.Washer	2		
929-01081-00-00	.Washer	2		
988-01081-00-00	.Nut	2		
288-84510-60-00	.Taillamp Unit Assy	1		
288-84551-09-00	.Bracket	1		
152-84518-00-00	.Grommet	2		
912-01060-12-00	.Bolt	3		
988-01061-00-00	.Nut	3		
922-01061-00-00	.Washer	3		
290-82530-00-00	.Stop Switch	1		
290-82539-00-00	.Stay, Switch	1		
288-83973-00-00	.Switch, Handle	1		
214-83974-00-00	.Holder, Switch	1		
985-03050-18-00	.Screw	1		
288-81313-10-00	.Coil, Lighting	1		
288-82590-20-00	.Wire, Harness	1		
803-82591-00-00	.Clamp, Wiring	1		

TOTAL PIECES: 39

NOTE: Suggested retail price for the above unit is: $25.95.
Installation will require approximately 2 hours.

Available: Feb. 10 @ Bellmawr
Mar. 1 @ Los Angeles

PLEASE MAKE NOTE OF THIS BULLETIN IN YOUR JT1 PARTS BOOK

MOTORCYCLE PARTS NEWS

YAMAHA INTERNATIONAL CORPORATION
BUENA PARK, CALIFORNIA 90620

NUMBER **310**

DATE 7/10/71

JT1   STEERING BEARING RACES/CARBURETOR CAP

#1: Steering bearing races (Fig. No. 18-1)

Both inner races (referred to as RACE #2 in Parts Book) have been modified to provide greater strength. Originally, top and bottom inner races were identical, but are now two differently sized races. There is no change, however, in bearing balls.

These parts have been included in standard models after engine #26308, and should be used as replacement parts on all JT1's.

NOTE: The front fork guide (Fig. No. 17-27, JT1 Parts Book) cannot be used with these newer bearing races because the inner race holes are now too small to let the guide pass through. This part is not absolutely needed as its only purpose is to help align the underbracket during installation.

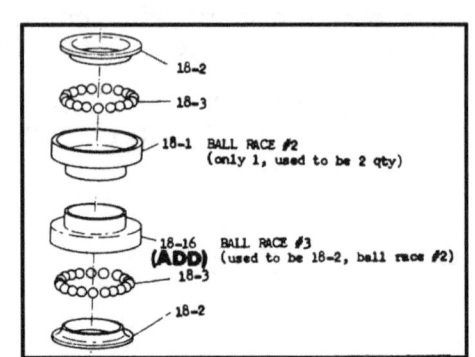

PARTS BOOK CORRECTION: Original JT1 Parts Book picture on page 49 shows top and bottom bearing assemblies upside down. Rearrange as in picture above.

Fig.No.	Description	Old Part Number	New Part Number	Qty.	Retail/Disc.	Remarks
18-1	BALL RACE #2	282-23412-00-00	282-23412-01-00	1	$.94/ A	Qty used to be 2.
18-16 (add)	BALL RACE #3	282-23412-00-00	288-23413-00-00	1	$.94/ A	E/N26309

#2: Carburetor cap (Fig. No. 2-20)

The carburetor cap design has been changed to permit an elastic steel band to be installed around its outer edge. This will help to hold the cap more securely in place.

These parts are standard equipment on JT1's after engine number 025908.

New and old caps are available, but the new cap can be interchanged on earlier machines without modification.

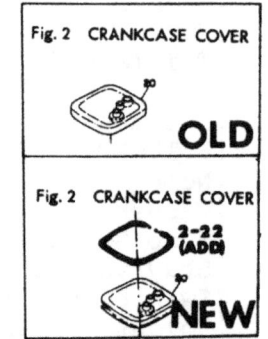

Fig.No.	Description	Old Part Number	New Part Number	Qty.	Retail/Disc.	Remarks
2-20	CAP, carburetor	288-14481-00-00	288-14481-01-00	1	$.62/ A	E/N25909
2-22 (add)	BAND, spring	----------------	288-14455-00-00	1	$.26/ A	E/N25909

<u>PLEASE BRING YOUR PARTS BOOKS AND PRICE LIST UP TO DATE</u>

#####

MOTORCYCLE PARTS NEWS

YAMAHA INTERNATIONAL CORPORATION
BUENA PARK, CALIFORNIA 90620
DATE 8/22/72

NUMBER 347
PAGE 1 of 1

JT2/JT2-MX   AIR CLEANER COVER JOINT

The metal retaining cover for the rubber air cleaner joint is now available from the Parts Department. Please update your JT2/JT2-MX Parts List to include this part.

PARTS ORDERING

Ref. No.	Part Number	Description	Qty.	Price
9 - 15	288-14417-00-00	COVER, Joint	1	

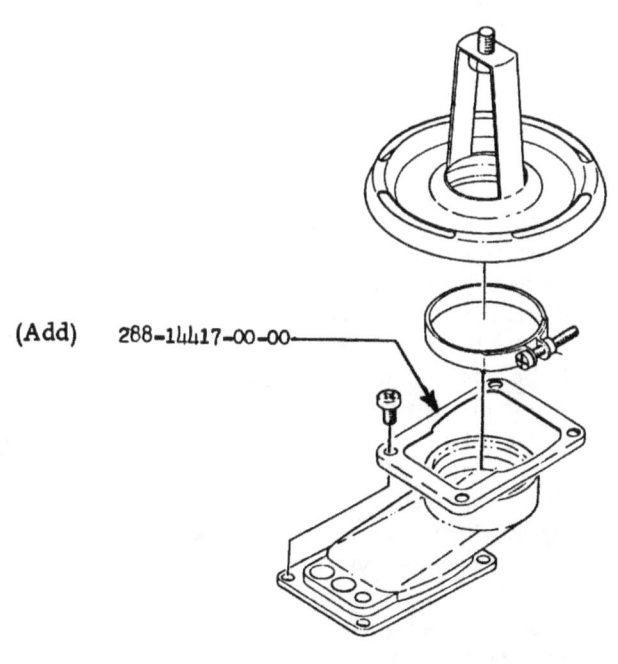

(Add) 288-14417-00-00

\# \# \# \#

LUBRICATION INTERVALS

Page	Item		Remarks	Type	Period				
					Initial (miles)			Thereafter every (miles)	
					250	500	1,000	500	1,000
7	Autolube	P R E O P C H K	See Service Notes	#1	See Service Notes				
—	Trans. Oil		Warm Engine Before Draining	#2	0	CHK	0	CHK	0
—	Drive Chain		Lube/Adjust as required	#3	See Service Notes				
—	Drive Chain		Remove/Clean/Lube/Adjust	#3		0		0	
44	Air Filter		Foam Type	#9	See Service Notes				
—	Throttle Grip & Housing		Light Application	#5	0				0
—	Rear Arm Pivot Shaft		Lube Periodically	#6			0		0
—	Brake Pedal Shaft		Light Application	#5			0		0
—	Change Pedal Shaft		Light Application	#5			0		0
55	Front Forks		Drain Completely-Ck Specs	#3	CHK		0		0
—	Steering Ball Races		Inspect Thoroughly/Med. Pack	#7			0		0
—	Point Cam Lubr. Wick		Very Light Application	#8			0		0
—	Wheel Bearings		Do not Over-Pack	#7			0		0

#1. Check tank level before each ride. Top off when oil level is at sight glass or before any prolonged use. Use the following lubricant (in order of preference):
Yamalube, or two-stroke oil labeled "BIA certified for service TC-W"
#2. At ambient temperatures of 45-90°F, use YAMALUBE 4-stroke. Do not use "additives" in oil.
#3. Use 10W/30 "SE" motor oil. (If desired, specialty type lubricants of quality manufacture may be used.)
"Drive Chain"—Lube every 150-200 miles. If severe usage, every 50-100 miles or daily.
#4. Use graphic base type (specialty types available—use name-brand, quality manufacturer).
#5. Light duty: smooth, lightweight, "White" grease. Heavy duty: standard 90wt. lube grease (do not use lube grease on throttle/housing).
#6. Use standard 90wt. lube grease—smooth, not coarse.
#7. Medium-weight wheel bearing grease of quality manufacturer—preferrably waterproof.
#8. Lightweight machine oil.
#9. Air filters—foam element air filters must be damp with oil at all times to function properly. Clean and lube monthly or per mileage. If hard usage, clean and lube daily. Do not over-oil. Use SAE 10W/30 "SE".

PERIODIC MAINTENANCE INTERVALS

Page	Item		Remarks	Initial (miles)		Thereafter every (miles)	
				250	500	500	1,000
48-49	Brake System (Complete)	A L S O P R E O P	Chk/Adj. as required-Repair as required	0		0	
22-26	Clutch		Check/Adjust as required	0		0	
69-70	Spark Plug		Inspect/Clean or replace as required	0	0	0	
46-54	Wheels and Tires		Pressure/Spoke Tension/Runout	0	0	0	
—	Fittings and Fasteners		Tighten before each trip	0	0	0	
—	Grip wire		Cable Oper/Adj. (incl. Autolube)	0	0		0
54	Drive Chain		Tension/Alignment	0	0	0	
—	Transmission Oil Level Check	C H K	Includes Trans./Autolube Tank (See Note #1)	0	0	0	
44	Air Filter		Foam Type (See Service Notes #2 & #4)	0	0	0	
—	Fuel Petcock		Clean/Flush Tank as required	0	0		0
63	Ignition Timing		Adjust/Clean/Replace points as required		0		0
43-44	Carburetor Adjustment		Check Operation/Synch./Fittings		0		0
42-43	Carburetor Overhaul		Clean/Repair as required/Refit/Adjust		0		0
16	Cylinder Compression		Preventive Maintenance Check		0		0
—	Decarbonize Engine		Includes Exhaust System		0		0

SERVICE NOTES:

#1. Check Autolube tank level before each ride. Top off when oil level shows at the sight glass or before any prolonged use. See "Lubrication Intervals" for type of oil to use.

#2. Foam elements air filters must be damp with oil at all times to function properly. Remove, clean, and oil filter at least once per month or every 250 ~ 500 miles; whichever occurs first. (If extremely hard usage, such as dirt riding, clean and lube daily.) See "Lubrication Intervals" for additional details.

#3. Pre-operational checks should be made each time the machine is used. Such an inspection can be thoroughly accomplished in a very short time, and the added safety it assures the rider is more than worth the minimal time involved.

#4. For additional information regarding drive chain, transmission oil level, wet-type air filter, see "Lubrication Intervals".

PRE-OPERATION CHECK CHART

ITEM	ROUTINE	PAGE
BRAKES	Check operation/adjustment	
CLUTCH	Check operation/lever adjustment	
AUTOLUBE TANK	Check oil level/top-off as required	
TRANSMISSION	Top-off as required	
DRIVE CHAIN	Check alignment/adjustment/lubrication	
BATTERY (JT2)	Check electolyte level weekly/top-off monthly	
SPARK PLUG(S)	After break-in - check color/cond'n weekly/1,000 mi.	
AUTOLUBE PUMP	Check for proper cable operation	
AIR FILTER	Foam type - must be clean and damp w/oil always	
WHEELS & TIRES	Check pressure/runout/spoke tightness/axle nuts	
FITTINGS/FASTENERS	Check all - tighten as necessary	
LIGHTS/SIGNALS (JT1L/JT2)	Check headlight/tail - stop lights	

Pre-operation checks should be made each time the machine is used. Such an inspection can be thoroughly accomplished in a very short time; and the added safety it assures is more than worth the time involved.

Torque Specifications

The list below covers those stud/bolt sizes with standard I.S.O. pitch threads. Torque specifications for components with thread pitches other than standard are given within the applicable chapter.

Torque specifications call for dry, clean threads. Components such as the cylinder or cylinder head should be at room temperature prior to torquing. A cylinder head or any other item with several fasteners should be torqued down in a cross-hatch pattern in successive stages until torque specification is reached. The method is similar to installing an automobile wheel and will avoid warping the component.

A (NUT)	B (BOLT)	TORQUE SPECIFICATION		
		Kg-m	Ft-lbs	In-lbs
10mm	6mm	1.0	7.2	85
13mm	8mm	2.0	15	175
14mm	8mm	2.0	15	175
17mm	10mm	3.5~4.0	25~29	300~350
19mm	12mm	4.0~4.5	29~33	350~400
22mm	14mm	4.5~5.0	33~36	400~440
26mm	17mm	5.8~7.0	42~50	500~600
27mm	18mm	5.8~7.0	42~50	500~600
30mm	20mm	7.0~8.3	50~60	600~700
SPARK PLUG		2.7~2.9	19~21	230~250

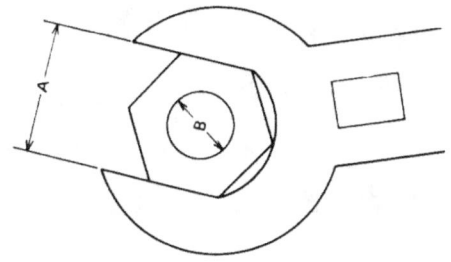

CLEANING AND STORAGE

A. Cleaning

Frequent thorough cleaning of your motorcycle will not only enchance it's appearance but will improve general performance and extend the useful life of many components.

1. Before cleaning the machine:
    a. Block off end of exhaust pipe to prevent water entry; a plastic bag and strong rubber band may be used.
    b. Remove air cleaner or protect it from water with plastic covering.
    c. Make sure spark plug(s), gas cap, oil tank cap, transmission oil filler cap and battery caps are properly installed.
2. If engine case is excessively greasy, apply degreaser with a paint brush. Do not apply degreaser to chain, sprockets, or wheel axles.
3. Rinse dirt and degreaser off with garden hose, using only enough hose pressure to do the job. Excessive hose pressure may cause water seepage and contamination of wheel bearings, front forks, brake drums, and transmission seals. Many expensive repair bills have resulted from improper high-pressure detergent applications such as those available in coin-operated car washes.
4. Once the majority of the dirt has been hosed off, wash all surfaces with warm water and mild, detergent-type soap. An old tooth brush or bottle brush is handy to reach those hard-to-get-to places.
5. Rinse machine off immediately with clean water and dry all surfaces with a chamois, clean towel, or soft absorbent cloth.
6. Immediately after washing, remove excess moisture from chain and lubricate to prevent rust.
7. Chrome-plated parts such as handlebars, rims, spokes, forks, etc., may be further cleaned with automotive chrome cleaner.
8. Clean the seat with a vinyl upholstery cleaner to keep the cover pliable and glossy.
9. Automotive-type wax may be applied to all painted and chrome-plated surfaces. Avoid combination cleaner-waxes. Many contain abrasives which may mar paint or protective finish on fuel and oil tanks.
10. After finishing, start the engine immediately and allow to idle for several minutes.

B. Storage

Long term storage (30 days or more) of your motorcycle will require some preventive procedures to insure against deterioration. After cleaning machine thoroughly, prepare for storage as follows:

1. Drain fuel tank, fuel lines, and carburetor float bowl(s).
2. Remove empty fuel tank, pour a cup of 10W to 30W oil in tank, shake tank to coat inner surfaces thoroughly and drain off excess oil. Re-install tank.
3. Remove spark plug(s), pour about one tablespoon of 10W to 30W oil in spark plug hole(s) and re-install spark plugs. Kick engine over several times (with ignition off) to coat cylinder walls with oil.
4. Remove drive chain. Clean thoroughly with solvent and lubricate with graphite-base chain lubricant. Re-install chain or store in a plastic bag (tie to frame for safe-keeping).
5. Lubricate all control cables.
6. Remove battery and charge. Store in a dry place and re-charge once a month. Do not store battery in an excessively warm or cold place (less than 32°F or more than 90°F).
7. Block up frame to raise both wheels off ground. (Main stands can be used on machines so equipped.)
8. Deflate tires to 15psi.
9. Tie a plastic bag over exhaust pipe outlet(s) to prevent moisture entering.
10. If storing in humid or salt-air atmosphere, coat all exposed metal surfaces with a light film of oil. Do not apply oil to rubber parts or seat cover.

MILLIMETERS TO INCHES

	0	0.1	0.2	0.3	0.4	0.5	0.6	0.7	0.8	0.9
0		0.0039	0.0079	0.0018	0.0157	0.0197	0.0236	0.0276	0.0315	0.0354
1	0.0394	0.0433	0.0472	0.0512	0.0551	0.0591	0.0630	0.0669	0.7099	0.0748
2	0.0787	0.0827	0.0866	0.0906	0.0945	0.0984	0.1024	0.1063	0.1102	0.1142
3	0.1181	0.1200	0.1260	0.1299	0.1339	0.1378	0.1417	0.1457	0.1496	0.1535
4	0.1575	0.1614	0.1654	0.1693	0.1732	0.1772	0.1811	0.1850	0.1890	0.1929
5	0.1969	0.2000	0.2047	0.2087	0.2126	0.2165	0.2205	0.2244	0.2283	0.2323
6	0.2362	0.2402	0.2441	0.2480	0.2520	0.2559	0.2598	0.2638	0.2677	0.2717
7	0.2756	0.2795	0.2835	0.2874	0.2913	0.2953	0.2992	0.3031	0.3071	0.3110
8	0.3150	0.3189	0.3228	0.3268	0.3307	0.3346	0.3386	0.3425	0.3465	0.3504
9	0.3542	0.3583	0.4016	0.3661	0.3701	0.3740	0.3780	0.3819	0.3858	0.3898
10	0.3937	0.3976	0.4016	0.4055	0.4094	0.4134	0.4173	0.4213	0.4252	0.4291

0.01mm=0.004   0.03mm=0.0012   0.05mm=0.0020   0.07mm=0.0028   0.09mm=0.0035
0.02mm=0.008   0.04mm=0.0016   0.06mm=0.0024   0.08mm=0.0031   0.10mm=0.0039

INCHES TO MILLIMETERS

	0	0.01	0.02	0.03	0.04	0.05	0.06	0.07	0.08	0.09
0		0.254	0.508	0.762	1.016	1.270	1.524	1.778	2.032	2.286
0.1	2.540	2.794	3.048	3.302	3.556	3.810	4.064	4.318	4.572	4.826
0.2	5.080	5.334	5.588	5.842	6.096	6.350	6.604	6.858	7.112	7.366
0.3	7.620	7.874	8.128	8.382	8.636	8.890	9.144	9.398	9.652	9.906
0.4	10.160	10.414	10.668	10.922	11.176	11.430	11.684	11.938	12.192	12.446
0.5	12.700	12.954	13.208	13.462	13.716	13.970	14.224	14.478	14.732	14.986
0.6	15.240	15.494	15.748	16.002	16.256	16.510	16.764	17.018	17.272	17.526
0.7	17.780	18.034	18.288	18.542	18.796	19.050	19.304	19.558	19.812	20.066
0.8	20.320	20.574	20.828	21.082	21.336	21.590	21.844	22.098	22.352	22.606
0.9	22.860	23.114	23.368	23.622	23.876	24.130	24.384	24.638	24.892	25.146
1.0	25.400	25.654	25.908	26.162	26.416	26.670	26.924	27.178	27.432	27.686

0.001"=0.0254mm   0.003"=0.0762mm   0.005"=0.1270mm   0.007"=0.1778mm   0.009"=0.2286mm
0.002"=0.0508mm   0.004"=0.1016mm   0.006"=0.1524mm   0.008"=0.2032mm   0.010"=0.254mm

Conversion Tables

Metric to Inch System

	Known	Multiplier (Rounded Off)	Result
Torque	kg-m	7.235	ft-lbs
	kg-m	86.82	in.-lbs
	kg-cm	.0724	ft-lbs
	kg-cm	.8682	in.-lbs
Weight	kg	2,205	lb
	g	.03527	oz
Flow/Distance	Km/ℓ	2.352	mpg
	Km/hr	0.6214	mph
	Km	0.6214	mi
	m	3.281	ft
	m	1.094	yd
	cm	0.3937	in.
	mm	0.03937	in.
Volume/Capacity	cc (cm^3)	0.03381	oz (U.S. liq.)
	cc (cm^3)	0.06102	cu in.
	ℓ (Liter)	2.1134	pt (U.S. liq.)
	ℓ (Liter)	1.057	qt (U.S. liq.)
	ℓ (Liter)	0.2642	gal (U.S. liq.)
Misc.	kg/mm	56.007	lb/in.
	kg/cm^2	14.2234	psi (lb/in.^{2})
	Centigrade (°C)	9/5(°C+32)	Fahrenheit (°F)

Inch to Metric System

	Known	Multiplier (Rounded Off)	Result
Torque	ft-lbs	0.13826	kg-m
	in.-lbs	0.01152	kg-m
	ft-lbs	13.825	kg-m
	in.-lbs	1.1518	kg-m
Weight	lb	0.4536	kg
	oz	28.35	g
Flow/Distance	mpg	0.4252	Km/ℓ
	mph	1.609	Km/hr
	mi	1.609	Km
	ft	0.3048	m
	yd	0.9144	m
	in.	2.54	cm
	in.	25.4	mm
Volume/Capacity	oz (U.S. liq.)	29.57	cc (cm^3)
	cu in.	16.387	cc (cm^3)
	pt (U.S. liq.)	0.4732	ℓ (Liter)
	qt (U.S. liq.)	0.9463	ℓ (Liter)
	gal (U.S. liq.)	3.7853	ℓ (Liter)
Misc.	lb/in.	0.017855	kg/mm
	psi (lb/in.^{2})	0.07031	kg/cm^2
	Fahrenheit (°F)	5/9(°F-32)	Centigrade (°C)

Definition of Terms:

m-kg	=	Meter Kilograms: Usually torque.
g	=	Gram(s).
kg	=	Kilogram(s): 1,000 grams.
km	=	Kilometer(s).
l	=	Liter(s).
km/l	=	Kilometer(s) Per Liter: Mileage.
cc	=	Cubic Centimeter(s) (cm^3): Volume or Capacity.
kg/mm	=	Kilogram(s) Per Millimeter: Usually Spring Compression Rate.
kg/cm^2	=	Kilogram(s) Per Square Centimeter: Pressure.

MINI ENDURO JT1 AND JT1L

MINI ENDURO JT2 AND JT2·MX

MODIFICATIONS FOR TRAIL RIDING

JT 1 AND 2 ENDURO

    Displacement: 58cc
    Bore and Stroke: . . . . 42 x 42mm
    Number of Cylinders: 1
    Use: . . . . Trail
    Cylinder Head Volume: 7.8cc
        P/N 259-11111-01-94
    Carburetor Size: . . . . Y 16 P
        P/N 288-14301-00-00
    Ignition Timing: . . . . 1.8mm BTDC
    Spark Plug Heat Range: . . . . NGK B 7 HS

Special Parts:

    Wide Ratio Transmission

JT 1 AND 2 ENDURO

Port Diagram
Cylinder Part No. 259-11311-00-00
All Dimensions in Millimeters:
Tolerance: ±0.5mm

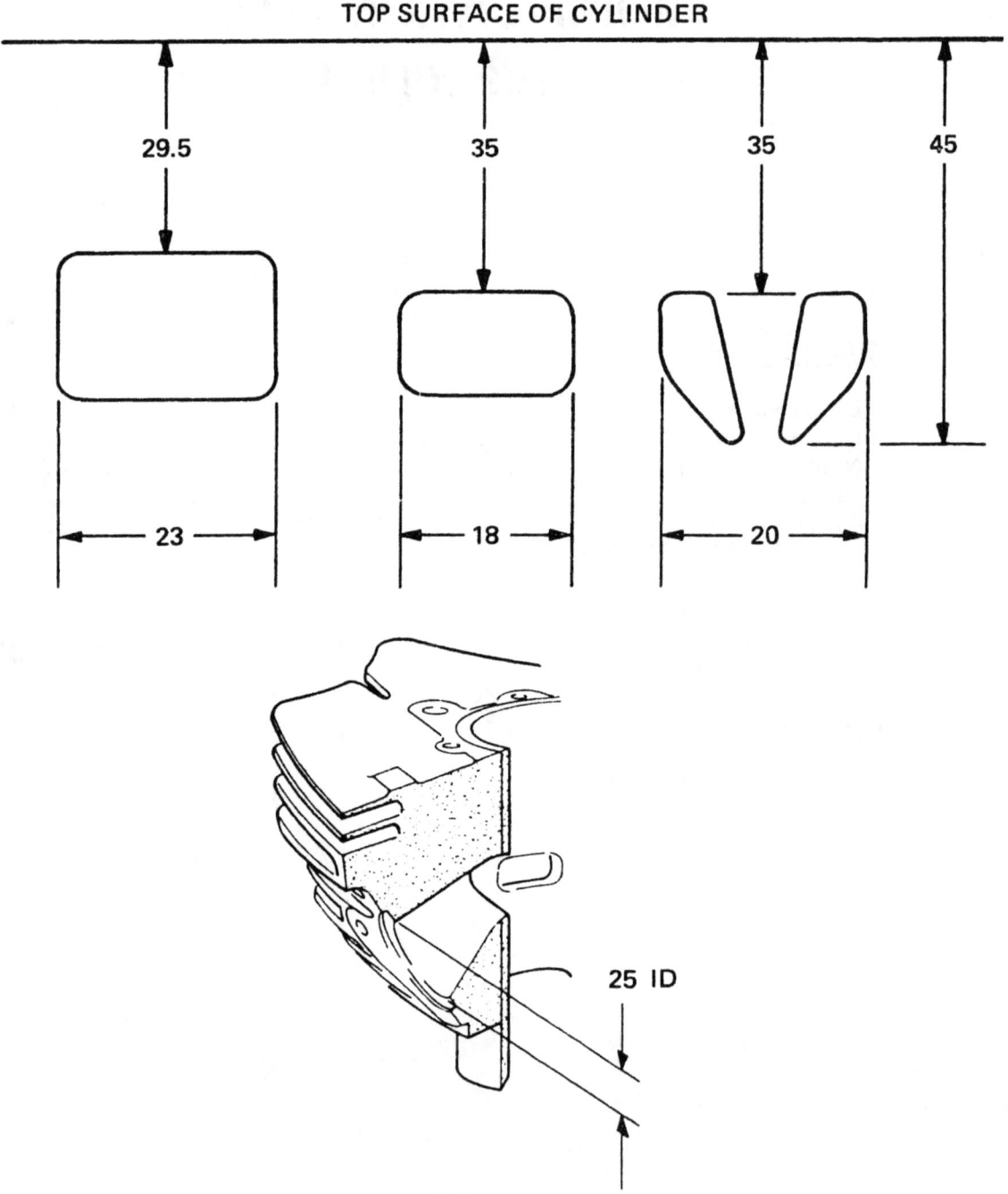

JT 1 AND 2 ENDURO

Piston Diagram
Piston Part No. 289-11631-00-96
All Dimensions in Millimeters:
Tolerance: ± 0mm

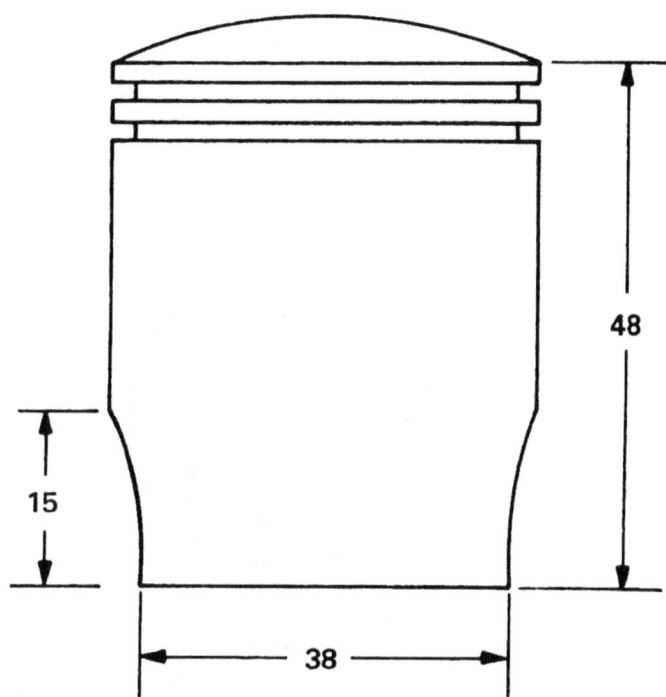

JT 1 AND 2 ENDURO

Rotary Valve Diagram
Rotary Valve Part No. 257-13512-00-00

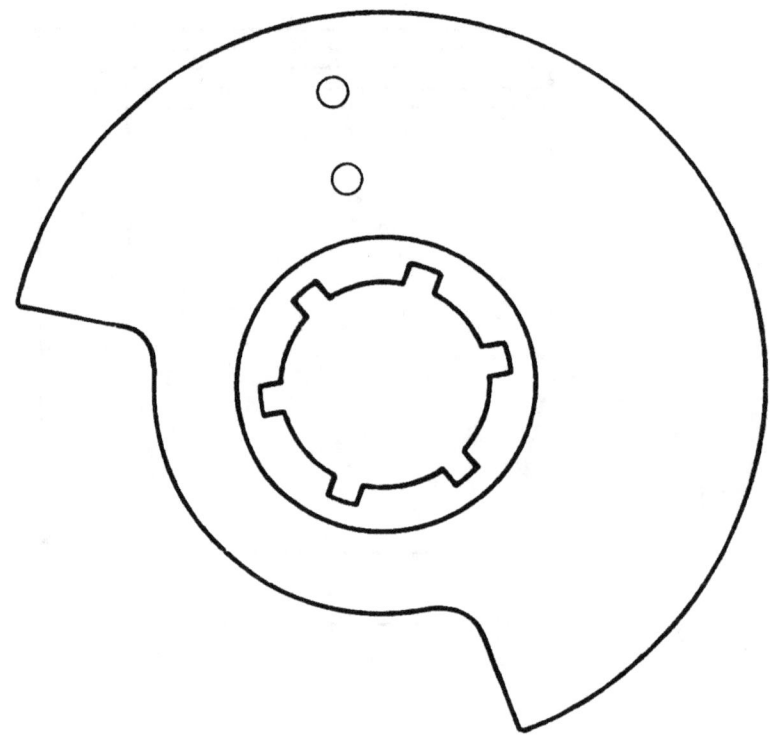

MINI ENDURO JT1 AND JT1L

MINI ENDURO JT2 AND JT2·MX

MODIFICATIONS FOR MOTOCROSS SHORT TRACK AND TT RACING

JT 1 AND 2 SPECIAL

    Displacement: 58cc
    Bore and Stroke: . . . . 42 x 42mm
    Number of Cylinders: 1
    Use: . . . . Motocross, Short Track and TT
    Cylinder Head Volume: 5.4cc
        P/N 109-11111-70-00 – Special.
    Carburetor Size: 18mm
        P/N 109-14101-70-00 – VM 18 SC Special.
    Ignition Timing: . . . . 2.0mm BTDC
    Spark Plug Heat Range: . . . . NGK B 9 HN

Special Parts:

    Rod: . . . . Slotted, 2mm wide, 10mm long
    Wide Ratio Transmission.
    Expansion Chamber: . . . . P/N 109-14610-10-00
    Shift Lever: . . . . P/N 241-18111-00-93

If rotary valve cover is modified to accept a larger carburetor, and an air cleaner is to be installed, the air cleaner should be of the wet filtron type. The air cleaner may be mounted to right side of engine by means of a rubber elbow.

If larger carburetor is used, the oil pump must be removed.

If oil pump is removed:

- Fuel-to-oil ratio of approximately 20:1 or 24:1 will be required.

- New throttle cable will be required.

JT 1 AND 2 SPECIAL

Port Diagram
Cylinder Part No. 109-11311-70-00
All Dimensions in Millimeters:
Tolerance: ± 0.5mm

CAUTION

When modifying rear booster port, be careful not to remove center bridge [A] since this would damage the piston ring.

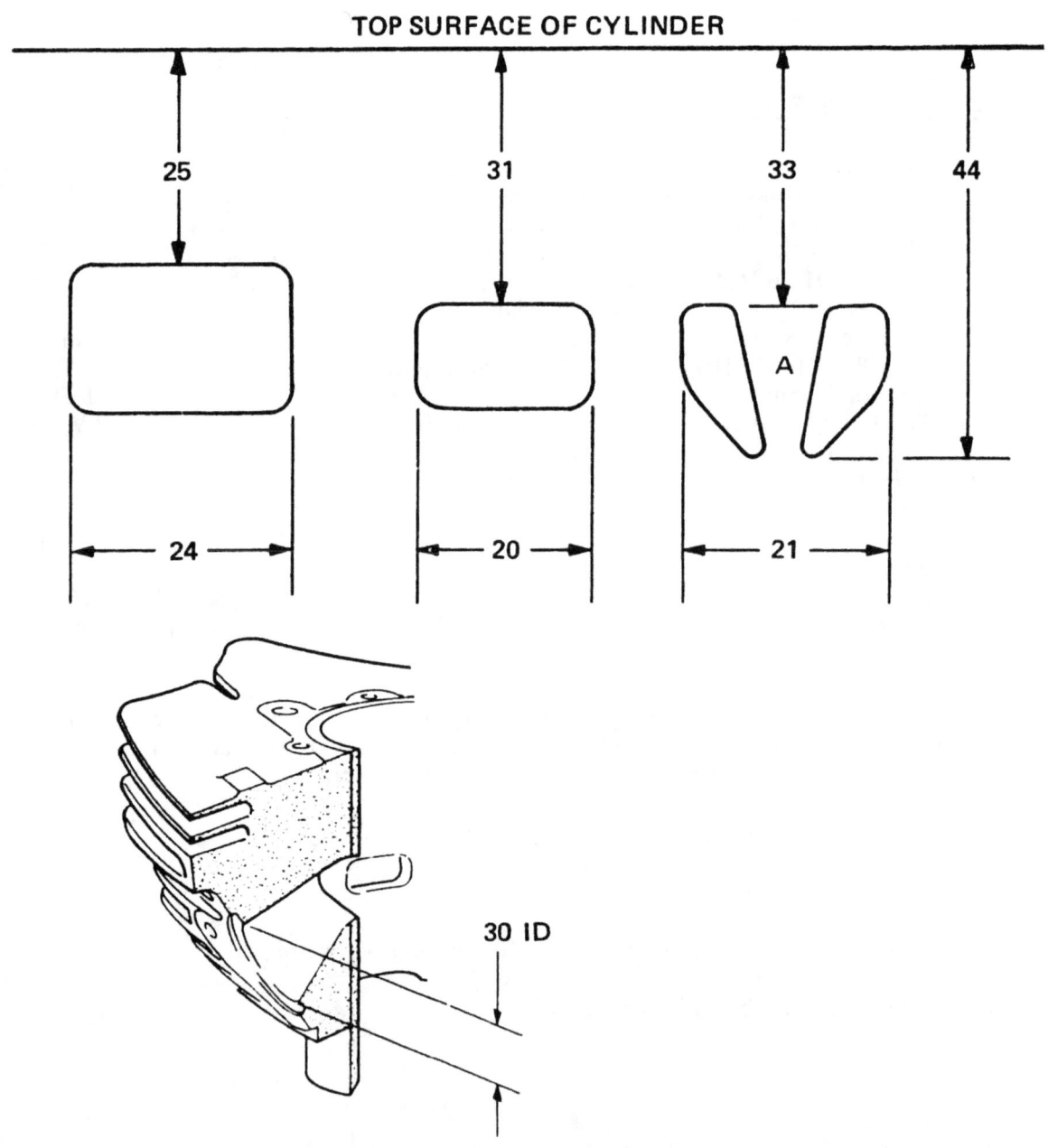

JT 1 AND 2 SPECIAL

Piston Diagram
Piston Part No. 109-11631-70-00
Piston Ring Part No. 109-11602-01-00
All Dimensions in Millimeters:
Tolerances: ± 0mm

CAUTION

After cutting off a portion of the piston skirt, be sure to check for cracks along edge of skirt and around intake ports after each race.

If there is evidence of cracks or extreme wear, replace piston.

NOTE

When modifying piston skirt, be sure to modify the intake side only. This will change port timing.

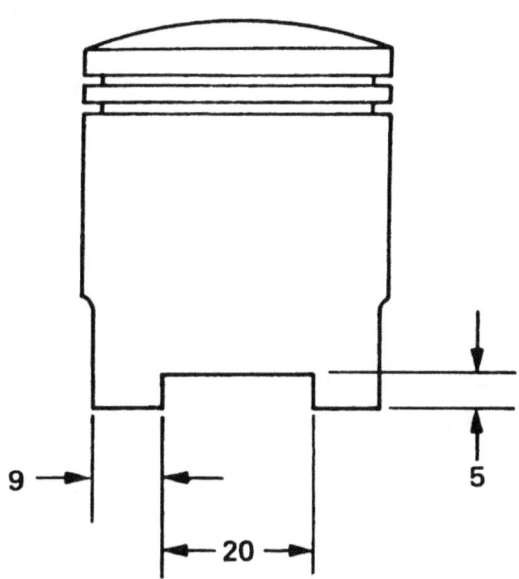

JT 1 AND 2 SPECIAL

Rotary Valve Cover.

If special type 18mm carburetor is to be used, rotary valve cover [1] must be modified.

If the special type 18mm carburetor cannot be obtained, do not modify rotary valve cover.

If rotary valve cover is modified, be sure intake port [4] on crankcase housing is also enlarged to 18mm ID.

The throat opening on the rotary valve cover is 16mm ID on outer end [3] and 17mm ID on inner end [2]. Modification of rotary valve cover consists of enlarging throat opening to 18mm ID.

There are two methods available for modifying rotary valve cover:

Method one does not allow cover to be returned to stock configuration.

Method One:

- Measure and cut 14mm from outer end of throat.

- Weld or braze 23mm wide and 44mm long tubular stock to rotary valve cover.

- Drill center of stock to 18mm ID.

Method Two:

- Weld or braze 23mm wide and 30mm long tubular stock to outer end of throat.

- Using braze, fill in step area between rotary valve cover and stock.

- Drill center of stock to 18mm ID.

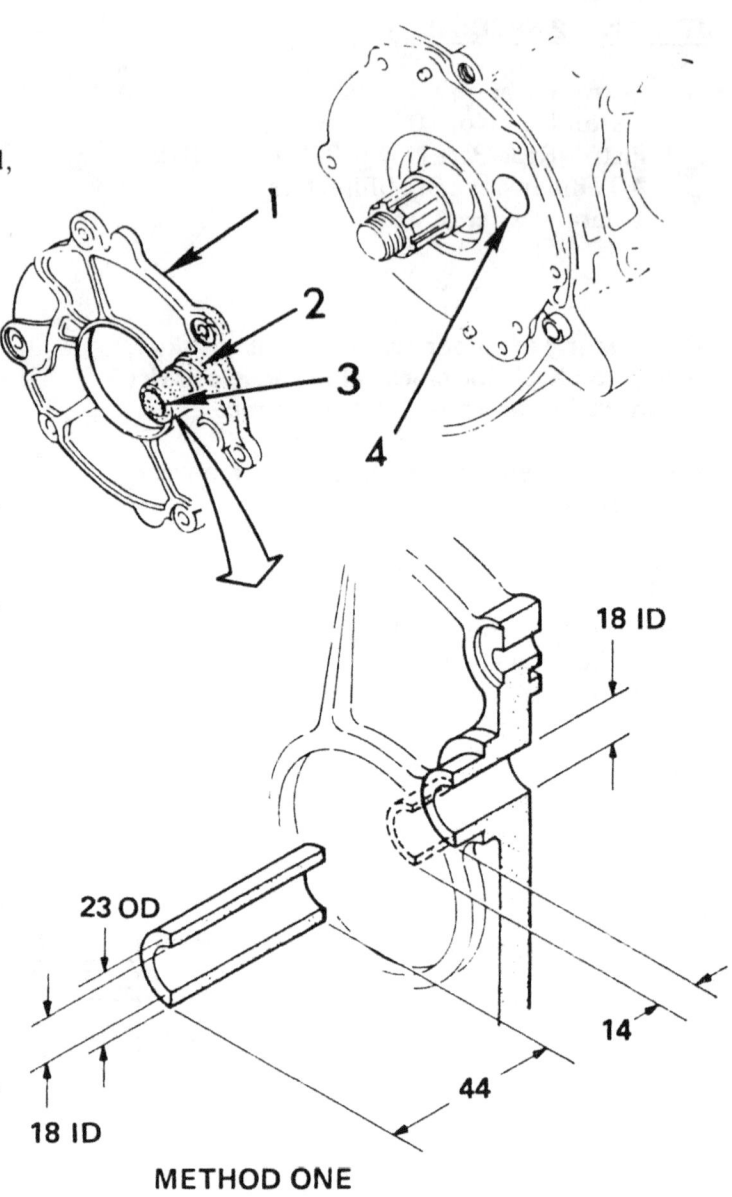

METHOD ONE

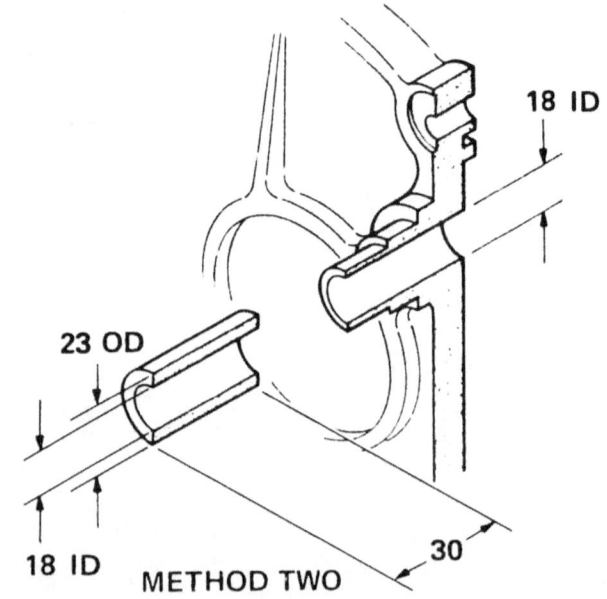

METHOD TWO

JT 1 AND 2 SPECIAL

Rotary Valve Diagram
Rotary Valve Part No. 257-13512-00-00

NOTE

The rotary valve diagram is drawn to actual size and may be used as a template when modifying valve.

When installing rotary valve:

- Be sure that piston is at bottom of stroke.

- Be sure that two indent marks [1] on valve are aligned with shear pin on crankshaft.

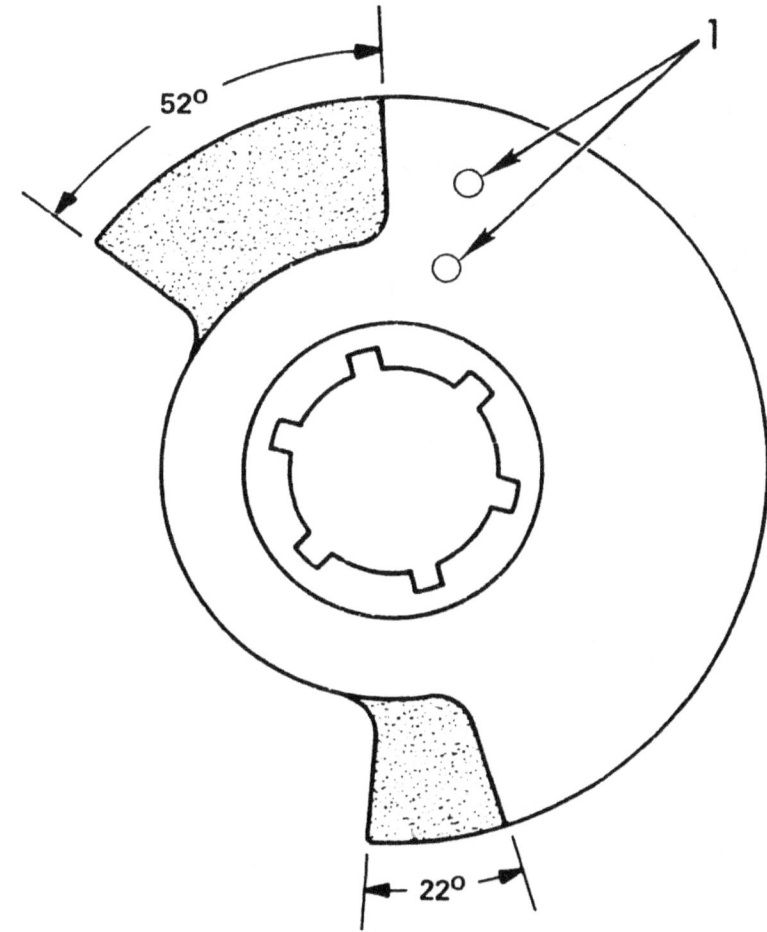

JT 1 AND 2 SPECIAL

Expansion Chamber P/N 109-14610-10-00
Material Thickness 1mm
All Dimensions in Millimeters:
Tolerance: ± 1.0mm

NOTE

Modify stock expansion chamber as shown in sketch.

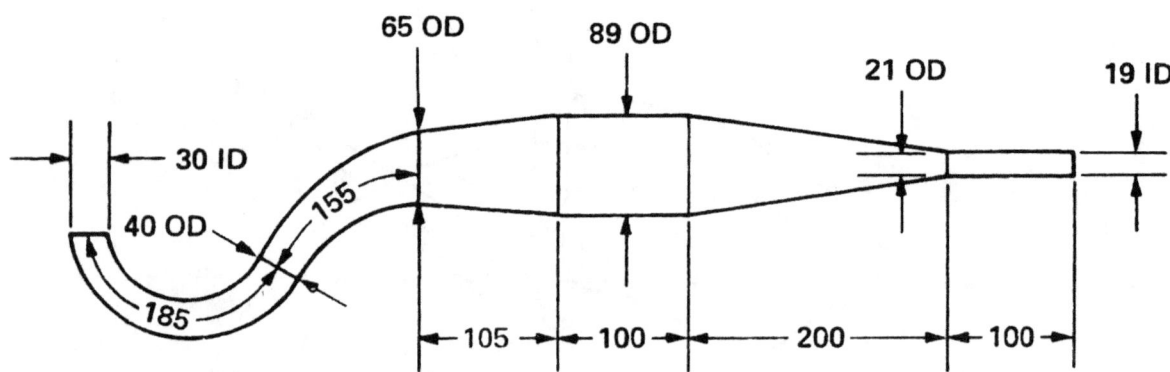

PARTS LISTS

MINI ENDURO JT1 AND JT1L

MINI ENDURO JT2 AND JT2·MX

NOTES

JT1L Electrical component parts are shown
at the end of the JT1 parts list.

The Part Numbers in these parts lists were generated in
the early 1970's when these models were new and they may
have changed since they were published.
However, they are a good starting point when seeking
replacement parts, and your YAMAHA dealer will likely be
able to provide you with updated part numbers which should be
noted in the list.

NOTICE

ALL PART NUMBERS CONTAINED IN THIS CATALOGUE ARE COMPRISED OF TEN DIGITS. WHEN ORDERING, PLEASE ADD TWO ZEROS TO THE END OF EACH PART NUMBER REQUIRED TO CONVERT THE TEN DIGITS INTO THE NEW TWELVE DIGIT NUMBERS.

JT1

JT2

JT2-MX

FOREWORD

This Parts List relates to the parts in use for the Yamaha JT1, JT1L, JT2 & JT2-MX. When you are ordering replacement parts, refer to this Parts List and quote both part numbers and part names correctly.

1. Structure of Part No.

   Yamaha parts are divided largely into two categories; general parts and standard parts, and each part No. has the following structure:

   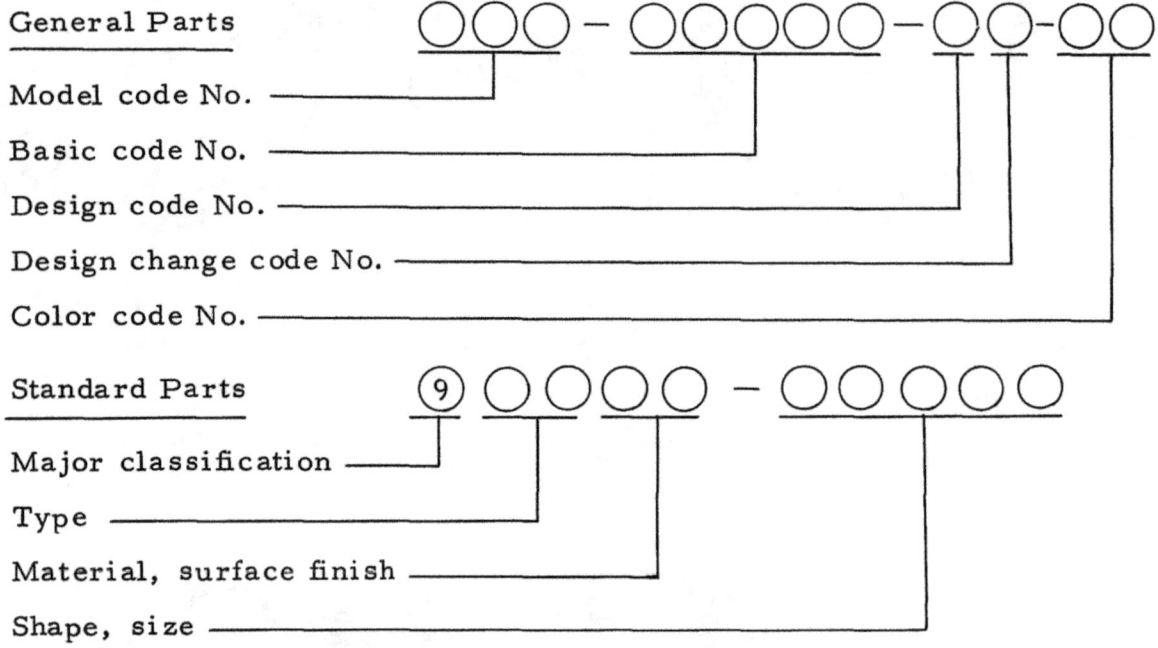

   General Parts
   - Model code No.
   - Basic code No.
   - Design code No.
   - Design change code No.
   - Color code No.

   Standard Parts
   - Major classification
   - Type
   - Material, surface finish
   - Shape, size

   Note: Every standard No. begins with 9.

2. How to Use this Parts List

   (1) Except for steel balls (whose size is indicated in inches), the size of all parts is indicated in millimeters in the following manner.

       Pipe (rubber or vinyl) ..... Inside diameter - length

       O-ring .... Sectional area - inside diameter

       Washer, shim, collar ...... Inside diameter - outside diameter - thickness (length)

   (2) Parts, which are to be supplied in the form of assemblies, are listed with an indention of one letter's space, and a dot (.) is put

against the name of each part. If any two different assemblies (e.g., right and left side components) consist of almost the same type components, these two assemblies are listed in two lines, and then the names of component parts are listed in the subsequent lines with an indention as mentioned earlier. The quantity of parts is given in the following manner; that is, in the case of parts being the same in type between the right and left, a total quantity of parts is given. On the other hand, if the right and left side parts are different in type, the quantity of part(s) on each side is given.

Example

Description	Q'ty
CARBURETOR ASS'Y, left	1
CARBURETOR ASS'Y, right	1
. JET, pilot	2
. NOZZLE, main	2
⋮	
. LEVER, starter, left	1
. LEVER, starter, right	1

(3) Key to Symbols

U.R.	.....	Use size (thickness) and/or number as required
T	.....	Number of teeth in a gear
V	......	Voltage for light bulbs
S	......	"S" type oil seal or "S" type circlip
SD	......	"SD" type oil seal
SO	......	"SO" type oil seal
SW	......	"SW" type oil seal
E	......	"E" type circlip
R	......	"R" type circlip

F/No. .... Frame No. (Applicable machine No.)
S.R .... Suggested retail price
☆ .... Government inspected parts
L.H .... Left hand side (viewed from rider's seat facing forward).
R.H .... Right hand side (viewed from rider's seat facing forward).

(4) The right and left in relation to parts are determined on the basis of the rider facing toward the front.

(5) This Parts List is based on the models in production between June 1970 and July 1971. Accordingly, any modifications which have been made to parts will be announced in the Yamaha Parts News. It is advisable that according to the Yamaha Parts News, you will make necessary corrections to the Parts List on hand to keep it up-to-dated.

YAMAHA
PARTS LIST
MINI ENDURO JT1
MINI ENDURO JT1L

Fig. 1 CRANKCASE & CYLINDER

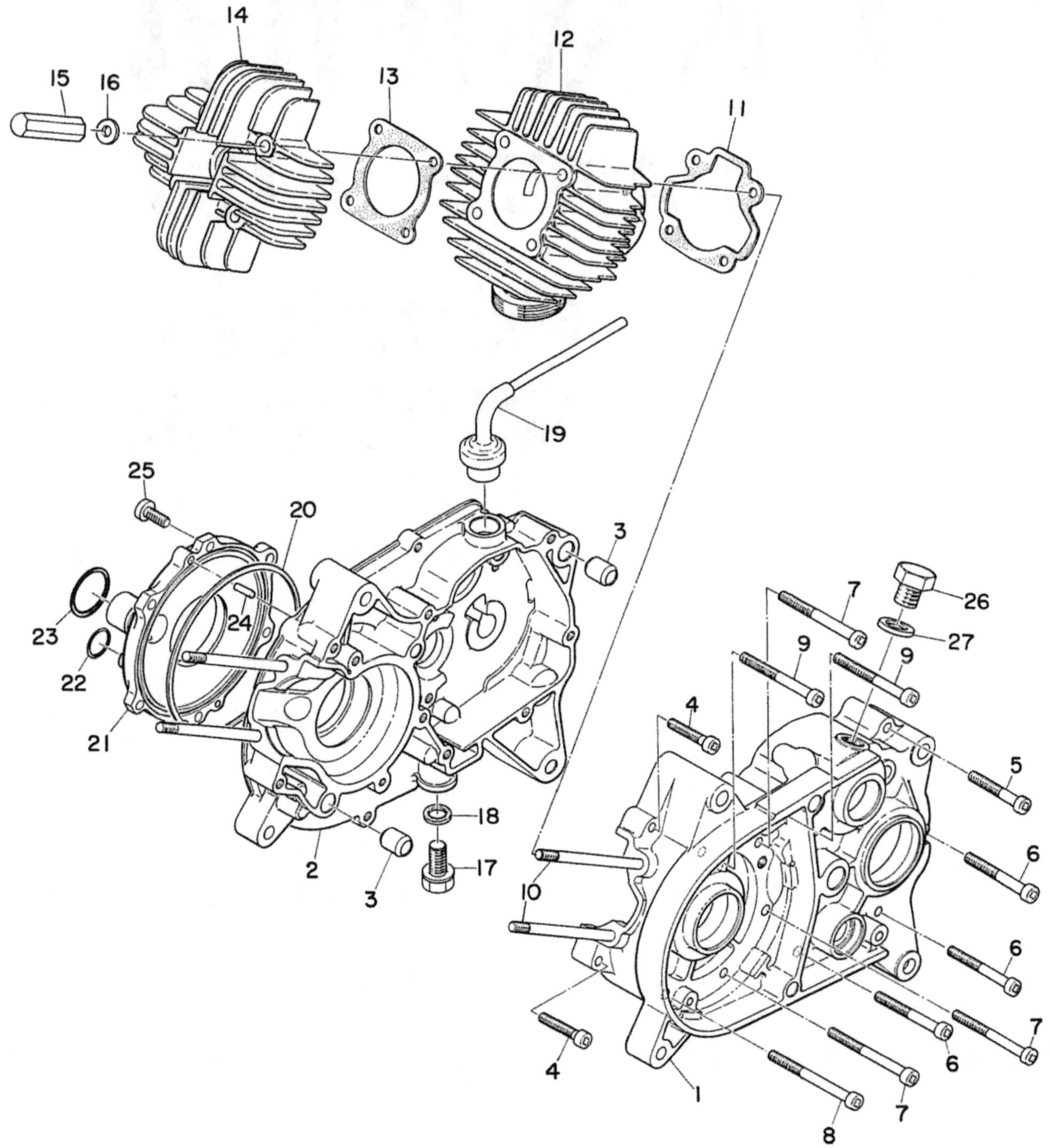

CRANKCASE & CYLINDER

Ref. No.	Part No.	Description	Q'ty	Applicable Machine No.	Remarks
1- 1	257-15111-00	CASE, crank left	1		
1- 2	257-15121-00	CASE, crank right	1		
1- 3	91810-08016	PIN, dowel (9.8-12-16)	2		
1- 4	92501-06030	SCREW, pan head	2		
1- 5	92501-06045	SCREW, pan head	1		
1- 6	92501-06050	SCREW, pan head	3		
1- 7	92501-06060	SCREW, pan head	3		
1- 8	92501-06065	SCREW, pan head	1		
1- 9	92501-06055	SCREW, pan head	2		
1-10	109-11361-00	BOLT, cylinder holding	4		
1-11	109-11351-00	GASKET, cylinder	1		
1-12	259-11311-00	CYLINDER	1		
1-13	107-11181-01	GASKET, cylinder head	1		
1-14	259-11111-01-94	HEAD, cylinder	1		
1-15	126-11171-60	NUT, cylinder holding	4		
1-16	92901-06200	WASHER, plain	4		
1-17	132-15351-00	PLUG, drain	1		
1-18	132-15353-00	GASKET, drain plug	1		
1-19	288-15371-00	BREATHER	1		
1-20	180-13554-00	RING, rubber	1		
1-21	257-13551-00	COVER, valve	1		
1-22	93210-23029	O-RING (3.53-21.82)	1		
1-23	93210-12014	O-RING (2.62-10.77)	1		
1-24	93604-14012	PIN, dowel (4-13.8)	2		

CRANKCASE & CYLINDER

Ref. No.	Part No.	Description	Q'ty	Applicable Machine No.	Remarks
1-25	92501-06015	SCREW, pan head	6		
1-26	288-18588-00	PLUG, blind	1		
1-27	136-82543-00	GASKET (11.6-18-1)	1		

Fig. 2 CRANKCASE COVER

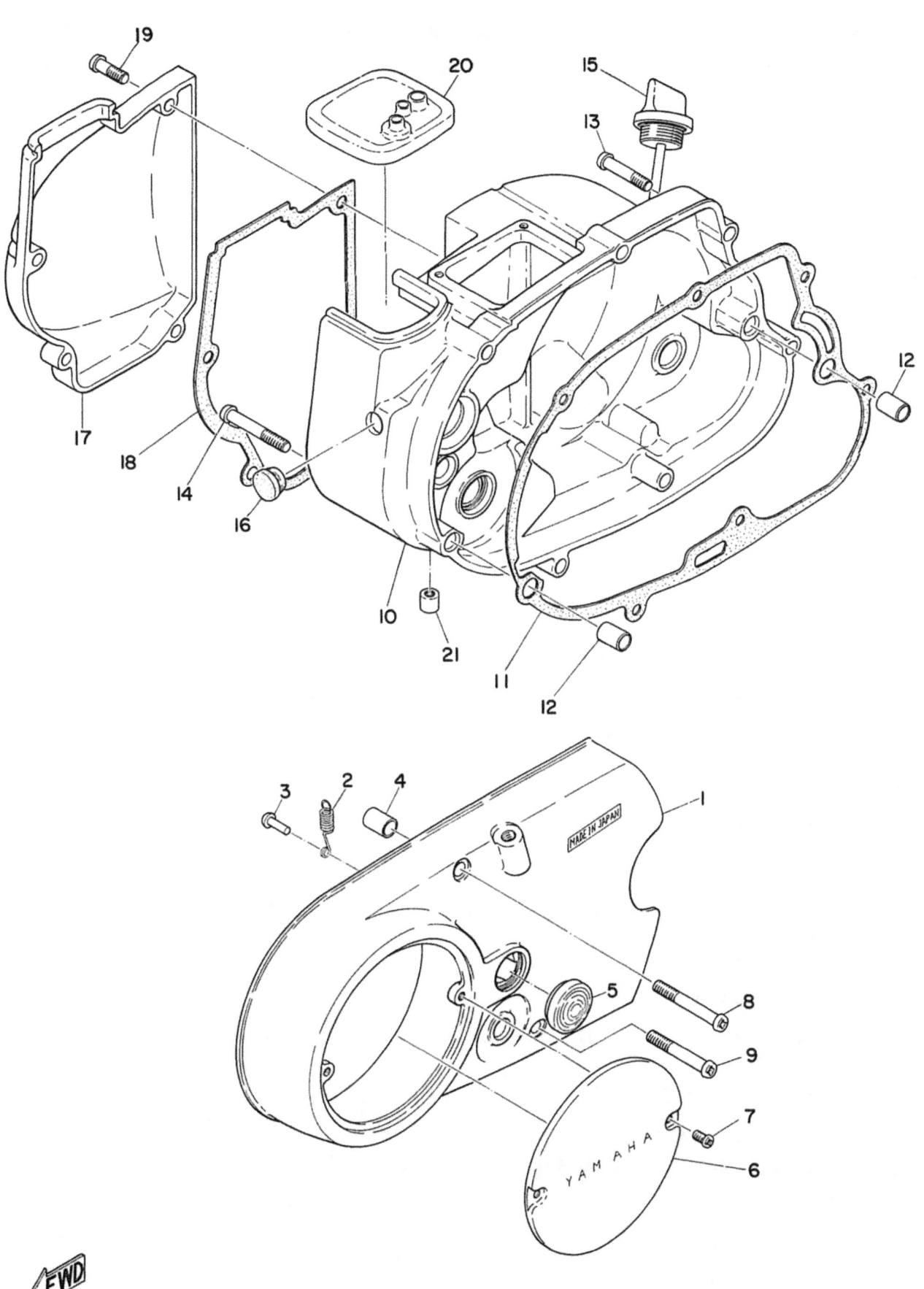

CRANKCASE COVER

Ref. No.	Part No.	Description	Q'ty	Applicable Machine No.	Remarks
2- 1	257-15410-00	CRANKCASE COVER ASS'Y, left	1		
2- 2	257-16345-00	. SPRING, lever return	1		
2- 3	132-16346-00	. HOOK, spring	1		
2- 4	91810-03014	PIN, dowel (8.5-10-14)	2		
2- 5	257-15417-01	COVER, cap	1		
2- 6	164-15415-00	COVER, generator	1		
2- 7	98501-04008	SCREW, pan head	2		
2- 8	92501 06045	SCREW, pan head	2		
2- 9	92501-06040	SCREW, pan head	1		
2-10	257-15421-00	COVER, crankcase, right	1		
2-11	257-15451-00	GASKET, crankcase cover	1		
2-12	91810-03014	PIN, dowel (8.5-10-14)	2		
2-13	92501-06030	SCREW, pan head	6		
2-14	92501-06040	SCREW, pan head	1		
2-15	180-15362-00	PLUG, oil level	1		
2-16	122-15486-00	GROMMET	1		
2-17	257-15413-00	COVER, carburetor	1		
2-18	257-15463-00	GASKET, caburetor cover	1		
2-19	92501-06018	SCREW, pan head	4		
2-20	288-14481-00	CAP, carburetor	1		
2-21	257-15433-00	CLEANER, drain	1		

Fig. 3 CRANK & PISTON

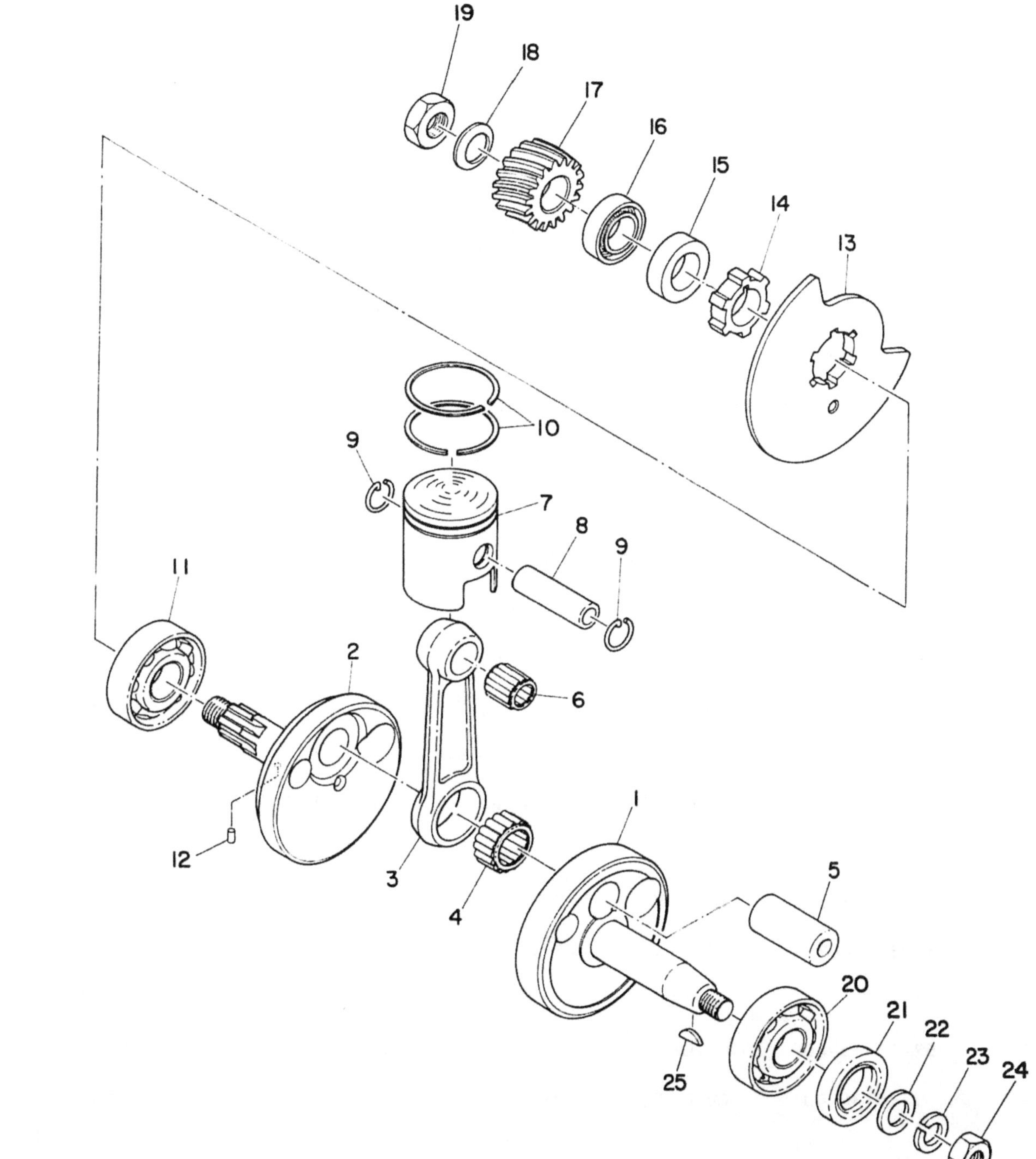

CRANK & PISTON

Ref. No.	Part No.	Description	Q'ty	Applicable Machine No.	Remarks
3- 0-1	259-11400-00	CRANK ASS'Y	1		
3- 1	259-11412-00	. CRANK, left	1		
3- 2	259-11422-00	. CRANK, right	1		
3- 3	126-11651-00	. ROD, connecting	1		
3- 4	93310-41810	. BEARING, con-rod big end	1		
3- 5	257-11681-00	. PIN, crank	1		
3- 6	93310-11202	BEARING, con-rod smallend	1		
3- 7	289-11631-00-96	PISTON (.96)	U.R. 1		STD
	289-11631-00-97	PISTON (.97)			
	289-11631-00-98	PISTON (.98)			
	289-11631-00-99	PISTON (.99)			
	289-11635-00	PISTON (1st o.s)	1		
	289-11636-00	PISTON (2nd o.s)	1		
3- 8	102-11633-01	PIN, piston	1		
3- 9	132-11634-00	CLIP, piston pin	2		
3-10	113-11601-02	PISTON RING SET	1s		STD
	113-11601-12	PISTON RING SET (1set o.s)	1s		
	113-11601-22	PISTON RING SET (2nd o.s)	1s		
3-11	93306-30302	BEARING (6303C3)	1		
3-12	93603-08067	PIN, dowel (3-8)	1		
3-13	257-13512-00	VALVE	1		
3-14	257-13515-00	COLLAR, valve	1		
3-15	257-16136-00	COLLAR, distance	1		
3-16	93103-28012	OIL SEAL (SW-27-47-8)	1		
3-17	257-16111-00	GEAR, primary drive (19T)	1		

CRANK & PISTON

Ref. No.	Part No.	Description	Q'ty	Applicable Machine No.	Remarks
3-18	164-16119-00	SPRING, bellevile	1		
3-19	137-16377-00	NUT, clutch boss	1		
3-20	93306-20408	BEARING (6204C3)	1		
3-21	93102-20009	OIL SEAL (SD-20-35-7)	1		
3-22	214-11557-01	WASHER (12.2-22-2.9)	1		
3-23	92901-12100	WASHER, spring	1		
3-24	98801-12200	NUT	1		
3-25	146-11545-00	KEY, woodruff	1		

Fig. 4 CLUTCH

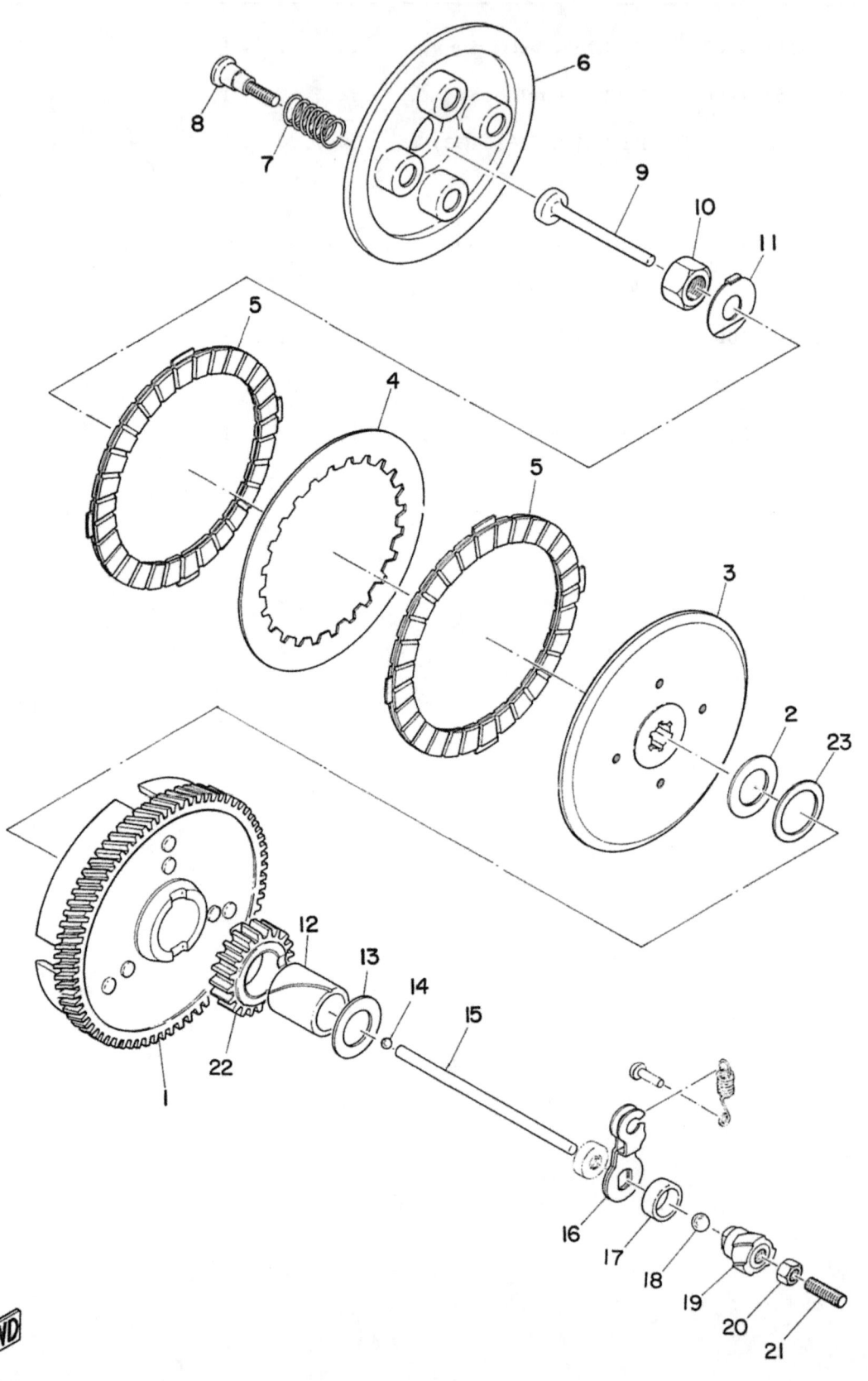

CLUTCH

Ref. No.	Part No.	Description	Q'ty	Applicable Machine No.	Remarks
4- 0-1	257-16301-01	CLUTCH ASS'Y	1		
4- 1	257-16150-01	. DRIVEN GEAR COMP. (74T)	1		
4- 2	122-16164-00	. PLATE, thrust (17.2-30-2)	1		
4- 3	257-16371-00	. BOSS, clutch	1		
4- 4	257-16324-00	. PLATE, clutch	1		
4- 5	131-16321-00	. PLATE, friction	2		
4- 6	257-16351-00	. PLATE, pressure	1		
4- 7	137-16333-00	. SPRING, clutch	4		
4- 8	137-16337-01	. SCREW, spring	4		
4- 9	137-16356-00	ROD, push 1	1		
4-10	137-16377-00	NUT, clutch boss	1		
4-11	137-16378-00	WASHER, clutch boss	1		
4-12	257-16181-00	SPACER	1		
4-13	122-16164-00	PLATE, thrust (17.2-30-2)	1		
4-14	93503-16003	BALL (3/16 inch)	1		
4-15	257-16357-00	ROD, push 2	1		
4-16	257-16342-00	LEVER, push	1		
4-17	93108-15001	OIL SEAL (OSO-15-22-7)	1		
4-18	93501-04004	BALL (1/4 inch)	1		
4-19	257-16341-00	SCREW, push	1		
4-20	92801-06300	NUT	1		
4-21	257-16343-00	SCREW, adjusting	1		
4-22	164-15631-01	GEAR, kick pinion (19T)	1		
4-23	116-16153-00	WASHER, thrust (23-30-1.5)	1		

Fig. 5 TRANSMISSION

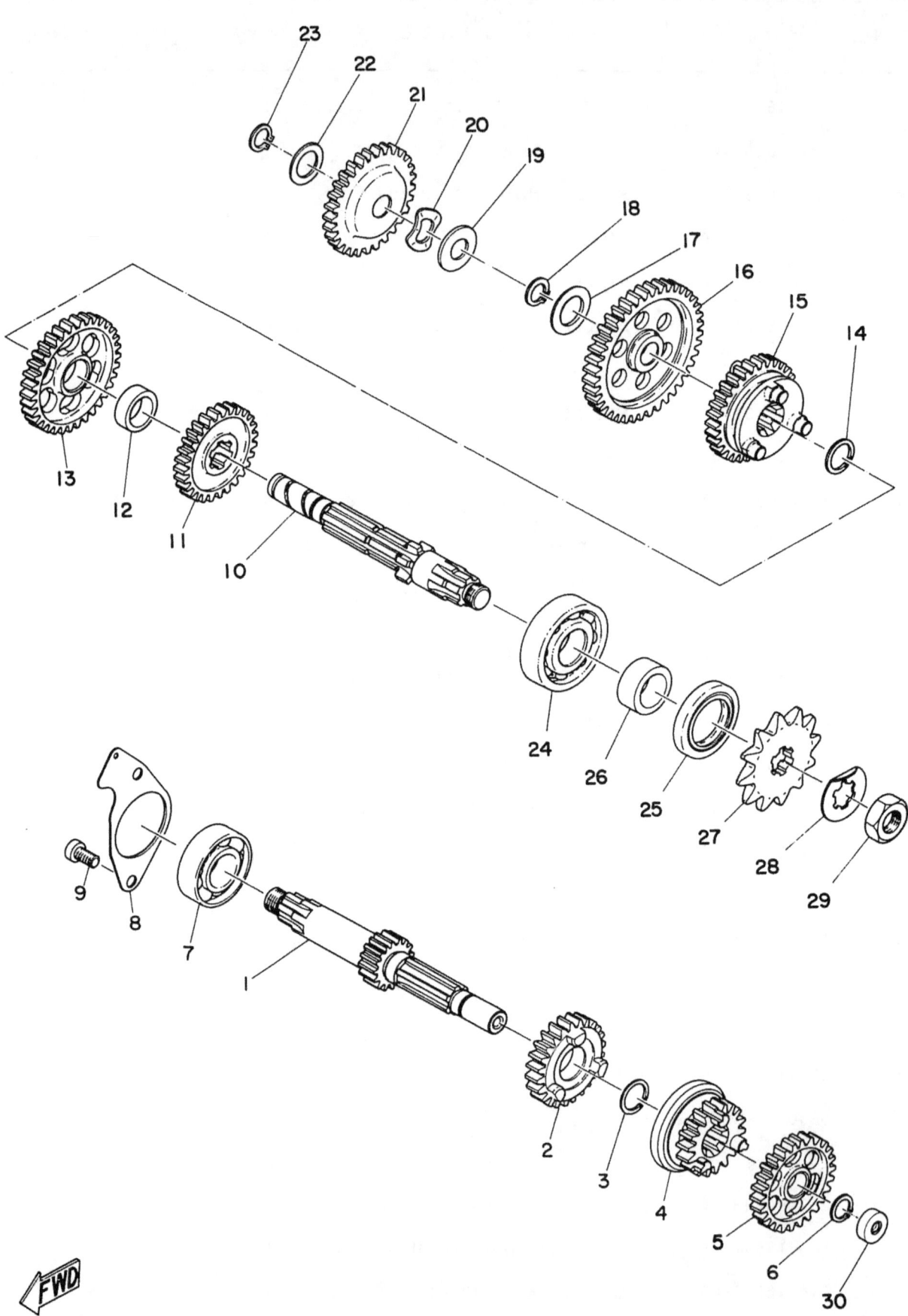

TRANSMISSION

Ref. No.	Part No.	Description	Q'ty	Applicable Machine No.	Remarks
5- 1	257-17411-01	AXLE, main (13T)	1		
5- 2	257-17131-01	GEAR, 3rd pinion (23T)	1		
5- 3	257-17414-00	CLIP	1		
5- 4	257-17121-00	GEAR, 2nd pinion (18T)	1		
5- 5	257-17141-00	GEAR, 4th pinion (26T)	1		
5- 6	93410-13004	CIRCLIP (S-13)	1		
5- 7	93306-20301	BEARING (6203)	1		
5- 8	257-17471-00	PLATE, bearing cover	1		
5- 9	92501-06012	SCREW, pan head	2		
5-10	257-17421-01	AXLE, drive	1		
5-11	257-17241-00	GEAR, 4th wheel (27T)	1		
5-12	257-17258-00	COLLAR, distance	1		
5-13	257-17221-01	GEAR, 2nd wheel (34T)	1		
5-14	257-17414-00	CLIP	1		
5-15	257-17231-00	GEAR, 3rd wheel (30T)	1		
5-16	257-17211-00	GEAR, 1st wheel (40T)	1		
5-17	257-17219-00-06	SHIM (13.2-24-0.6)	1		
5-18	93410-13004	CIRCLIP (S-13)	1		
5-19	201-15653-00	WASHER, thrust (13.2-23-1)	1		
5-20	137-15643-00	WASHER, wave	1		
5-21	257-15651-00	GEAR, kick idle (28T)	1		
5-22	132-15653-00-10	WASHER, thrust (13.3-22-1.0)	1	U.R	
	132-15653-00-12	WASHER, thrust (13.3-22-1.2)			
	132-15653-00-14	WASHER, thrust (13.3-22-1.4)			

TRANSMISSION

Ref. No.	Part No.	Description	Q'ty	Applicable Machine No.	Remarks
5-23	93410-13004	CIRCLIP (S-13)	1		
5-24	93306-30305	BEARING (6303)	1		
5-25	93102-25017	OIL SEAL (SD-25-40-5)	1		
5-26	257-17462-00	COLLAR, distance	1		
5-27	257-17461-20	SPROCKET, drive (12T)	⎫		
	257-17461-30	SPROCKET, drive (13T)	⎬ 1	U.R	STD
	257-17461-40	SPROCKET, drive (14T)	⎬		
	257-17461-50	SPROCKET, drive (15T)	⎭		
5-28	257-17464-00	WASHER, lock	1		
5-29	257-17463-00	NUT, lock	1		
5-30	257-15389-00	SEAL, push rod	1		

Fig. 6 SHIFTER A

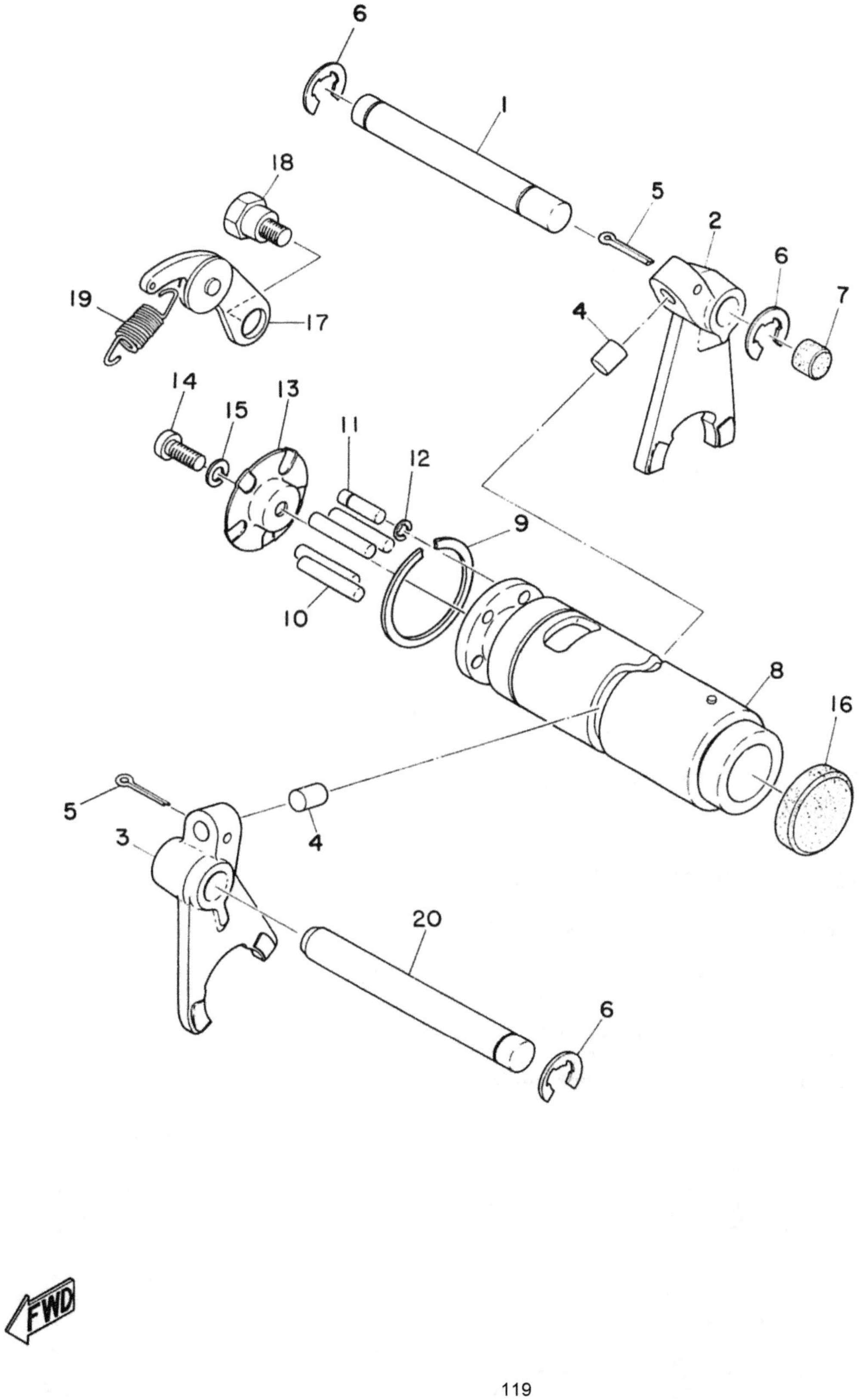

SHIFTER A

Ref. No.	Part No.	Description	Q'ty	Applicable Machine No.	Remarks
6- 1	257-18534-00	BAR, shift fork guide	1		
6- 2	259-18511-00	FORK, shift 1	1		
6- 3	257-18512-00	FORK, shift 2	1		
6- 4	257-18552-00	PIN, cam follower	2		
6- 5	91401-25017	PIN, cotter	2		
6- 6	93430-08006	CIRCLIP (E-8)	3		
6- 7	150-18328-00	PLUG, blind	1		
6- 8	257-18541-60	CAM, shaft	1		
6- 9	93440-32017	CIRCLIP	1		
6-10	93604-22050	PIN, dowel (4-21.8)	4		
6-11	174-18544-00	PIN, locating	1		
6-12	93430-03014	CIRCLIP (E-2.5)	1		
6-13	164-18561-00	PLATE, side	1		
6-14	98501-05012	SCREW, pan head	1		
6-15	92901-05100	WASHER, spring	1		
6-16	257-18589-00	PLUG, blind	1		
6-17	132-18140-00	STOPPER LEVER ASS'Y	1		
6-18	132-18177-00	BOLT, stopper	1		
6-19	132-18143-00	SPRING, stopper	1		
6-20	257-18531-00	BAR, shift fork guide	1		

Fig. 7 SHIFTER B

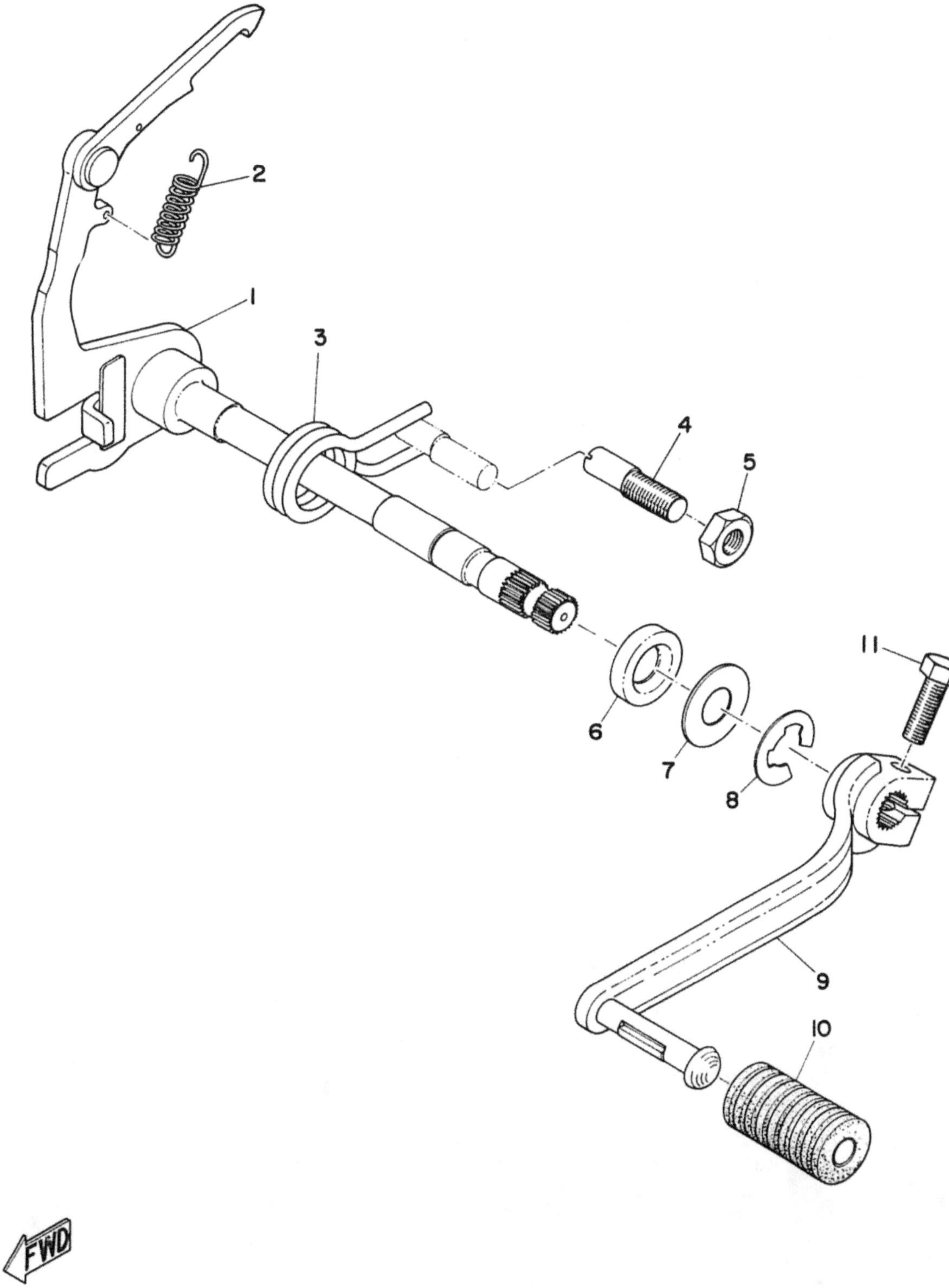

SHIFTER B

Ref. No.	Part No.	Description	Q'ty	Applicable Machine No.	Remarks
7- 1	257-18101-00	CHANGE SHAFT ASS'Y	1		
7- 2	132-18123-00	. SPRING, shift arm	1		
7- 3	132-18124-00	SPRING, shaft return	1		
7- 4	132-18133-00	SCREW, adjusting	1		
7- 5	98800-08100	NUT	1		
7- 6	93101-12004	OIL SEAL (S-12-22-5)	1		
7- 7	132-18137-00	WASHER, change axle (14.1-28-1.6)	1		
7- 8	93430-10016	CIRCLIP (E-10)	1		
7- 9	248-18111-00-93	PEDAL, change	1		
7-10	132-18113-01	COVER, change pedal	1		
7-11	91201-06020	BOLT	1		

Fig. 8   KICK

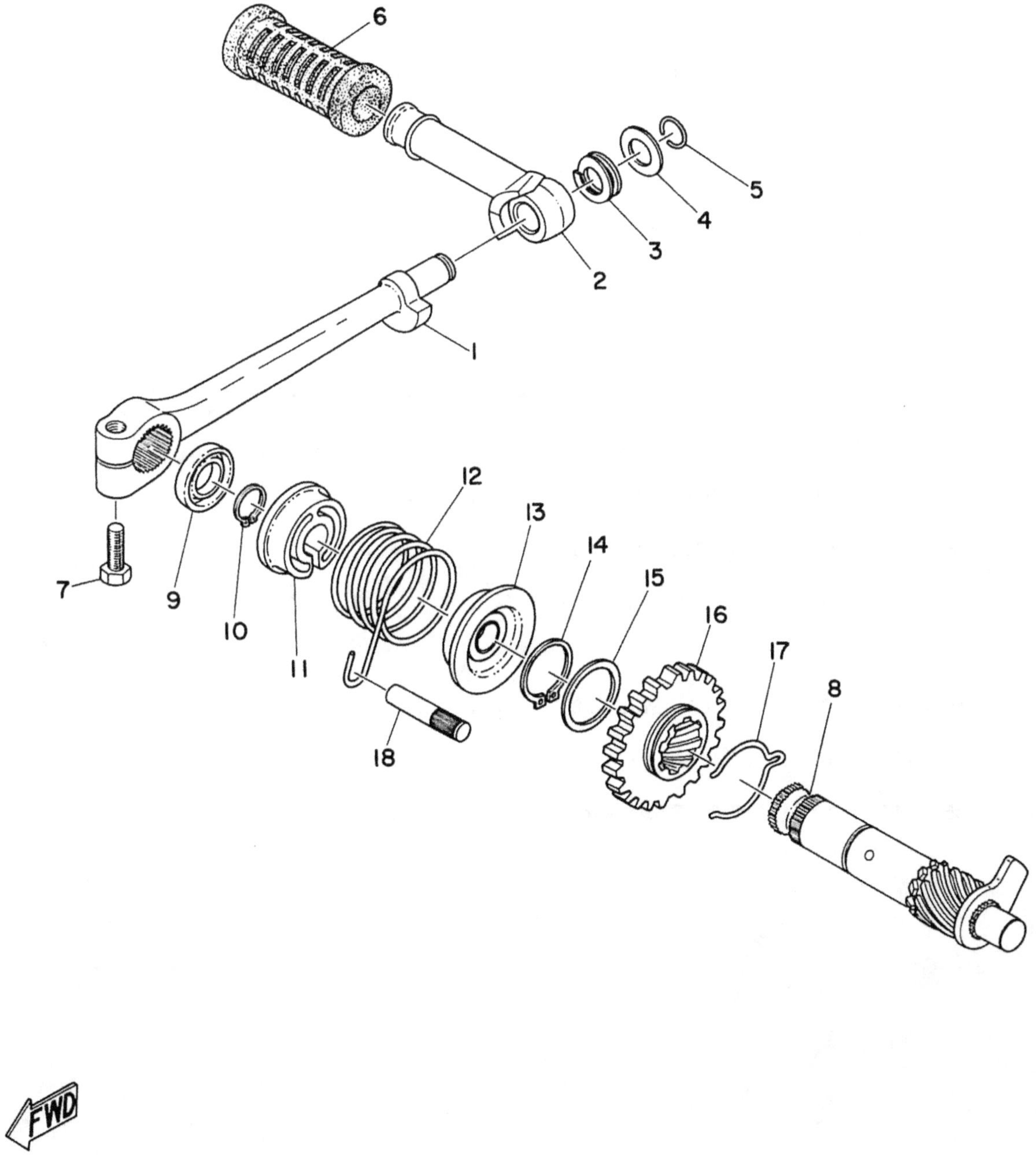

KICK

Ref. No.	Part No.	Description	Q'ty	Applicable Machine No.	Remarks
8- 0-1	276-15610-00-93	KICK CRANK ASS'Y	1		
8- 1	276-15611-00	. CRANK, kick	1		Not for sale
8- 2	122-15612-01	. LEVER, kick	1		
8- 3	214-15625-00	. SPRING, kick crank	1		
8- 4	132-15616-00	. WASHER, kick lever	1		
8- 5	132-15617-00	. CLIP, kick lever	1		
8- 6	156-15618-01	COVER, kick lever	1		
8- 7	91101-06020	BOLT	1		
8- 8	180-15660-00	KICK AXLE ASS'Y	1		
8- 9	93109-15001	OIL SEAL (SDO-15-26-6)	1		
8-10	93410-15005	CIRCLIP (S-15)	1		
8-11	132-15676-00	COVER, kick spring	1		
8-12	132-15665-00	SPRING, kick	1		
8-13	132-15664-00	GUIDE, kick spring	1		
8-14	93410-25017	CIRCLIP (S-25)	1		
8-15	117-15644-00	SHIM (25.1-32-1)	1		
8-16	180-15641-00	GEAR, kick (28T)	1		
8-17	180-15687-00	CLIP, kick	1		
8-18	257-15668-00	STOPPER, kick spring	1		

Fig. 9 AIR CLEANER

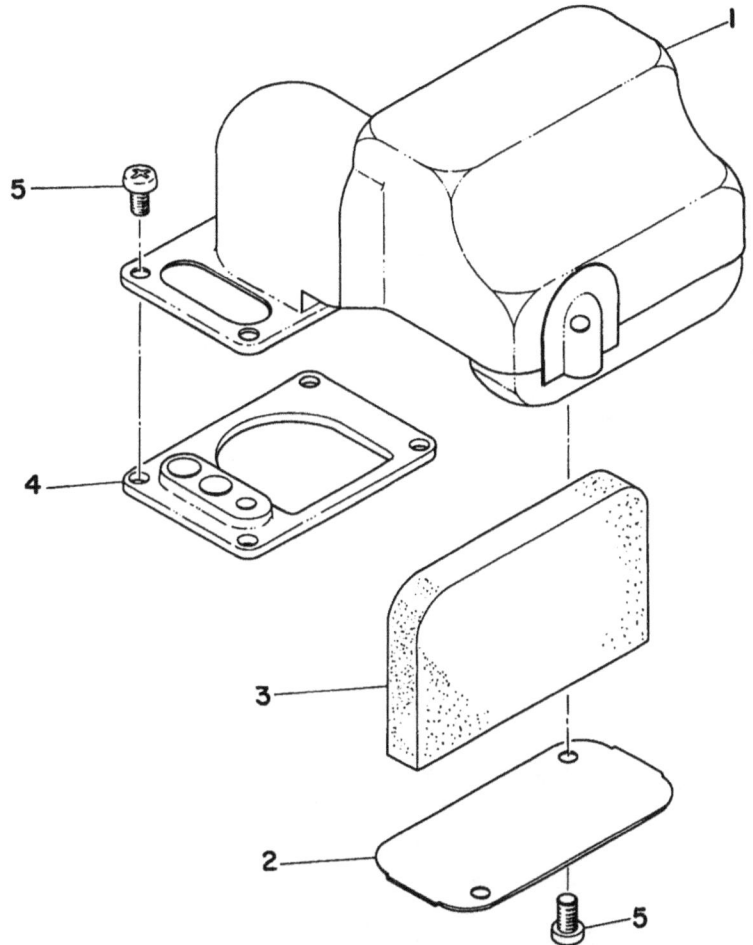

AIR CLEANER

Ref. No.	Part No.	Description	Q'ty	Applicable Machine No.	Remarks
9- 1	288-14411-00	CASE, air cleaner	1		
9- 2	288-14412-00	CAP, case	1		
9- 3	288-14451-00	ELEMENT, air cleaner	1		
9- 4	288-14453-00	JOINT, air cleaner	1		
9- 5	98501-04008	SCREW, pan head	6		

Fig. 10 CARBURETOR

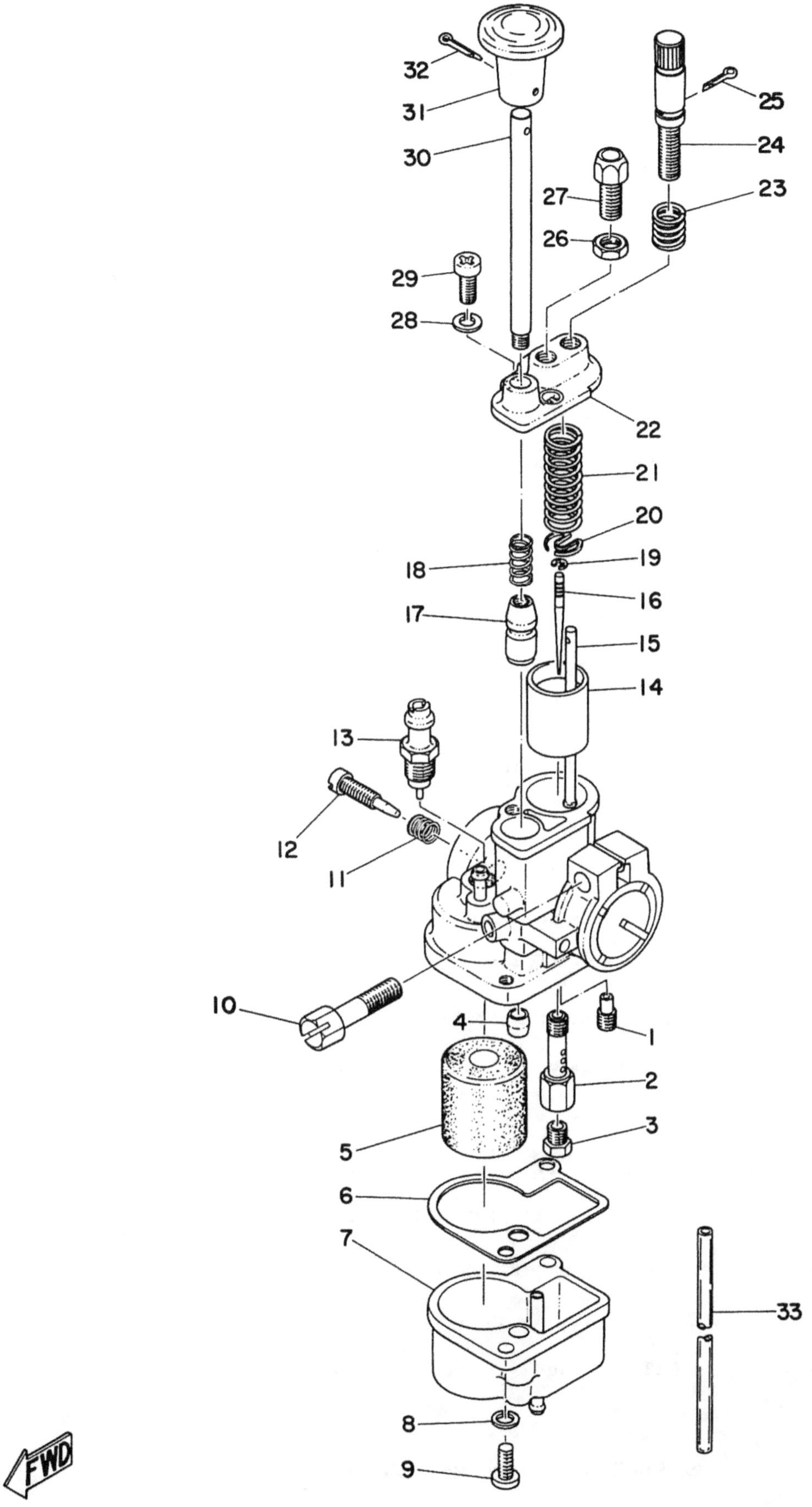

CARBURETOR

Ref. No.	Part No.	Description	Q'ty	Applicable Machine No.	Remarks
10- 0-1	288-14301-00	CARBURETOR ASS'Y	1		
10- 1	288-14342-38	. JET, pilot (#38)	1		
10- 2	288-14341-00	. NOZZLE, main	1		
10- 3	288-14343-42	. JET, main (#84)	1		
	288-14343-43	. JET, main (#86)	1		STD
	288-14343-44	. JET, main (#88)	1		
10- 4	288-14344-25	. JET, starter (#50)	1		
10- 5	288-14385-00	. FLOAT	1		
10- 6	288-14384-00	. GASKET	1		
10- 7	288-14381-00	. BODY, float chamber	1		
10- 8	92901-04100	. WASHER, spring	2		
10- 9	98501-04010	. SCREW, pan head	2		
10-10	288-14125-00	. SCREW, body fitting	1		
10-11	288-14334-00	. SPRING, air adjusting	1		
10-12	288-14323-00	. SCREW, air adjusting	1		
10-13	288-14390-10	. VALVE SEAT ASS'Y (#1.0)	1		
10-14	288-14312-15	. VALVE, throttle (#6.5)	1		
10-15	288-14314-00	. BAR, throttle	1		
10-16	288-14336-00	. NEEDLE	1		
10-17	288-14371-00	. PLUNGER STARTER ASS'Y	1		
10-18	288-14335-00	. SPRING, plunger	1		
10-19	288-14137-00	. CLIP	1		
10-20	288-14136-00	. SEAT, spring	1		
10-21	288-14331-00	. SPRING, throttle valve	1		

CARBURETOR

Ref. No.	Part No.	Description	Q'ty	Applicable Machine No.	Remarks
10-22	288-14158-00	. TOP, mixing chamber	1		
10-23	288-14333-00	. SPRING, throttle stop	1		
10-24	288-14321-00	. SCREW, throttle	1		
10-25	91401-12010	. PIN, cotter	1		
10-26	288-14161-00	. NUT, wire adjusting	1		
10-27	288-14124-00	. SCREW, wire adjusting	1		
10-28	92901-04100	. WASHER, spring	1		
10-29	98501-04010	. SCREW, pan head	1		
10-30	288-14379-00	. ROD, starter	1		
10-31	288-14118-00	KNOB, starter	1		
10-32	91401-16012	PIN, cotter	1		
10-33	288-14197-00	PIPE, air vent	1		

Fig. 11 MUFFLER

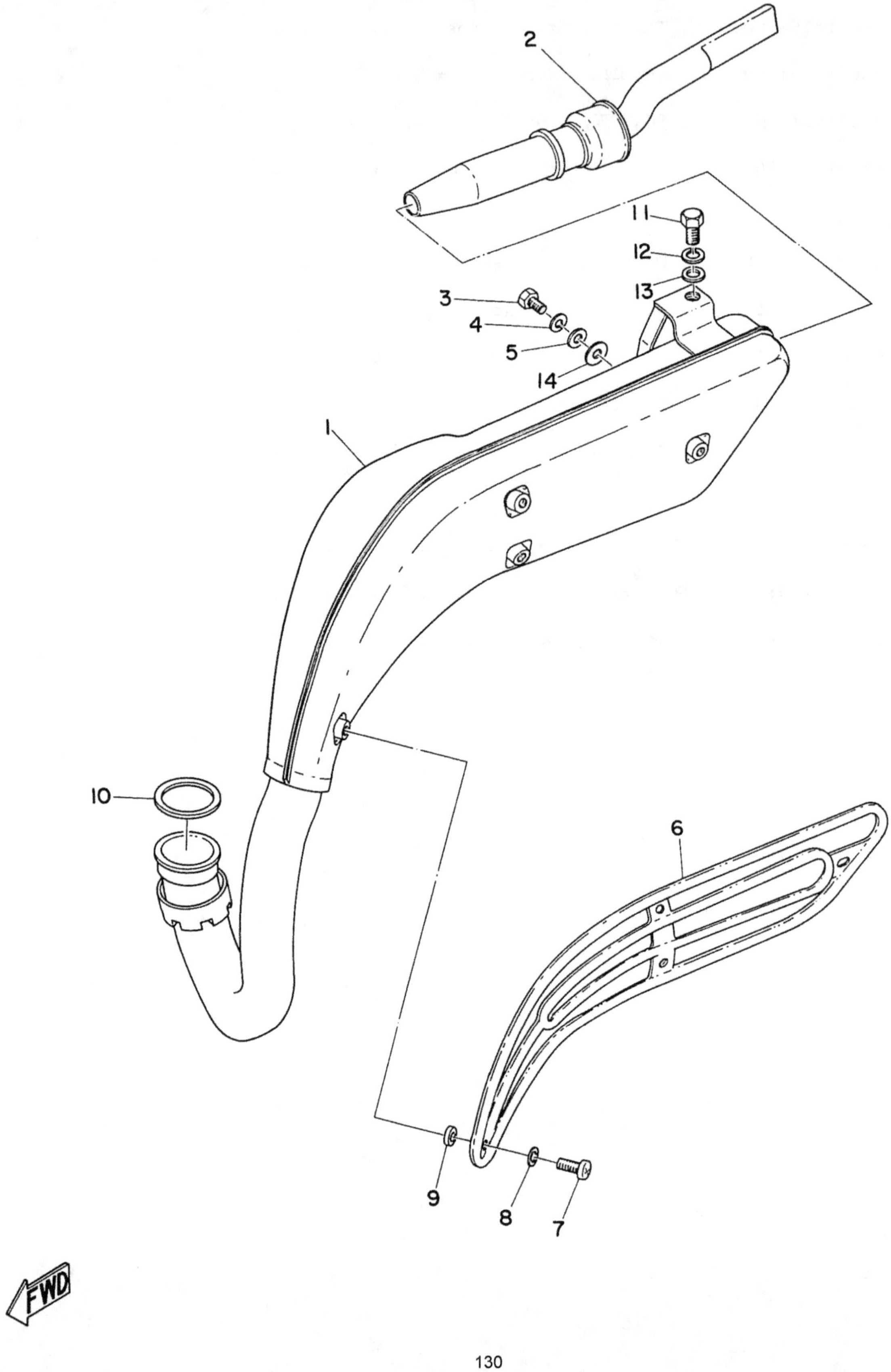

MUFFLER

Ref. No.	Part No.	Description	Q'ty	Applicable Machine No.	Remarks
11- 1	288-14610-30	EXHAUST PIPE ASS'Y	1		
11- 2	288-14752-30	. PIPE, outlet	1		
11- 3	91201-06015	. BOLT	1		
11- 4	92901-06100	. WASHER, spring	1		
11- 5	136-22316-00	. WASHER, chain case (6.5-15-1.2)	1		
11- 6	288-14718-30	PROTECTOR, muffler	1		
11- 7	91903-06010	SCREW, bind	4		
11- 8	178-14766-00	WASHER, protector (6.2-12-3.0)	4		
11- 9	214-14766-00	WASHER, protector (6.2-12-1.5)	4		
11-10	132-14613-00	GASKET, exhaust	1		
11-11	97201-08012	BOLT	1		
11-12	92901-08100	WASHER, spring	1		
11-13	92901-08200	WASHER, plain	1		
11-14	288-14623-00	GASKET	1		

Fig. 12 OIL PUMP

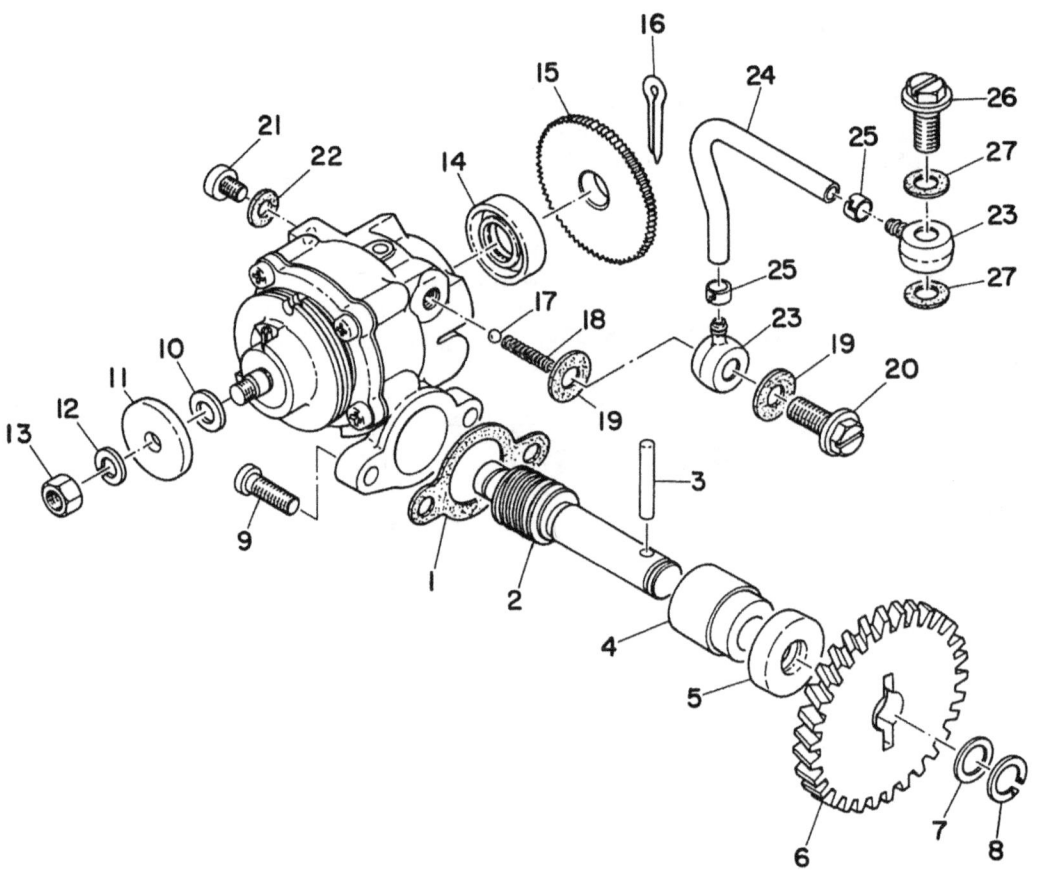

OIL PUMP

Ref. No.	Part No.	Description	Q'ty	Applicable Machine No.	Remarks
12- 1	126-13116-00	GASKET, pump case	1		
12- 2	257-13175-00	SHAFT, worm	1		
12- 3	93603-22028	PIN, dowel	1		
12- 4	137-13176-00	METAL, worm shaft outer	1		
12- 5	93101-10001	OIL SEAL (S-10-21-5)	1		
12- 6	257-13178-00	GEAR, drive (30T)	1		
12- 7	101-18137-00	WASHER (10.5-20-1.0)	1		
12- 8	93440-08001	CIRCLIP	1		
12- 9	98501-05015	SCREW, pan head	2		
12- 0-1	257-13101-00	OIL PUMP ASS'Y	1		
12-10	137-13137-00	. SHIM, plunger (5.8-10-0.1)	1		
12-11	137-13138-01	. PLATE, adjusting	1		
12-12	92901-05100	. WASHER, spring	1		
12-13	98801-05200	. NUT	1		
12-14	93101-10001	. OIL SEAL (S-10-21-5)	1		
12-15	137-13128-00	. PLATE, starter	1		
12-16	91401-12018	. PIN, cotter	1		
12-17	93505-32002	. BALL (5/32 inch)	1		
12-18	137-13169-00	. SPRING, check ball	1		
12-19	137-13167-00	. GASKET, banjo bolt	2		
12-20	137-13165-00	. BOLT, banjo	1		
12-21	98901-04008	. SCREW, bind	1		
12-22	137-13187-00	. GASKET, breather	1		
12-23	214-13162-00	. BANJO	2		

OIL PUMP

Ref. No.	Part No.	Description	Q'ty	Applicable Machine No.	Remarks
12-24	257-13161-00	. PIPE, delivery	1		
12-25	214-13164-00	. CLIP, delivery pipe	2		
12-26	137-13165-00	BOLT, banjo	1		
12-27	137-13167-00	GASKET, banjo	2		

Fig. 13 FLYWHEEL MAGNETO

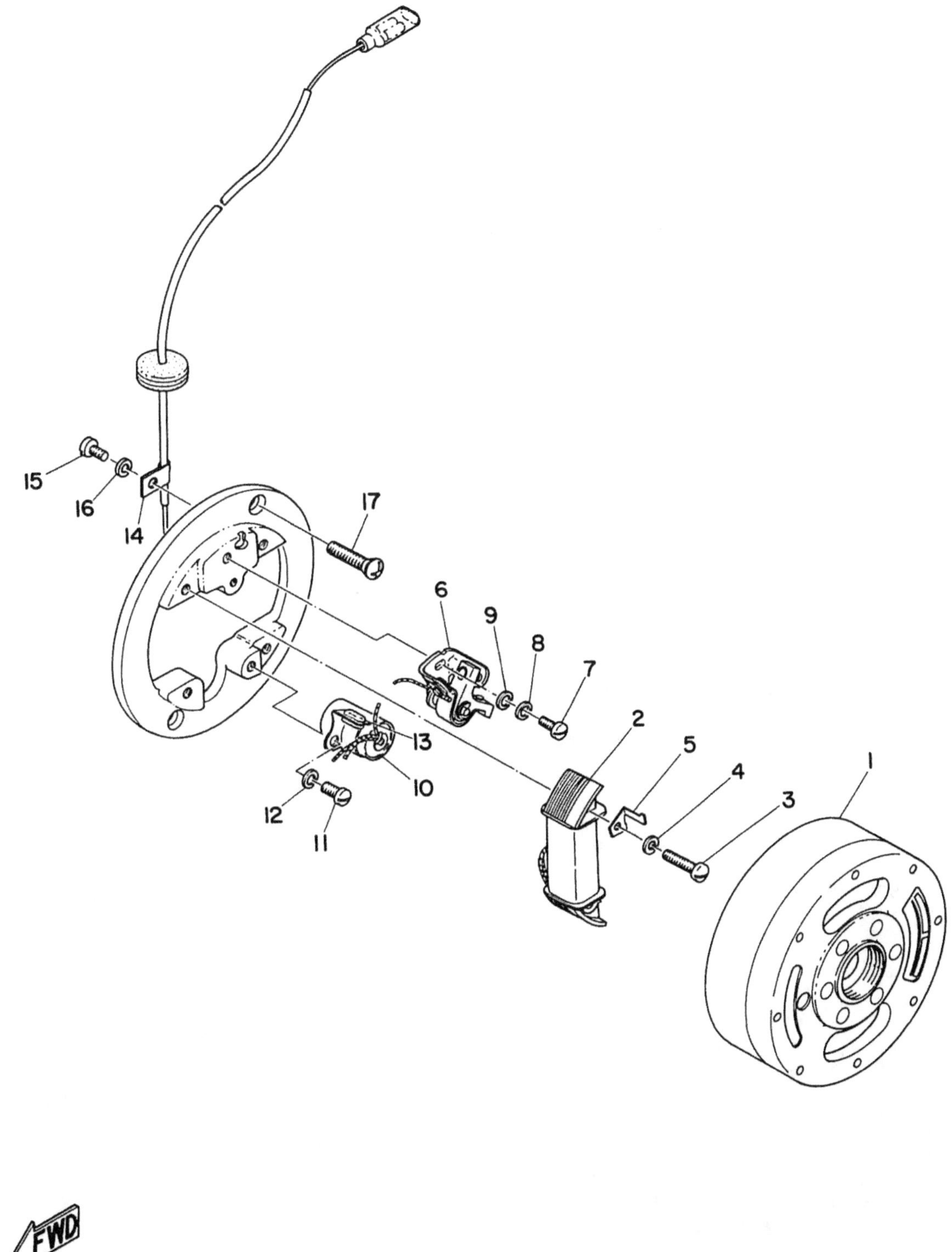

FLYWHEEL MAGNETO

Ref. No.	Part No.	Description	Q'ty	Applicable Machine No.	Remarks
13- 0-1	288-81300-10	FLYWHEEL MAGNETO ASS'Y	1		
13- 1	207-81350-10	. ROTOR ASS'Y	1		
13- 2	207-81312-10	. COIL, source	1		
13- 3	110-81348-20	. SCREW, pan head (4-25)	2		
13- 4	92901-04100	. WASHER, spring	2		
13- 5	257-81332-10	. PLATE, timing	1		
13- 6	207-81321-10	. CONTACT BREAKER ASS'Y	1		
13- 7	110-81347-20	. SCREW, pan head (4-12)	1		
13- 8	92901-04100	. WASHER, spring	1		
13- 9	92901-04200	. WASHER, plain	1		
13-10	207-81326-10	. CONDENSER	1		
13-11	110-81346-20	. SCREW, pan head (4-10)	1		
13-12	92901-04100	. WASHER, spring	1		
13-13	207-81331-10	. LUBRICATOR	1		
13-14	109-81328-10	. CLAMP, lead	1		
13-15	165-81145-21	. SCREW, pan head (4-8)	1		
13-16	92901-04100	. WASHER, spring	1		
13-17	98701-05015	SCREW, flat head	2		

Fig. 14 FRAME

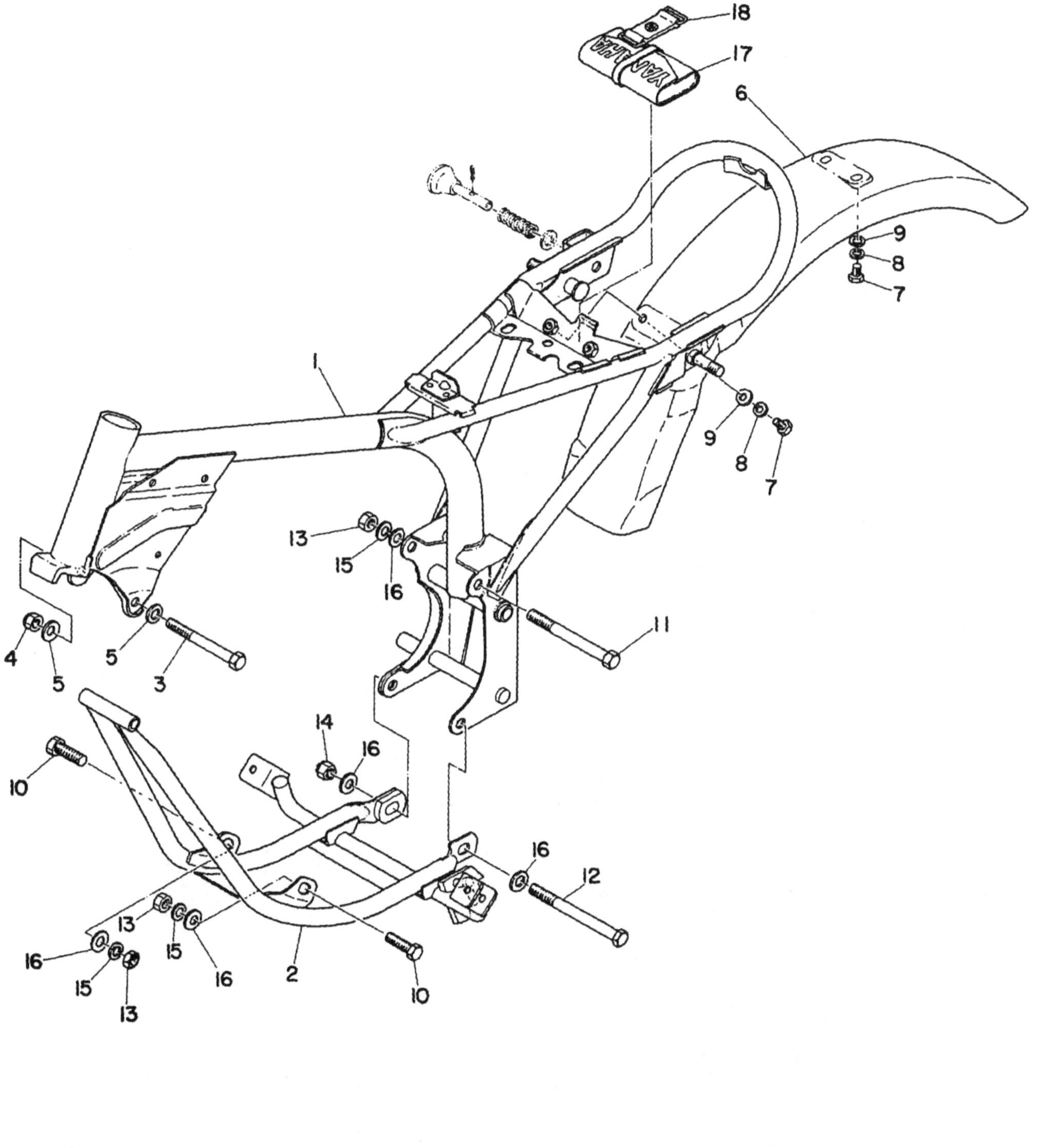

18
17
6
9
8
7
1
1
9
8
7
13
15
16
11
4
5
5
3
14
16
10
16
12
13
15
16
15
16
2
10
13
FWD

FRAME

Ref. No.	Part No.	Description	Q'ty	Applicable Machine No.	Remarks
14- 1	288-21110-00-33	FRAME COMP.	1		
14- 2	288-21280-00-33	DOWN TUBE COMP.	1		
14- 3	97201-08090	BOLT	1		
14- 4	183-22143-00	NUT	1		
14- 5	92901-08200	WASHER, plain	2		
14- 6	288-21610-00-74	REAR FENDER COMP.	1		Desert Orange
14- 7	91201-06010	BOLT	4		
14- 8	92901-06100	WASHER, spring	4		
14- 9	92901-06200	WASHER, plain	4		
14-10	97201-08030	BOLT	2		
14-11	97201-08100	BOLT	1		
14-12	97201-08115	BOLT	1		
14-13	98801-08100	NUT	3		
14-14	183-22143-00	NUT	1		
14-15	92901-08100	WASHER, spring	3		
14-16	92901-08200	WASHER, plain	4		
14-17	207-28100-00	TOOL ASS'Y	1		☆
14-18	288-21376-00	BAND, tool cover	1		

Fig. 15 REAR ARM & REAR CUSHION

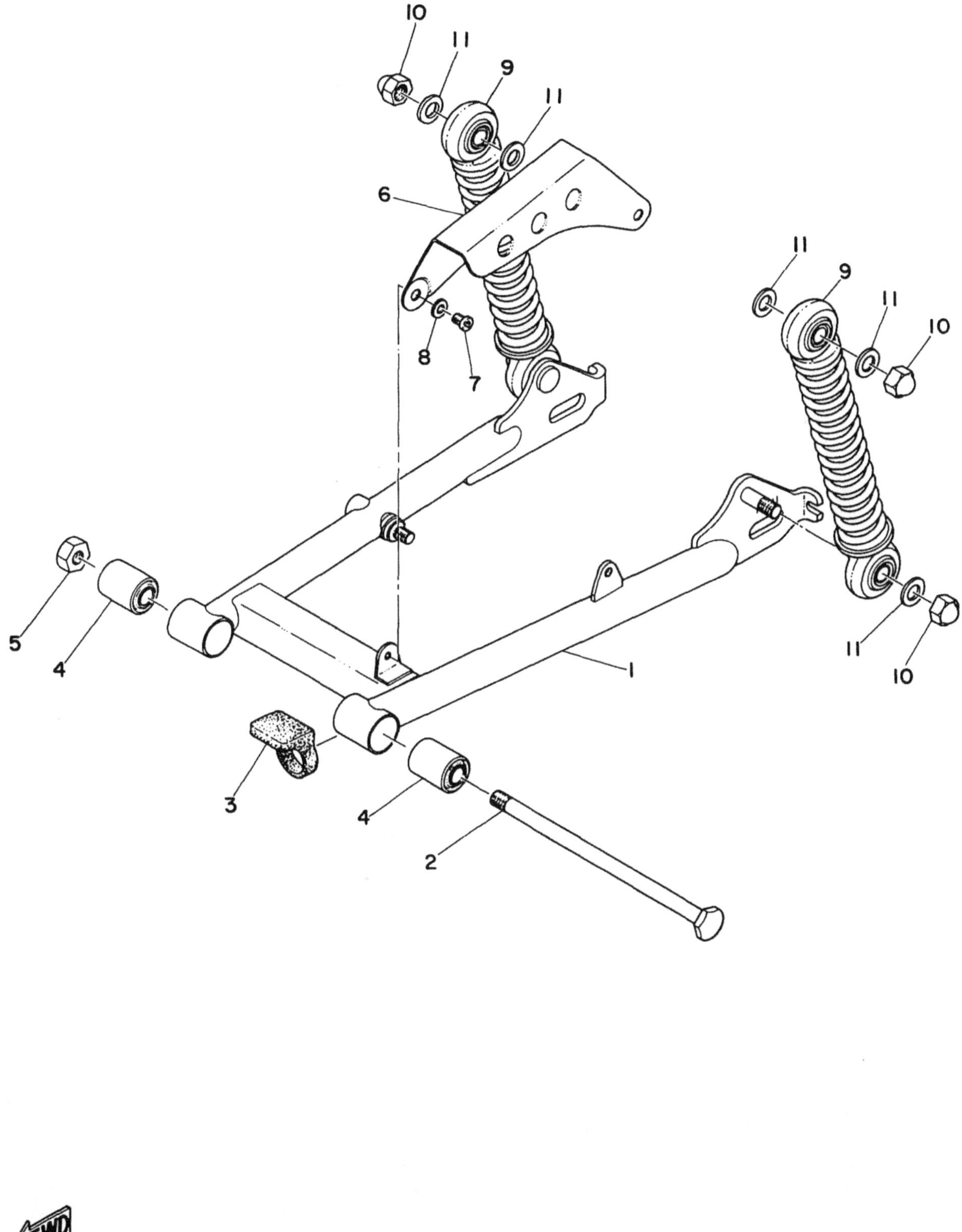

REAR ARM & REAR CUSHION

Ref. No.	Part No.	Description	Q'ty	Applicable Machine No.	Remarks
15- 1	288-22110-00-33	REAR ARM COMP.	1		
15- 2	288-22141-00	SHAFT, pivot	1		
15- 3	183-22151-00	SEAL, guard	1		
15- 4	102-22123-00	BUSHING, rear arm	2		
15- 5	92801-10100	NUT	1		
15- 6	288-22311-00-35	CHAIN CASE, half	1		
15- 7	98501-05008	SCREW, pan head	2		
15- 8	92901-05100	WASHER, spring	2		
15- 9	288-22210-00	REAR CUSHION ASS'Y	2		
15-10	92803-10700	NUT, crown	4		
15-11	102-22243-00	WASHER, rear cushion (10-25-2)	6		

Fig. 16 STAND & BRAKE PEDAL

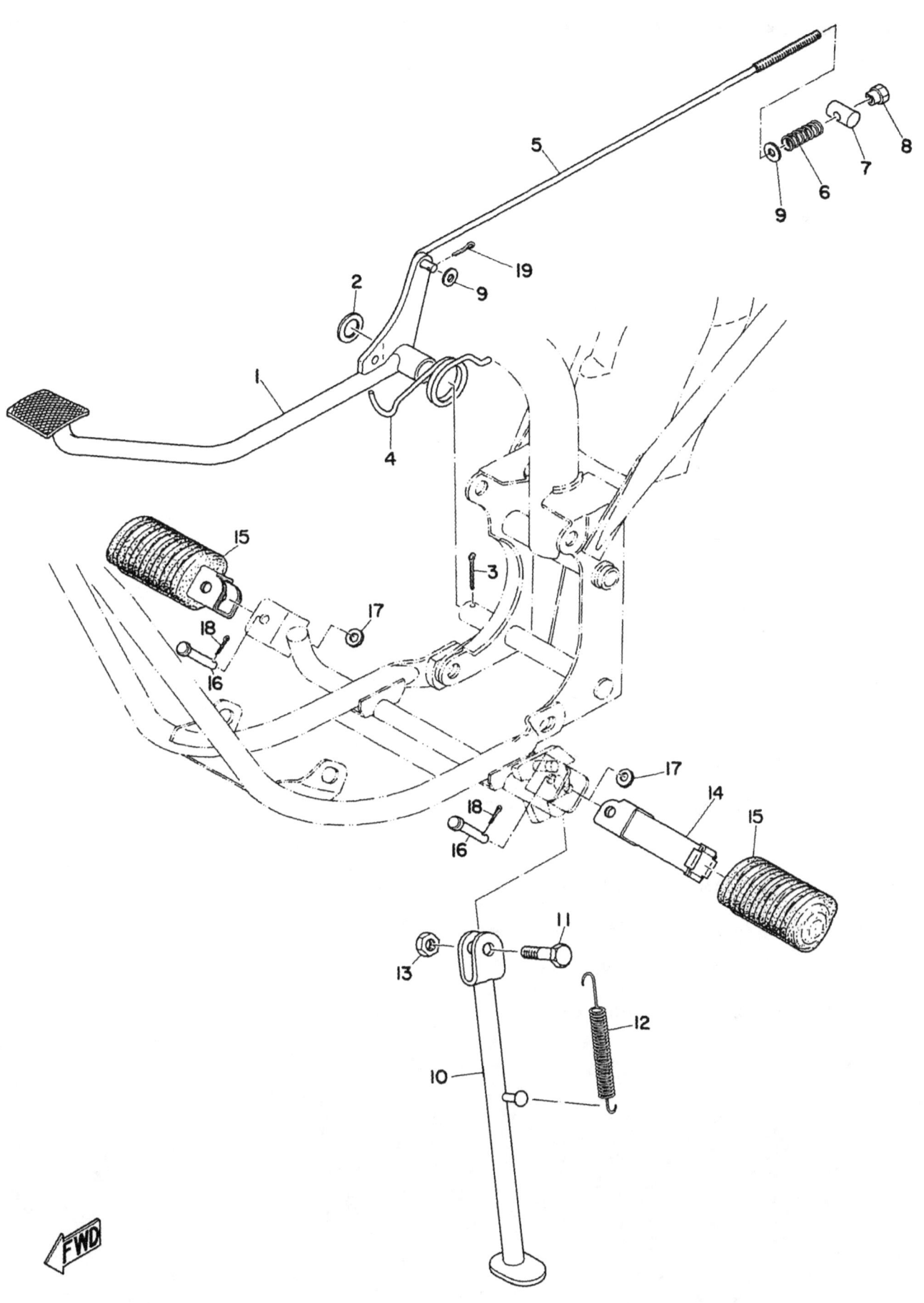

STAND & REAR BRAKE PEDAL

Ref. No.	Part No.	Description	Q'ty	Applicable Machine No.	Remarks
16- 1	288-27211-00-91	PEDAL, brake	1		
16- 2	135-22243-00	WASHER, rear cushion (14.8-27-2)	1		
16- 3	91401-30020	PIN, cotter	1		
16- 4	183-27216-00	SPRING, return	1		
16- 5	288-27231-00	ROD, brake	1		
16- 6	180-27236-00	SPRING, rod	1		
16- 7	156-27237-00	PIN, clevis	1		
16- 8	282-27238-00	NUT, adjusting	1		
16- 9	92901-06200	WASHER, plain	2		
16-10	288-27311-00	STAND, side	1		
16-11	137-27317-00	BOLT, side stand	1		
16-12	150-27316-00	SPRING, side stand	1		
16-13	98801-08300	NUT	1		
16-14	214-27421-00	FOOTREST	2		
16-15	214-27413-00	COVER, footrest	2		
16-16	91501-08038	PIN, clevis	2		
16-17	156-27226-00	WASHER, pedal link (8.2-13-0.6)	2		
16-18	91401-20015	PIN, cotter	2		
16-19	91401-20012	PIN, cotter	1		

Fig. 17 FRONT FORK & FRONT FENDER

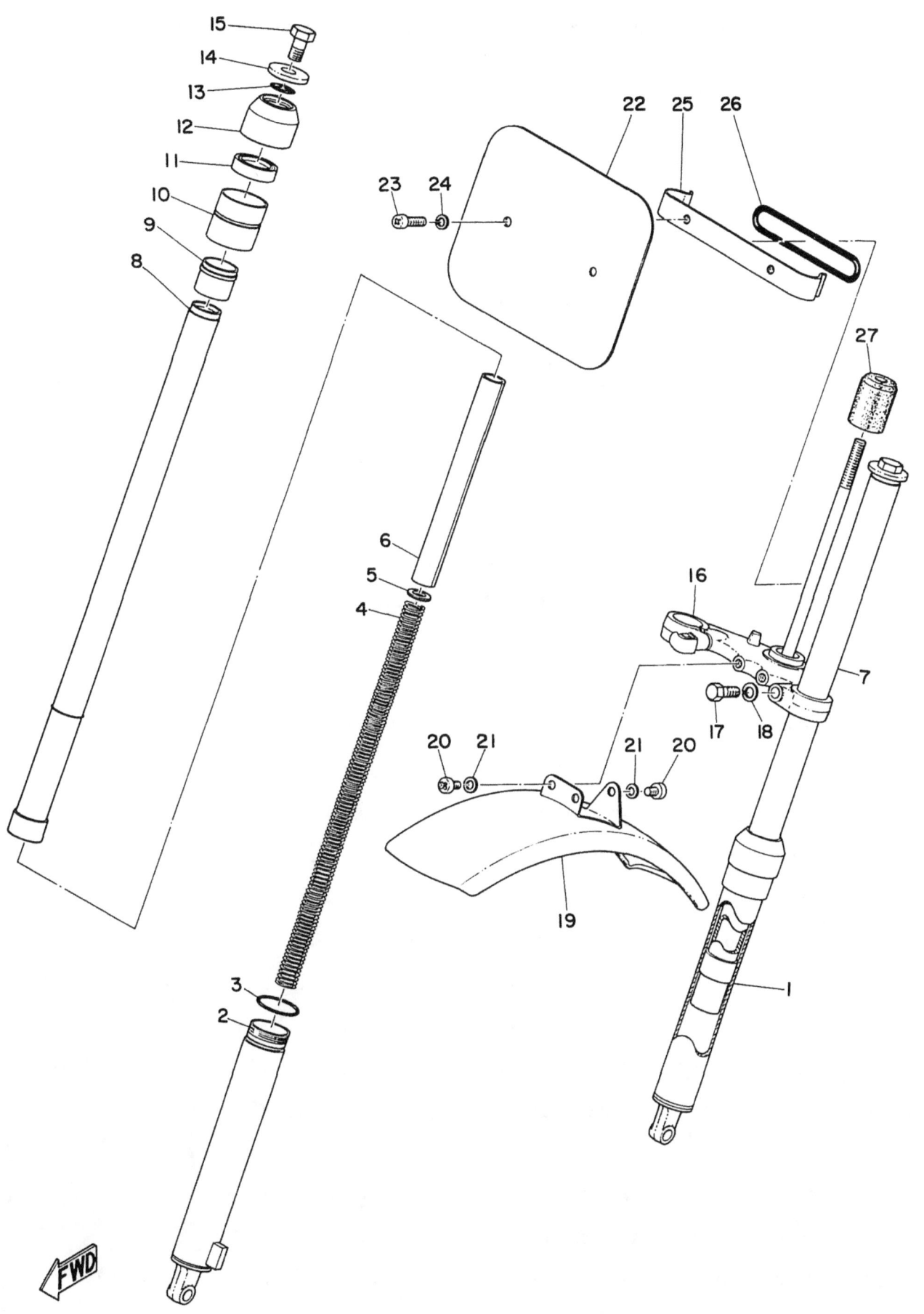

FRONT FORK & FRONT FENDER

Ref. No.	Part No.	Description	Q'ty	Applicable Machine No.	Remarks
17- 0-1	288-23100-00-74	FRONT FORK ASS'Y	1		Desert Orange
17- 1	288-23126-00-74	. TUBE, outer left	1		Desert Orange
17- 2	288-23136-00-74	. TUBE, outer right	1		Desert Orange
17- 3	207-23147-00	. O-RING	2		
17- 4	290-23141-00	. SPRING, fork	1		
17- 5	252-23149-00	. WASHER, spring upper	1		Only use the R.H.
17- 6	290-23118-00	. SPACER	1		
17- 7	290-23124-00	. TUBE, inner left	1		
17- 8	290-23134-00	. TUBE, inner right	1		
17- 9	109-23125-00	. METAL, slide	2		
17-10	290-23150-00	. OUTER NUT COMP.	2		
17-11	290-23145-00	. . OIL SEAL	2		
17-12	290-23144-00	. SEAL, dust	2		
17-13	122-23114-00	. PACKING	2		
17-14	207-23112-00	. WASHER, cap	2		
17-15	205-23111-40	. BOLT, cap	2		
17-16	290-23340-00	. UNDER BRACKET COMP.	1		
17-17	122-23346-00	. BOLT, under bracket	2		
17-18	92901-10100	. WASHER, spring	2		
17-19	288-21510-00-74	FRONT FENDER COMP.	1		Desert Orange
17-20	92501-06010	SCREW, pan head	3		
17-21	92901-06200	WASHER, plain	3		
17-22	288-23485-00	PLATE, number	1		
17-23	92501-06010	SCREW, pan head	2		

FRONT FORK & FRONT FENDER

Ref. No.	Part No.	Description	Q'ty	Applicable Machine No.	Remarks
17-24	92901-06200	WASHER, plain	2		
17-25	288-23486-00	STAY, plate	1		
17-26	288-23489-00	BAND	1		
17-27	288-23424-00	GUIDE, front fork	1		

Fig. 18 STEERING
IMPORTANT - SEE NEXT PAGE AND APPENDIX

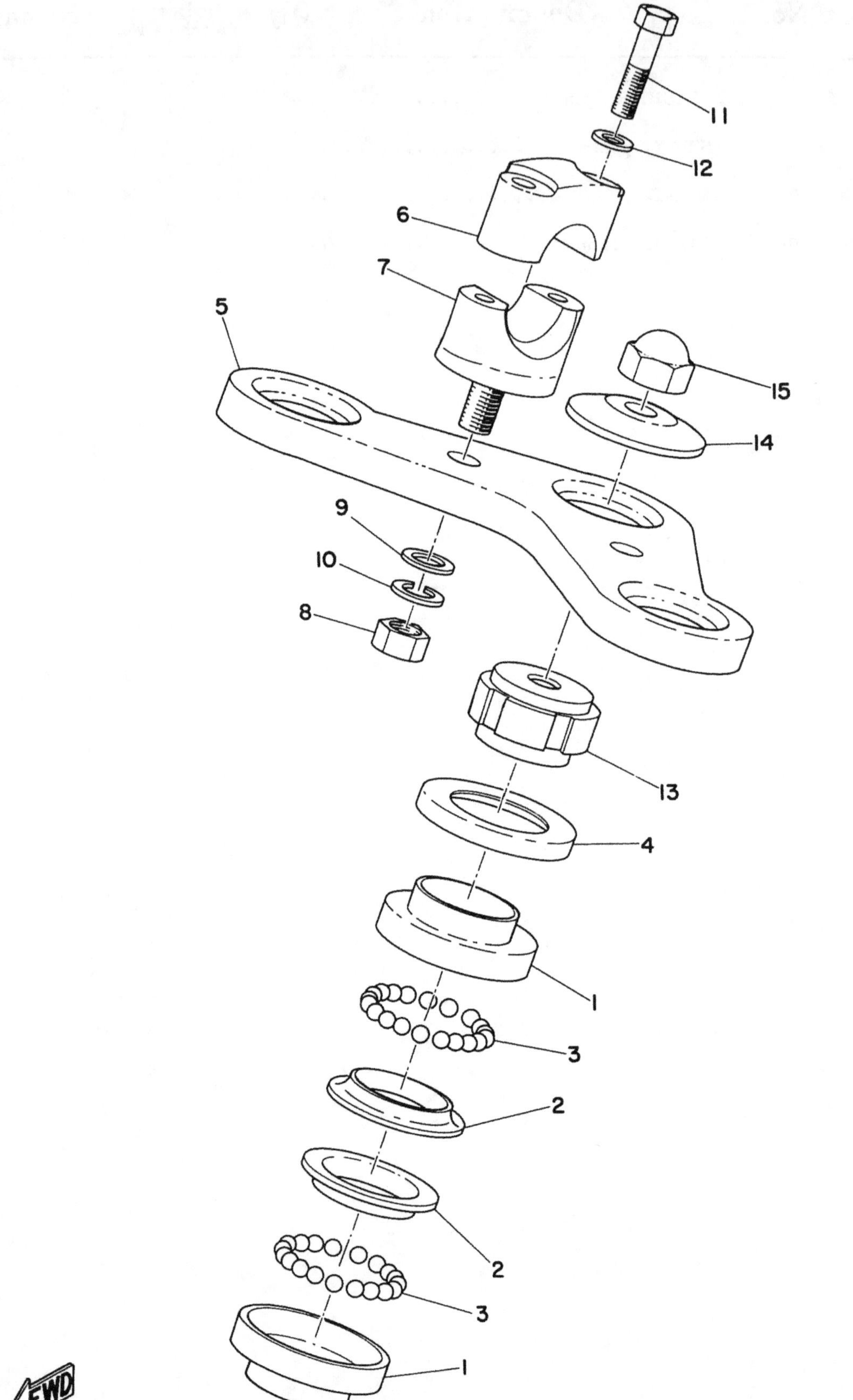

STEERING

Ref. No.	Part No.	Description	Q'ty	Applicable Machine No.	Remarks
18- 1	282-23412-00	RACE, ball 2	2		
18- 2	282-23414-00	RACE, ball 4	2		
18- 3	93503-16003	BALL (3/16 inch)	48		
18- 4	288-23415-00	COVER, ball race	1		
18- 5	185-23435-00	CROWN, handle	1		
18- 6	122-23441-00	HOLDER, handle upper	2		
18- 7	122-23442-02	HOLDER, handle under	2		
18- 8	92801-10100	NUT	2		
18- 9	92901-10200	WASHER, plain	2		
18-10	92901-10100	WASHER, spring	2		
18-11	91101-06035	BOLT	4		
18-12	92901-06100	WASHER, spring	4		
18-13	288-23454-00	NUT, fitting	1		
18-14	122-23443-00	WASHER, crown	1		
18-15	92804-10700	NUT, crown	1		

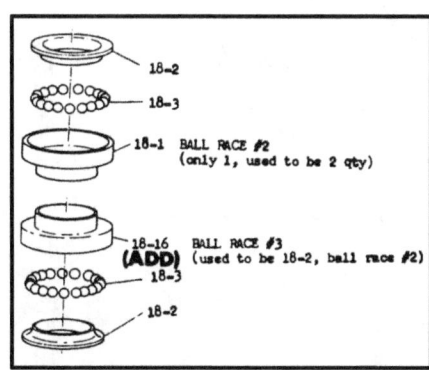

PARTS BOOK CORRECTION: Original JT1 Parts Book picture on previous page shows top and bottom bearing assemblies upside down. Rearrange as in picture above.

Fig. No.	Description	Old Part Number	New Part Number	Qty.	Retail/Disc.	Remarks
18-1	BALL RACE #2	282-23412-00-00	282-23412-01-00	1	$.94/ A	Qty used to be 2.
18-16 (add)	BALL RACE #3	282-23412-00-00	288-23413-00-00	1	$.94/ A	E/N26309

Fig. 19 HANDLE & WIRE

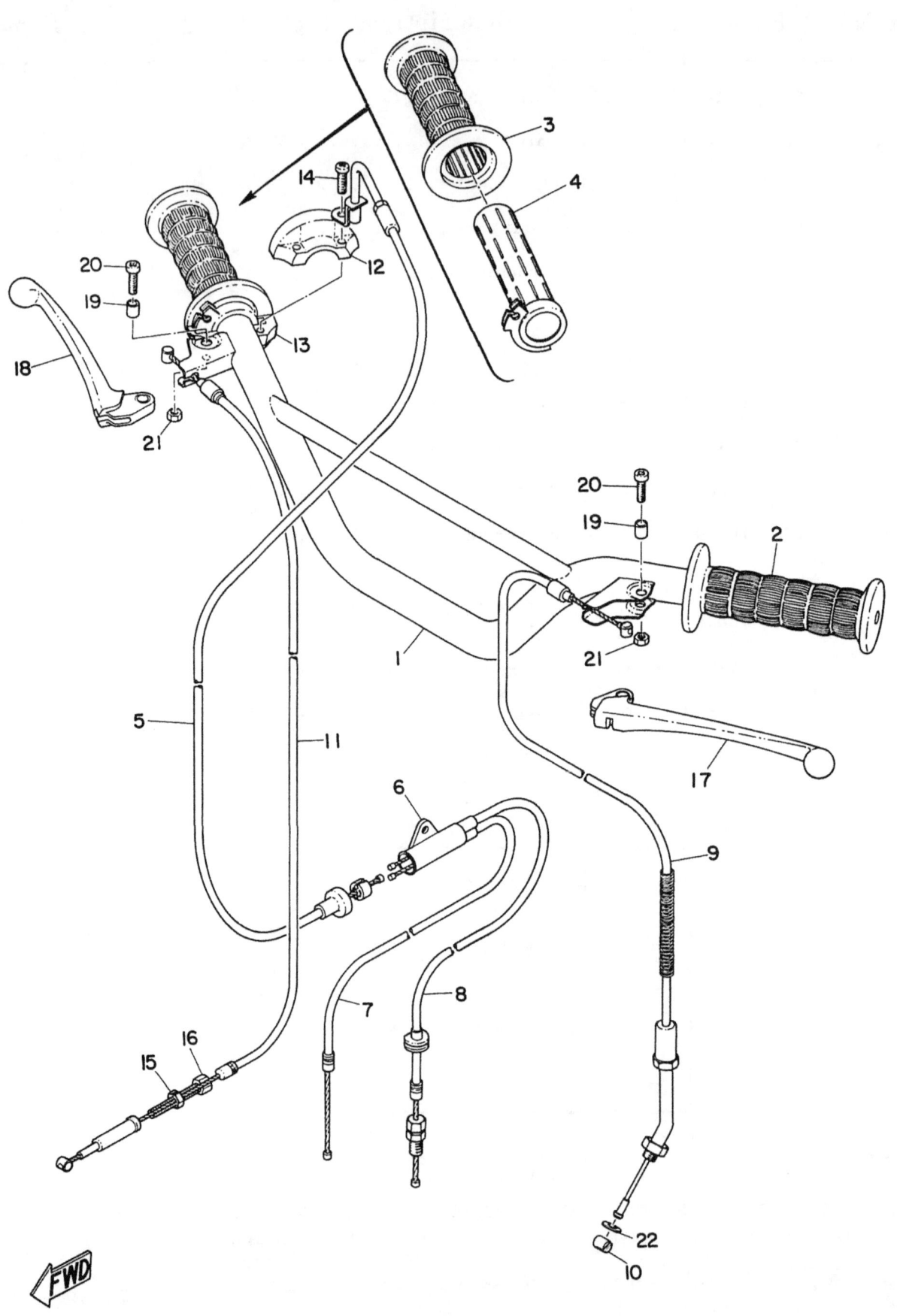

HANDLE & WIRE

Ref. No.	Part No.	Description	Q'ty	Applicable Machine No.	Remarks
19- 1	288-26111-00	HANDLE	1		
19- 2	214-26241-00	GRIP, left	1		
19- 3	214-26242-00	GRIP, right	1		
19- 4	214-26243-00	TUBE, guide	1		
19- 5	288-26311-00	WIRE, throttle 1	1		
19- 6	266-26261-00	CYLINDER	1		
19- 7	288-26312-00	WIRE, throttle 2	1		
19- 8	288-26321-00	WIRE, pump	1		
19- 9	288-26335-00	WIRE, clutch	1		
19-10	164-26363-00	. END, wire	1		
19-11	288-26341-00	WIRE, brake	1		
19-12	214-26281-01	CAP, grip upper	1		
19-13	248-26282-00	CAP, grip under	1		
19-14	98501-05018	SCREW, pan head	2		
19-15	109-26344-00	NUT, wire adjusting	1		
19-16	109-26345-00	BOLT, wire adjusting	1		
19-17	137-83912-01	LEVER, left	1		
19-18	137-83922-01	LEVER, right	1		
19-19	288-83913-00	COLLAR, lever	2		
19-20	98501-05018	SCREW, pan head	2		
19-21	98801-05100	NUT	2		
19-22	92901-06200	WASHER, plain	1		

Fig. 20 FUEL TANK

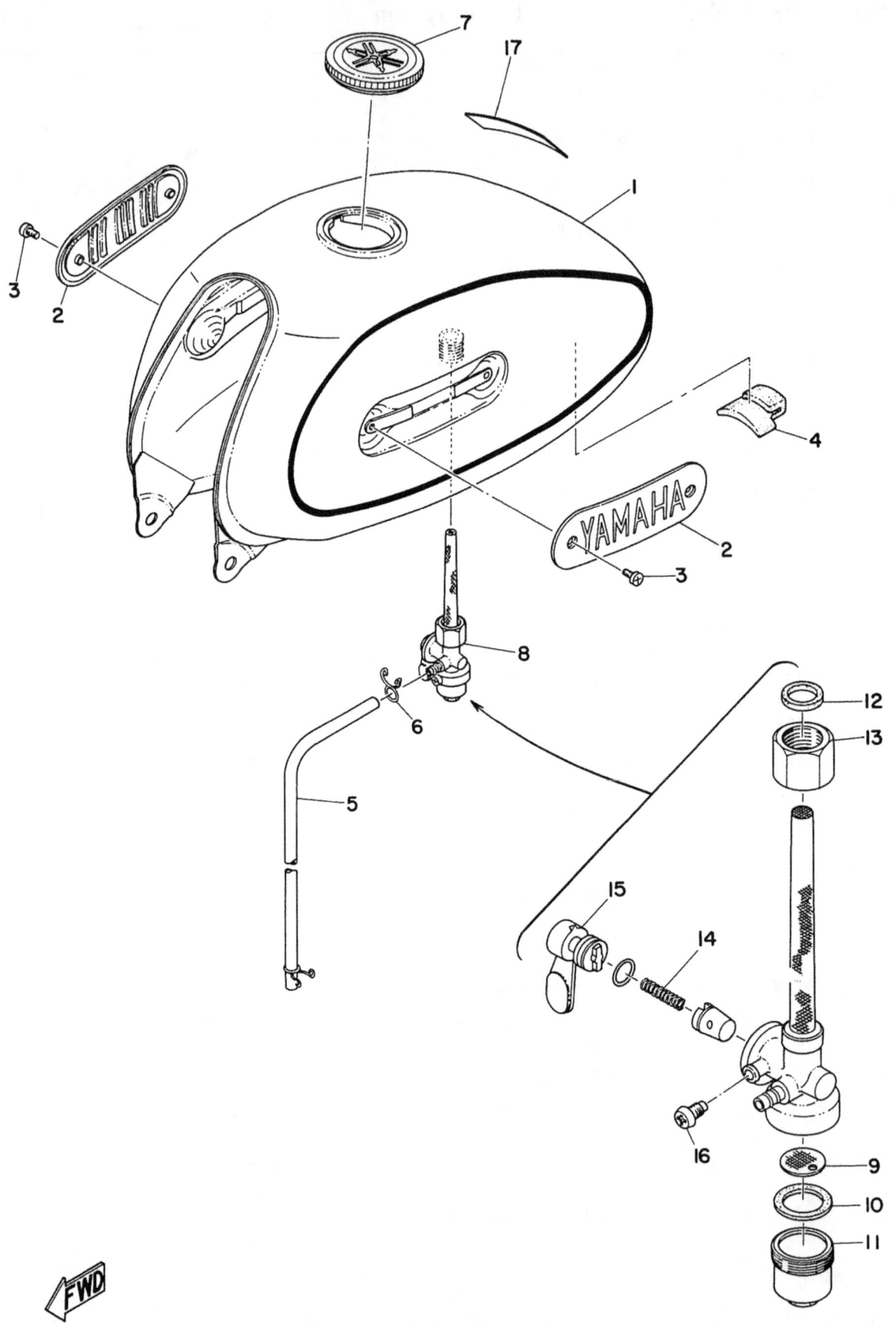

FUEL TANK

Ref. No.	Part No.	Description	Q'ty	Applicable Machine No.	Remarks
20- 1	288-24110-00-01	FUEL TANK COMP.	1		Desert Orange
20- 2	276-24161-00	EMBLEM	2		
20- 3	98501-04008	SCREW, pan head	4		
20- 4	288-24181-00	DAMPER, locating	1		
20- 5	626-24315-00	PIPE (5-235)	1		
20- 6	101-24356-00	CLIP, pipe	2		
20- 7	122-24610-01	CAP ASS'Y	1		
20- 8	127-24500-00	FUEL COCK ASS'Y	1		
20- 9	122-24515-00	. NET, filter	1		
20-10	102-24522-00	. GASKET, filter	1		
20-11	122-24521-00	. CUP, filter	1		
20-12	122-24532-00	. GASKET, nut	1		
20-13	122-24531-00	. NUT	1		
20-14	102-24529-00	. SPRING	1		
20-15	122-24524-00	. LEVER, cock	1		
20-16	127-24535-00	. SCREW, lever fitting	1		
20-17	288-21659-00	LABEL, warning	1		

Fig. 21 OIL TANK

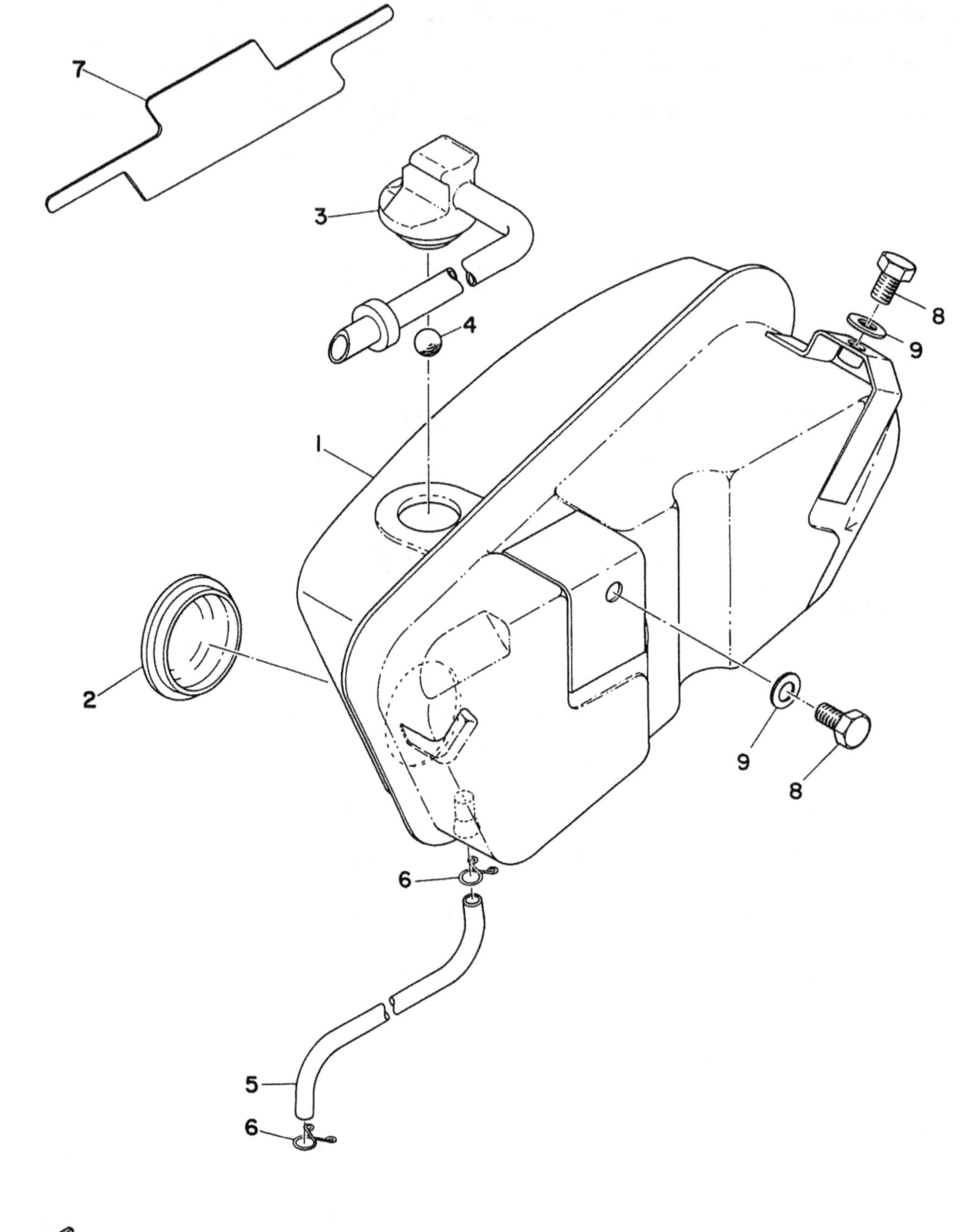

OIL TANK

Ref. No.	Part No.	Description	Q'ty	Applicable Machine No.	Remarks
21-1	288-21705-00-74	OIL TANK ASS'Y	1		Desert Orange
21-2	214-21761-00	. GAUGE, level	1		
21-3	288-21771-00	BODY, cap	1		
21-4	288-24684-00	BALL	1		
21-5	132-24319-01	PIPE, oil (5-380)	1		
21-6	101-24356-00	CLIP, oil	2		
21-7	288-21787-00	EMBLEM, enduro	1		
21-8	91201-06012	BOLT	2		
21-9	92901-06200	WASHER, plain	2		

Fig. 22 SEAT

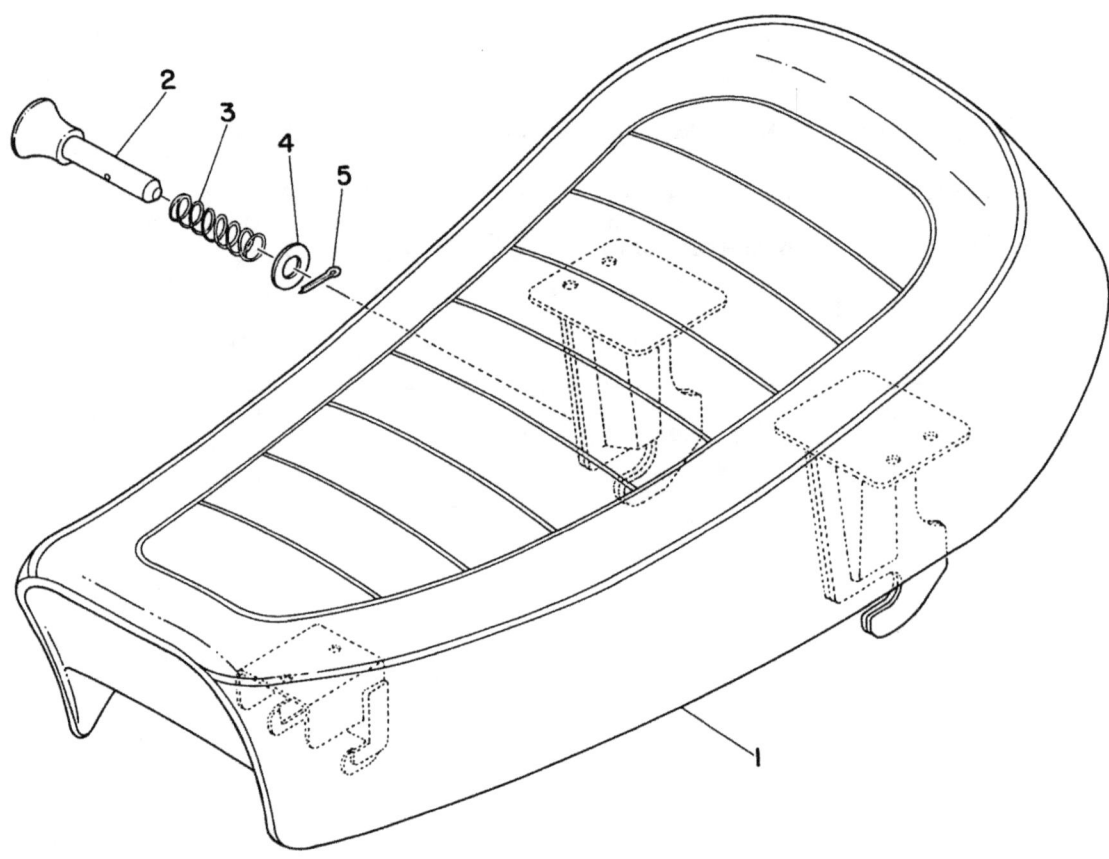

SEAT

Ref. No.	Part No.	Description	Q'ty	Applicable Machine No.	Remarks
22- 1	288-24770-00	SEMI-DOUBLE SEAT ASS'Y	1		
22- 1-1	288-24771-00	. COVER, seat	1		
22- 2	288-24727-00	PIN, seat fitting	1		
22- 3	288-24781-00	SPRING, seat	1		
22- 4	156-27226-00	WASHER (8.2-13-0.6)	1		
22- 5	91401-20012	PIN, cotter	1		

Fig. 23 FRONT WHEEL

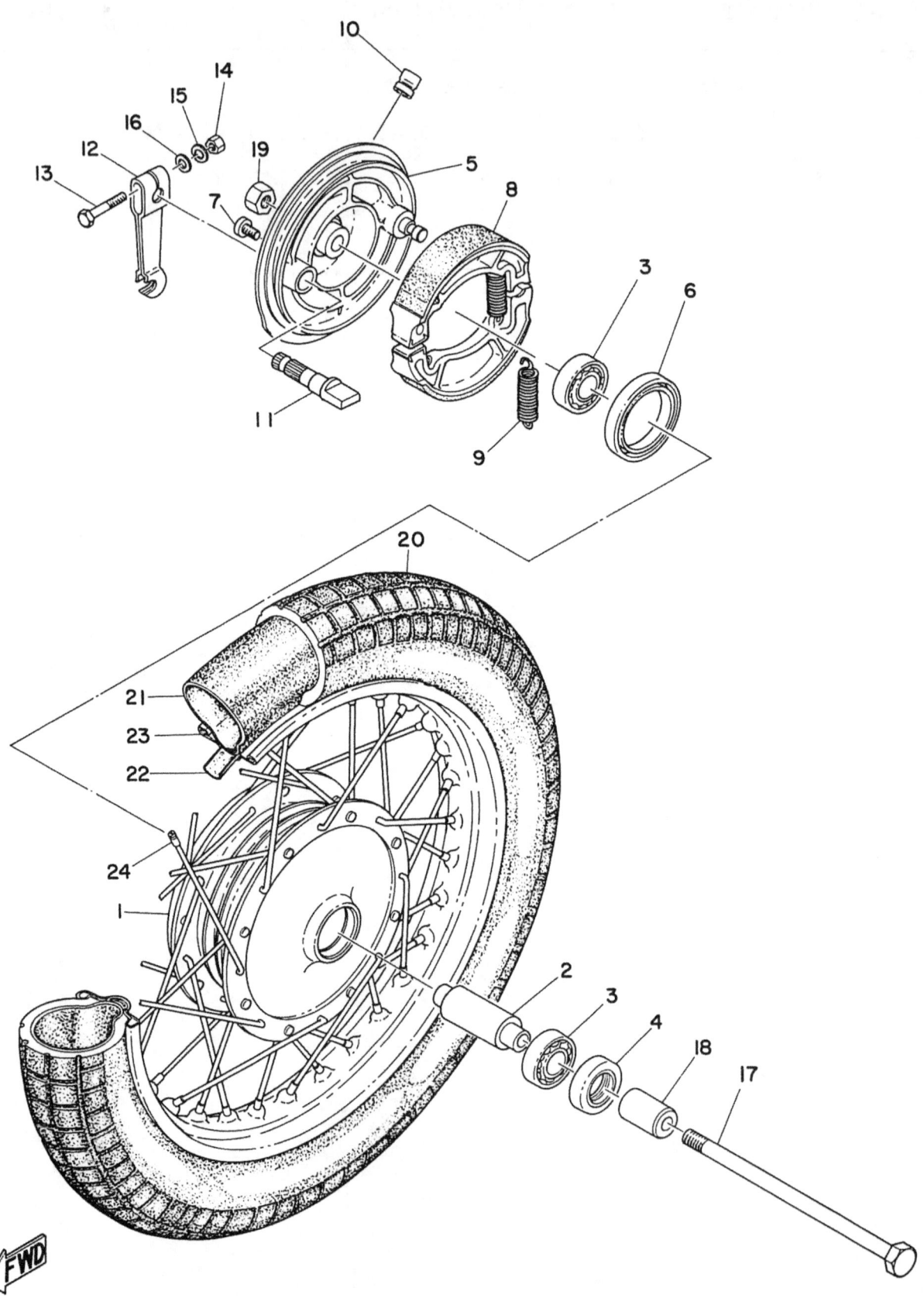

FRONT WHEEL

Ref. No.	Part No.	Description	Q'ty	Applicable Machine No.	Remarks
23- 1	288-25111-00	HUB, front	1		
23- 2	102-25117-00	SPACER, bearing	1		
23- 3	93306-20203	BEARING (6202)	2		
23- 4	93106-20001	OIL SEAL (DD20-35-7)	1		
23- 5	109-25121-01	PLATE, brake shoe	1		
23- 6	93107-42001	OIL SEAL (OS42-52.5-7)	1		
23- 7	92501-06010	SCREW, pan head	1		
23- 8	122-25330-00	BRAKE SHOE COMP.	2		
23- 9	102-25333-00	SPRING, return	2		
23-10	288-25139-00	PLUG, blind	1		
23-11	122-25351-01	CAM SHAFT	1		
23-12	109-25155-00	LEVER, cam shaft	1		
23-13	91201-06030	BOLT	1		
23-14	92801-06100	NUT	1		
23-15	92901-06100	WASHER, spring	1		
23-16	92901-06200	WASHER, plain	1		
23-17	128-25181-00	SHAFT, wheel	1		
23-18	128-25183-00	COLLAR, wheel shaft	1		
23-19	92801-10100	NUT	1		
23-20	94125-15091	TIRE (2.50-15-4PR)	1		☆
23-21	94225-15036	TUBE (2.50-15)	1		☆
23-22	94325-15028	BAND, rim (2.50-15)	1		
23-23	94414-15058	RIM (1.40-15)	1		
23-24	288-25104-00	SPOKE SET	1s		

Fig. 24 REAR WHEEL

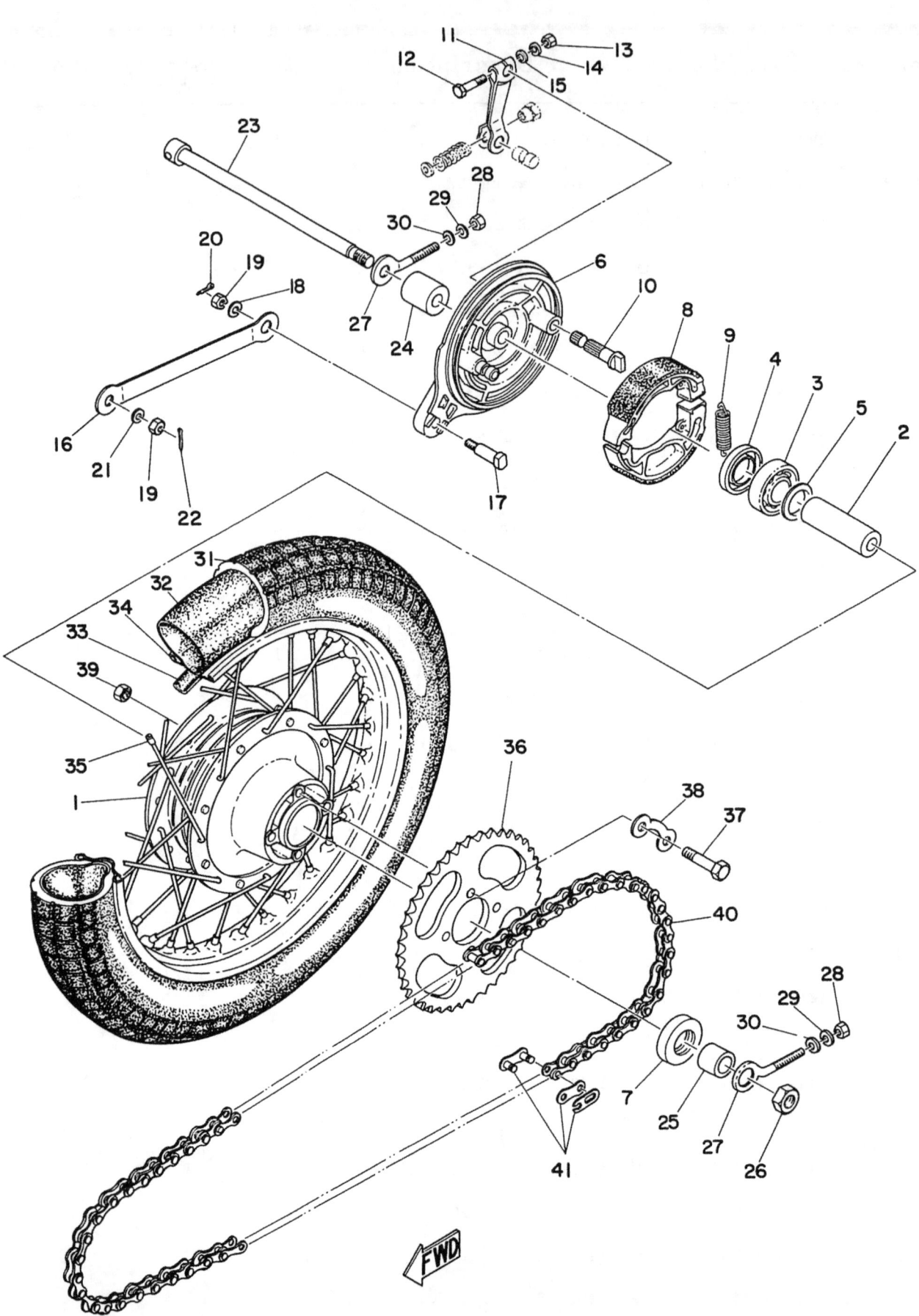

REAR WHEEL

Ref. No.	Part No.	Description	Q'ty	Applicable Machine No.	Remarks
24- 1	288-25311-00	HUB, rear	1		
24- 2	109-25317-00	SPACER, bearing	1		
24- 3	93306-30101	BEARING (6301)	1		
24- 4	93106-20002	OIL SEAL (DD-20-37-8)	1		
24- 5	102-25315-00	FLANGE, spacer	1		
24- 6	109-25321-02	PLATE, brake shoe	1		
24- 7	93102-18008	OIL SEAL (SD-18-37-8)	1		
24- 8	122-25330-00	BRAKE SHOE COMP.	2		
24- 9	102-25333-00	SPRING, return	2		
24-10	122-25351-01	CAM SHAFT	1		
24-10	122-25355-00	LEVER, cam shaft	1		
24-12	91201-06030	BOLT	1		
24-13	92801-06100	NUT	1		
24-14	92901-06100	WASHER, spring	1		
24-15	92901-06200	WASHER, plain	1		
24-16	102-25371-00	BAR, tension	1		
24-17	109-25373-00	BOLT, tension bar	1		
24-18	92901-08100	WASHER, spring	1		
24-19	98801-08300	NUT	2		
24-20	91401-20012	PIN, cotter	1		
24-21	92901-08200	WASHER, plain	1		
24-22	91401-20012	PIN, cotter	1		
24-23	288-25381-00	SHAFT, wheel	1		
24-24	102-25383-00	COLLAR, wheel shaft	1		

REAR WHEEL

Ref. No.	Part No.	Description	Q'ty	Applicable Machine No.	Remarks
24-25	109-25377-01	COLLAR, shaft	1		
24-26	183-25182-00	NUT, shaft	1		
24-27	102-25389-00	PULLER, chain	2		
24-28	92801-06100	NUT	2		
24-29	92901-06100	WASHER, spring	2		
24-30	92901-06200	WASHER, plain	2		
24-31	94125-15091	TIRE (2.50-15-4PR)	1		☆
24-32	94225-15036	TUBE (2.50-15)	1		☆
24-33	94325-15028	BAND, rim (2.50-15)	1		
24-34	94414-15058	RIM (1.40-15)	1		
24-35	288-25304-00	SPOKE SET	1s		
24-36	288-25441-10	GEAR, sprocket wheel (41T)	1		
24-37	109-25411-00	BOLT, fitting	4		
24-38	101-25412-00	WASHER, lock	2		
24-39	98801-08300	NUT	4		
24-40	94504-20090	CHAIN (DK420-90L)	1		
24-41	94604-20001	. JOINT, chain	1		

Fig. 25 ELECTRICAL

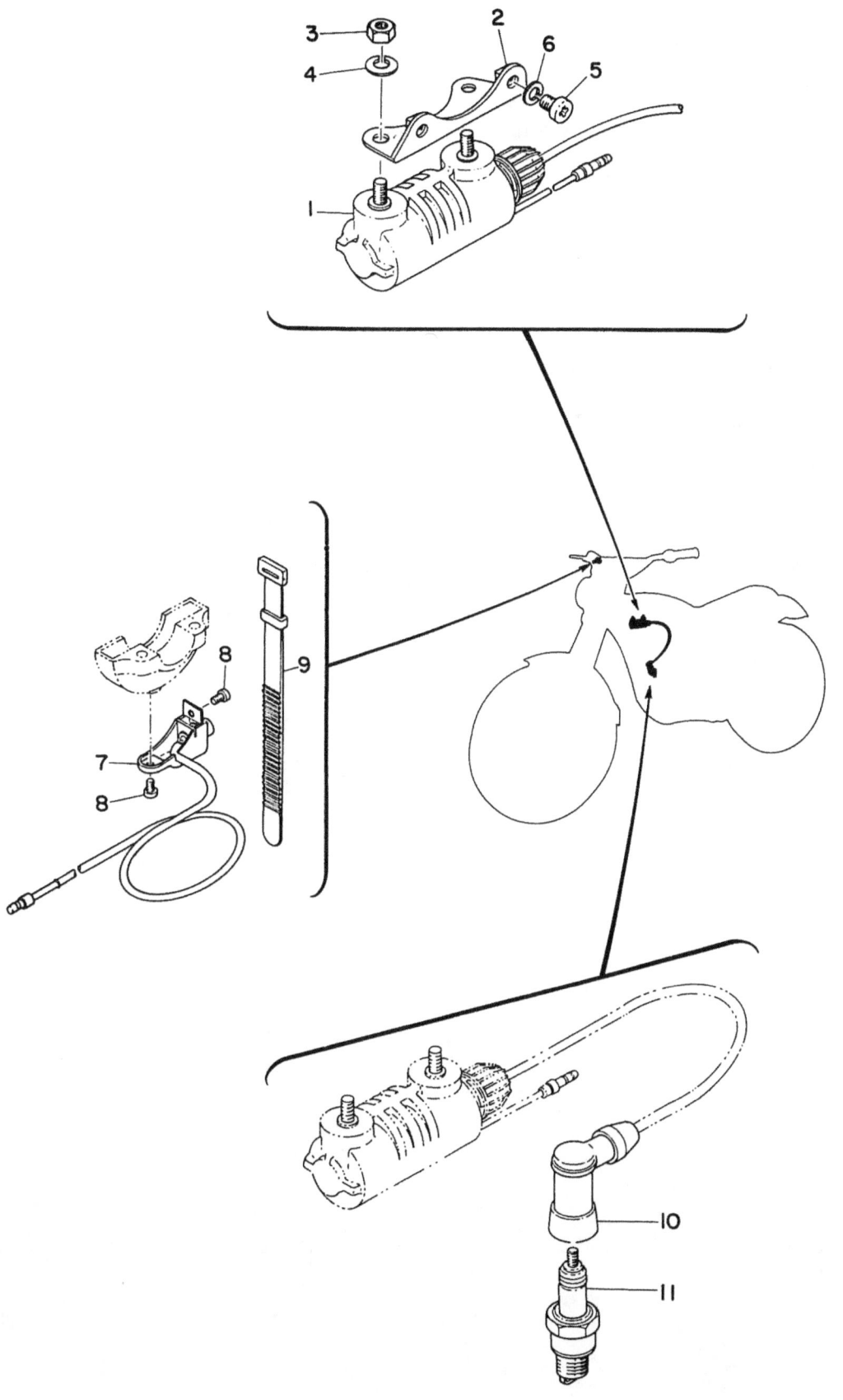

ELECTRICAL

Ref. No.	Part No.	Description	Q'ty	Applicable Machine No.	Remarks
25- 1	248-82310-10	IGNITION COIL ASS'Y	1		
25- 2	248-82316-00	BRACKET, ignition coil	1		
25- 3	92801-06100	NUT	2		
25- 4	92901-06100	WASHER, spring	2		
25- 5	92501-06012	SCREW, pan head	2		
25- 6	92901-06100	WASHER, spring	2		
25- 7	261-83976-00	SWITCH, handle 1	1		
25- 8	98501-05005	SCREW, pan head	2		
25- 9	168-83936-01	BAND, switch cord	1		
25-10	117-82370-20	PLUG CAP ASS'Y	1		
25-11	94700-00040	PLUG, spark (B-7HS)	1		

Fig. 26 HEAD LAMP & TAIL LAMP (JT1L)

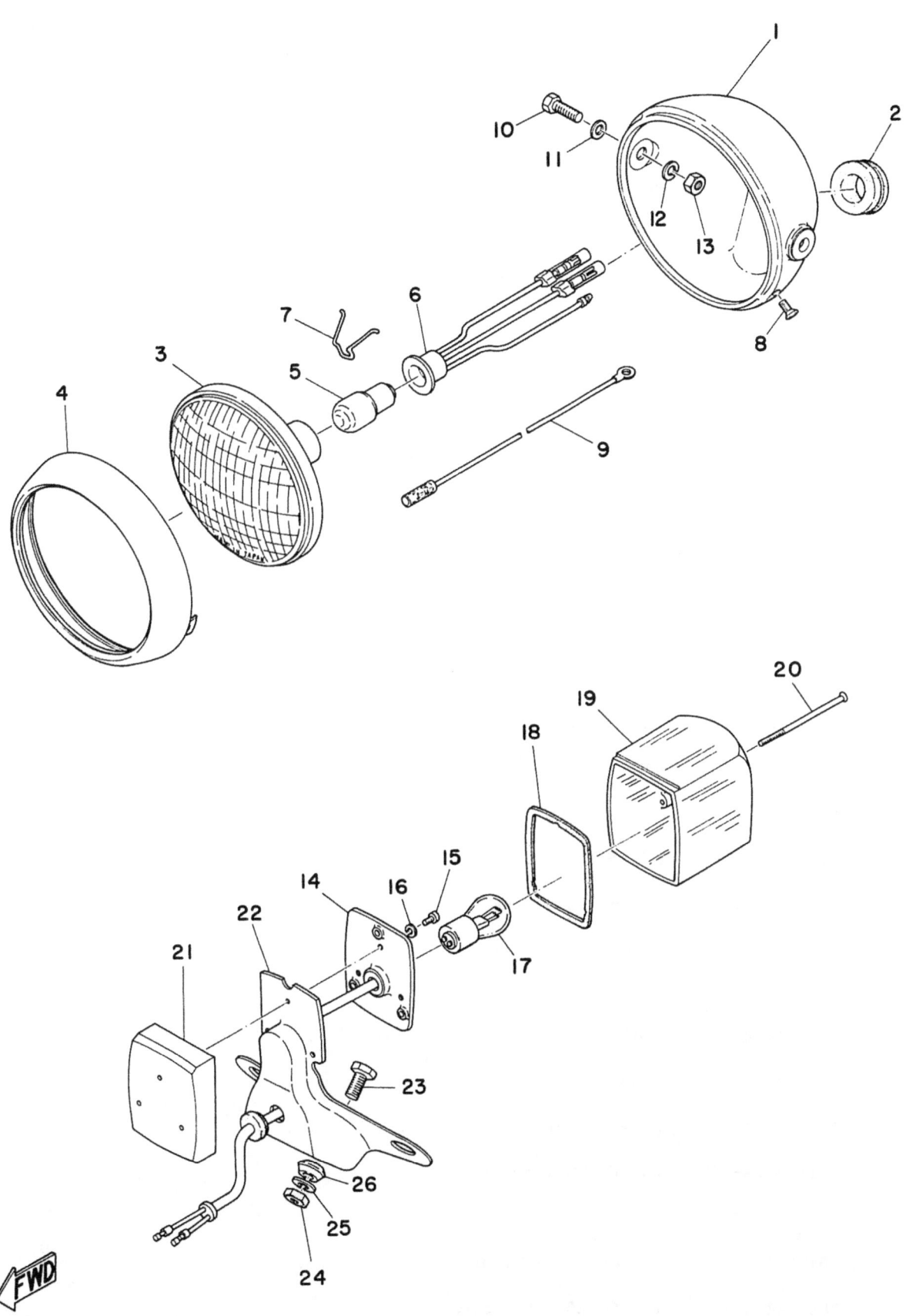

Fig. 26 HEAD LAMP & TAIL LAMP (JT1L)

Ref. No.	Parts No.	Description	Q'ty	Applicable Machine No.	Remarks
26- 1	241-84330-00-74	BODY ASS'Y	1		
26- 2	150-84153-00	. GROMMET	1		
26- 0-1	288-84110-60	HEAD LAMP UNIT ASS'Y	1		
26- 3	288-84120-60	. LENS ASSY	1		
26- 4	195-84315-01	. RIM, head lamp	1		
26- 5	104-84114-00	. BULB (6V 15W/15W)	1		
26- 6	241-84312-00	. SOCKET	1		
26- 7	195-84324-00	. SPRING, reflector set	3		
26- 8	195-84325-00	SCREW, rim fitting	1		
26- 9	173-84313-00	WIRE, earth	1		
26-10	97203-08020	BOLT	2		
26-11	92903-08200	WASHER, plain	2		
26-12	92901-08100	WASHER, spring	2		
26-13	98801-08100	NUT	2		
26- 0-2	288-84510-60	TAIL LAMP UNIT ASS'Y	1		
26-14	290-84511-00	. BASE	1		
26-15	98501-04010	. SCREW, pan head	3		
26-16	92901-04100	. WASHER, spring	3		
26-17	122-84514-00	. BULB, tail lamp (6V 10/3W)	1		
26-18	164-84723-00	. GASKET	1		
26-19	288-84521-09	. LENS, tail lamp	1		
26-20	201-84724-00	. SCREW, lens fitting	3		
26-21	201-84716-00	. COVER, tail lamp	1		
26-22	288-84551-09-35	BRACKET, license	1		

HEAD LAMP & TAIL LAMP (JT1L)

Ref. No.	Parts No.	Description	Q'ty	Applicable Machine No.	Remarks
26-23	91201-06012	BOLT	2		
26-24	92801-06100	NUT	2		
26-25	92901-06100	WASHER, spring	2		
26-26	152-84518-00	GROMMET	2		

Fig. 27 ELECTRICAL (JT1L)

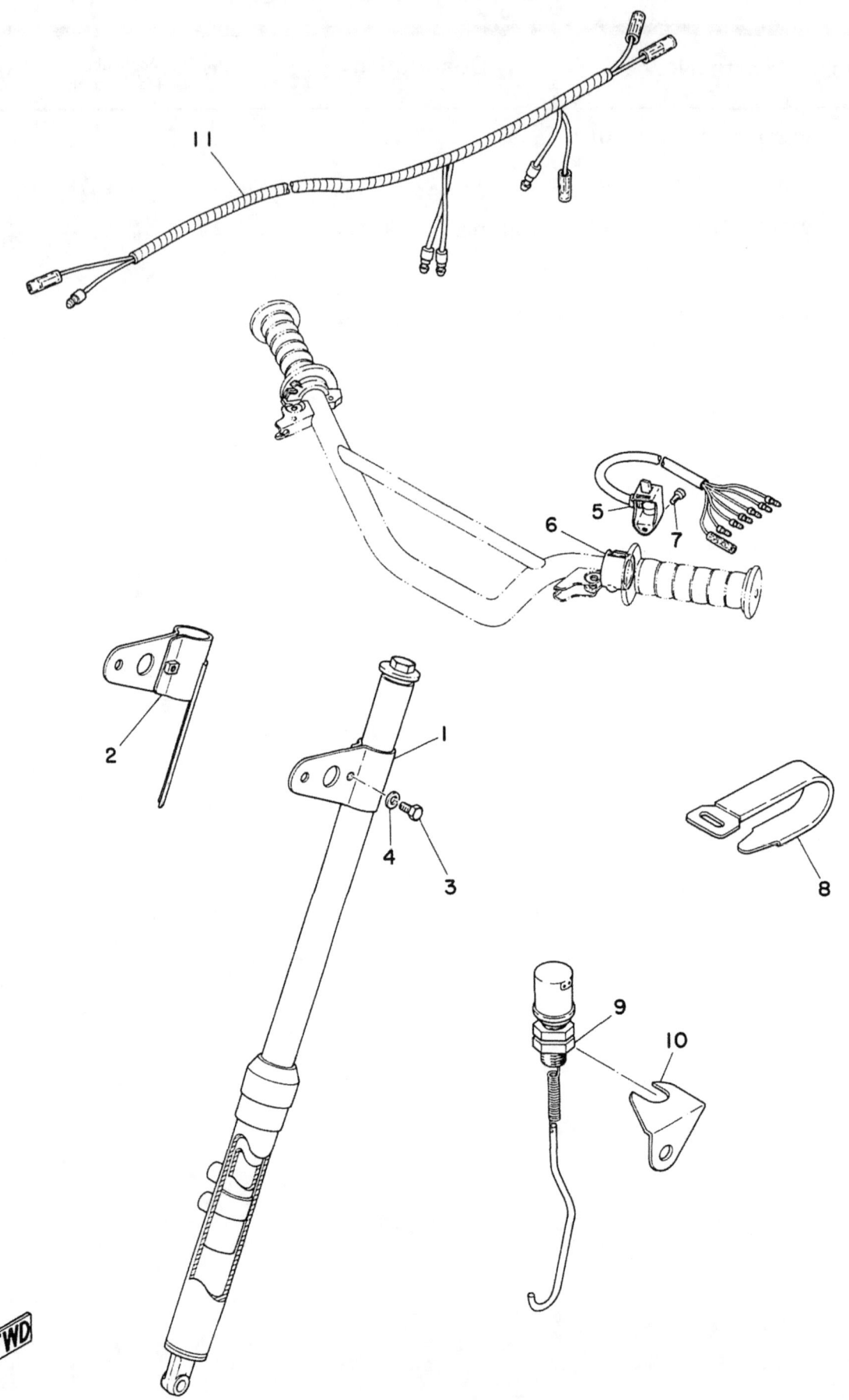

ELECTRICAL (JT1L)

Ref. No.	Parts No.	Description	Q'ty	Applicable Machine No.	Remarks
27- 1	290-84118-01	STAY, head lamp left	1		
27- 2	290-84119-01	STAY, head lamp right	1		
27- 3	91203-06015	BOLT	2		
27- 4	92901-06200	WASHER, plain	2		
27- 5	288-83973-00	SWITCH, handle 3	1		
27- 6	214-83974-00	HOLDER, handle switch	1		
27- 7	98503-05015	SCREW, pan head	1		
27- 8	168-83936-01	BAND, switch cord	1		
27- 9	290-83530-00	STOP SWITCH ASS'Y	1		
27-10	290-83539-00	STAY, stop switch	1		
27-11	288-82590-20	WIRE HARNESS ASS'Y	1		

Fig. 28 FLYWHEEL MAGNETO (JT1L)

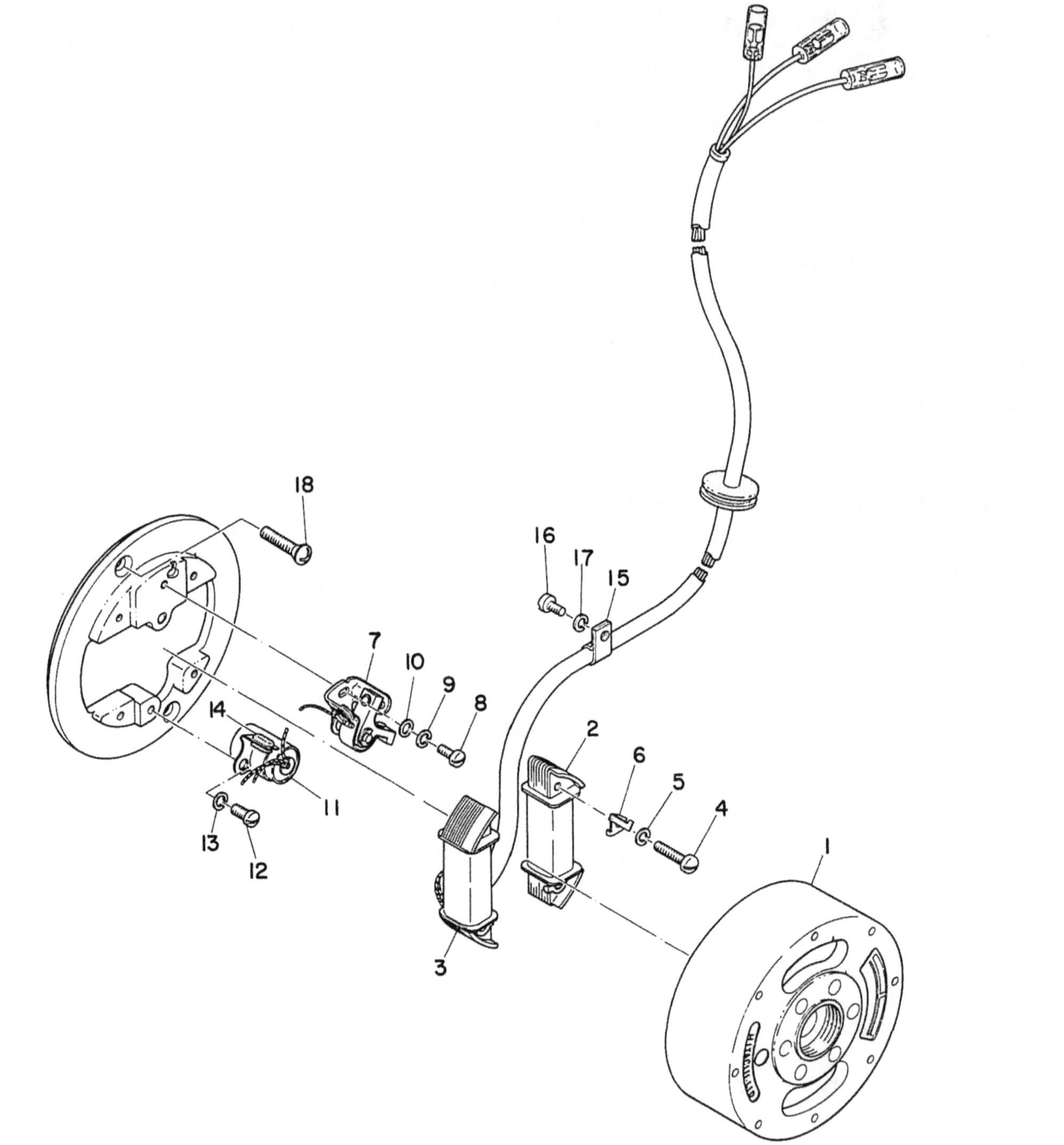

FLYWHEEL MAGNETO (JT1L)

Ref. No.	Part. No.	Description	Q'ty	Applicable Machine No.	Remarks
28- 0-1	288-81300-11	FLYWHEEL MAGNETO ASS'Y	1		
28- 1	207-81350-10	. ROTOR ASS'Y	1		
28- 2	207-81312-10	. COIL, source	1		
28- 3	288-81313-11	. COIL, lighting	1		
28- 4	110-81348-20	. SCREW, pan head	4		
28- 5	92901-04100	. WASHER, spring	4		
28- 6	257-81332-10	. PLATE, timing	1		
28- 7	207-81321-10	. CONTACT BREAKER ASS'Y	1		
28- 8	110-81347-20	. SCREW, pan head	1		
28- 9	92901-04100	. WASHER, spring	1		
28-10	92901-04200	. WASHER, plain	1		
28-11	207-81326-10	. CONDENSER	1		
28-12	110-81346-20	. SCREW, pan head	1		
28-13	92901-04100	. WASHER, spring	1		
28-14	207-81331-10	. LUBRICATOR	1		
28-15	109-81328-10	. CLAMP, lead	1		
28-16	165-81145-21	. SCREW, pan head (4-8)	1		
28-17	92901-04100	. WASHER, spring	1		
28-18	98701-05015	SCREW, flat head	2		

NOTES

YAMAHA
PARTS LIST
MODEL JT2
MODEL JT2·MX

Fig. 1 CRANKCASE · CYLINDER

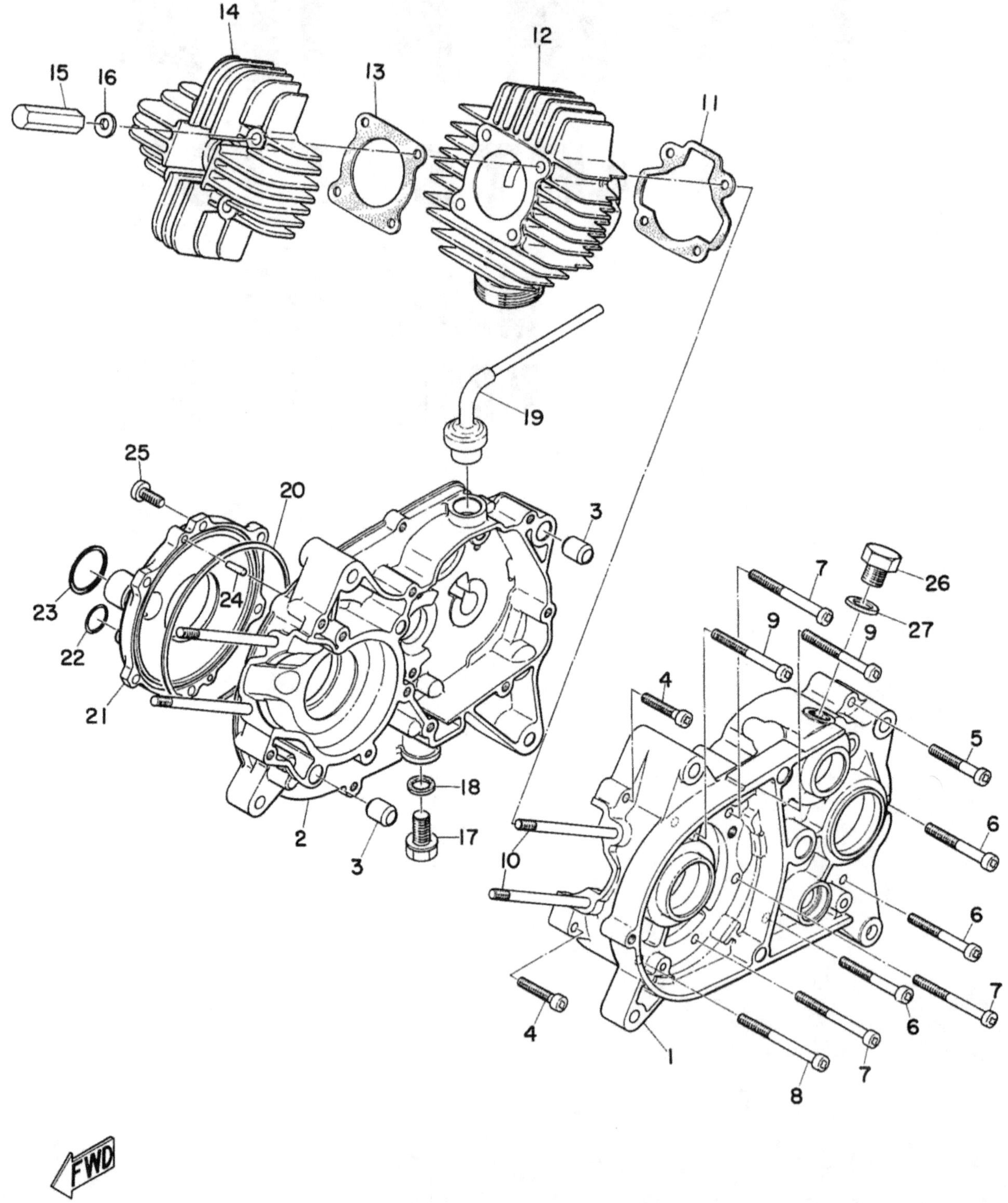

CRANKCASE · CYLINDER

Ref. No.	Part No.	Description	Q'ty JT	Q'ty MX	Applicable Machine No.	Remarks
1-1	257-15111-01	CASE, crank left	1	1		
1-2	257-15121-00	CASE, crank right	1	1		
1-3	91810-08016	PIN, dowel (9.8-12-16)	2	2		
1-4	92501-06030	SCREW, pan head	2	2		
1-5	92501-06045	SCREW, pan head	1	1		
1-6	92501-06050	SCREW, pan head	3	3		
1-7	92501-06060	SCREW, pan head	3	3		
1-8	92501-06065	SCREW, pan head	1	1		
1-9	92501-06055	SCREW, pan head	2	2		
1-10	109-11361-00	BOLT, cylinder holding	4	4		
1-11	109-11351-00	GASKET, cylinder	1	1		
1-12	259-11311-00	CYLINDER	1	1		
1-13	107-11181-01	GASKET, cylinder head	1	1		
1-14	259-11111-01-94	HEAD, cylinder	1	1		
1-15	126-11171-60	NUT, cylinder holding	4	4		
1-16	92901-06200	WASHER, plain	4	4		
1-17	132-15351-00	PLUG, drain	1	1		
1-18	132-15353-00	GASKET, drain plug	1	1		
1-19	288-15371-00	BREATHER	1	1		
1-20	180-13554-00	RING, rubber	1	1		
1-21	257-13551-00	COVER, valve	1	1		
1-22	93210-23029	O-RING (3.53-21.82)	1	1		
1-23	93210-12014	O-RING (2.6-10.77)	1	1		
1-24	93604-14012	PIN, dowel (4-13.8)	2	2		

CRANKCASE · CYLINDER

Ref. No.	Part No.	Description	Q'ty JT	Q'ty MX	Applicable Machine No.	Remarks
1-25	92501-06015	SCREW, pan head	6	6		
1-26	288-18588-00	PLUG, blind	1	1		
1-27	136-82543-00	GASKET (11.6-18-1)	1	1		

Fig. 2 CRANKCASE COVER

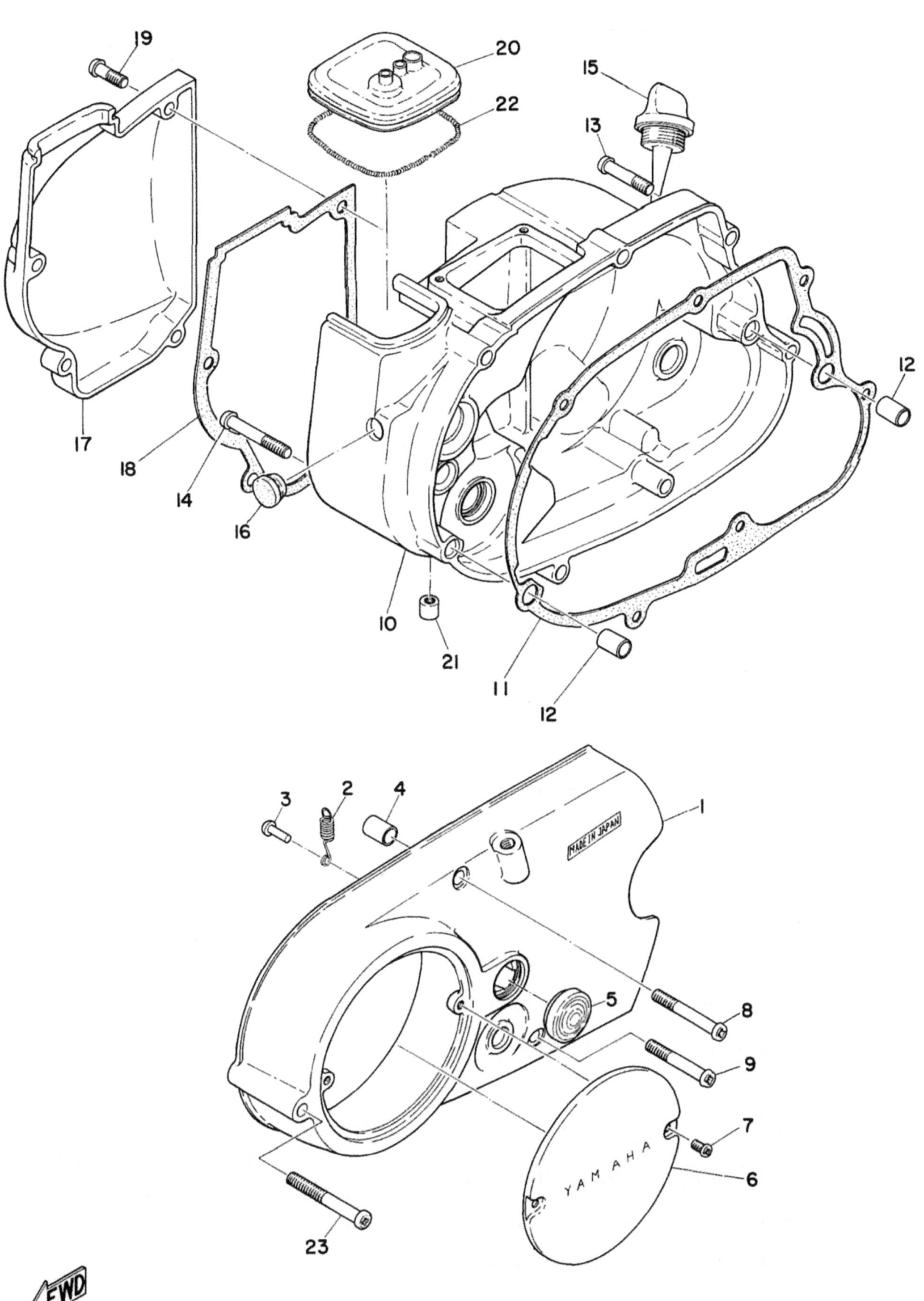

CRANKCASE COVER

Ref. No.	Part No.	Description	Q'ty JT	Q'ty MX	Applicable Machine No.	Remarks
2- 1	257-15410-01	CRANKCASE COVER ASS'Y, left	1	1		
2- 2	257-16345-00	. SPRING, lever return	1	1		
2- 3	132-16346-00	. HOOK, spring	1	1		
2- 4	91810-03014	PIN, dowel (8.5-10-14)	2	2		
2- 5	257-15417-01	COVER, cap	1	1		
2- 6	164-15415-00	COVER, generator	1	1		
2- 7	98501-04008	SCREW, pan head	2	2		
2- 8	92501-06045	SCREW, pan head	2	2		
2- 9	92501-06040	SCREW, pan head	1	1		
2-10	257-15421-01	COVER, crankcase right	1	1		
2-11	257-15451-00	GASKET, crankcase cover	1	1		
2-12	91810-03014	PIN, dowel (8.5-10-14)	2	2		
2-13	92501-06030	SCREW, pan head	6	6		
2-14	92501-06040	SCREW, pan head	1	1		
2-15	315-15362-00	PLUG, oil level	1	1		
2-16	122-15486-00	GROMMET	1	1		
2-17	257-15413-00	COVER, carburetor	1	1		
2-18	257-15463-00	GASKET, carburetor cover	1	1		
2-19	92501-06018	SCREW, pan head	4	4		
2-20	288-14481-01	CAP, carburetor	1	1		
2-21	257-15433-00	CLEANER, drain	1	1		
2-22	288-14455-00	BAND	1	1		
2-23	92501-06050	SCREW, pan head	1	1		

Fig. 3 CRANK·PISTON

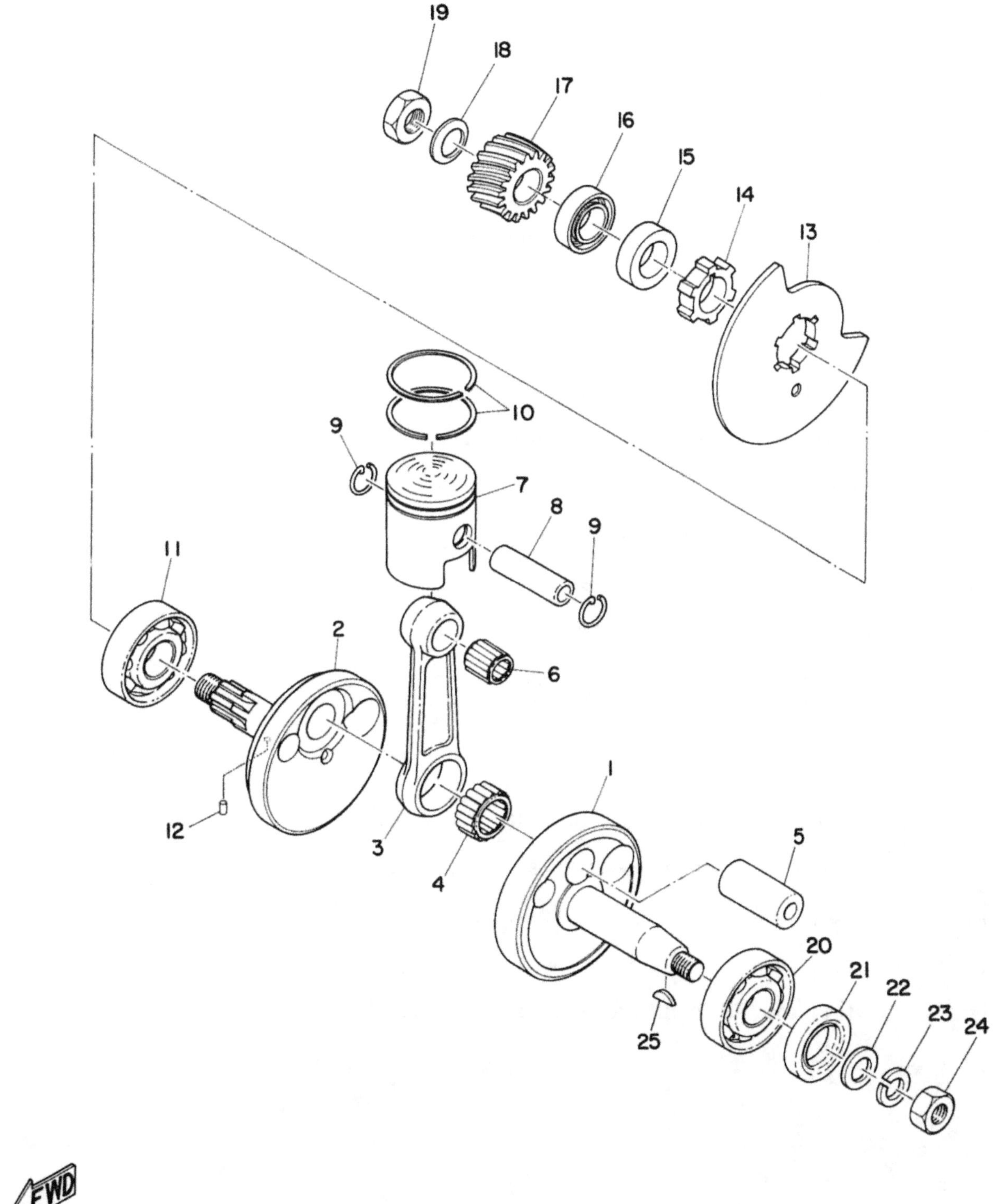

CRANK · PISTON

Ref. No.	Part No.	Description	Q'ty JT	Q'ty MX	Applicable Machine No.	Remarks
3-0-1	259-11400-00	CRANK ASS'Y	1	1		
3-1	259-11412-00	. CRANK, left	1	1		
3-2	259-11422-00	. CRANK, right	1	1		
3-3	126-11651-00	. ROD, connecting	1	1		
3-4	93310-41810	. BEARING, con-rod big end	1	1		
3-5	257-11681-00	. PIN, crank	1	1		
3-6	93310-11202	BEARING, con-rod smallend	1	1		
3-7	289-11631-00-96	PISTON (.96mm STD)	U.R 1	U.R 1		
	289-11631-00-97	PISTON (.97mm STD)				
	289-11631-00-98	PISTON (.98mm STD)				
	289-11635-00	PISTON (1st O.S)	1	1		Alternate Part
	289-11636-00	PISTON (2nd O.S)	1	1		Alternate Part
3-8	102-11633-01	PIN, piston	1	1		
3-9	132-11634-00	CLIP, piston pin	2	2		
3-10	113-11601-02	PISTON RING SET	1s	1s		STD
	113-11601-12	PISTON RING SET (1st o.s)	1s	1s		Alternate Part
	113-11601-22	PISTON RING SET (2nd o.s)	1s	1s		Alternate Part
3-11	93306-30302	BEARING (6303C3)	1	1		
3-12	93603-08067	PIN, dowel (3-8)	1	1		
3-13	257-13512-00	VALVE	1	1		
3-14	257-13515-00	COLLAR, valve	1	1		
3-15	257-16136-00	COLLAR, distance	1	1		

CRANK · PISTON

Ref. No.	Part No.	Description	Q'ty JT	Q'ty MX	Applicable Machine No.	Remarks
3-16	93103-28012	OIL SEAL (SW-27-47-8)	1	1		
3-17	257-16111-00	GEAR, primary drive (19T)	1	1		
3-18	164-16119-00	SPRING, bellevile	1	1		
3-19	137-16377-00	NUT, clutch boss	1	1		
3-20	93306-20412	BEARING (6204C3)	1	1		
3-21	93102-20009	OIL SEAL (SD-20-35-7)	1	1		
3-22	214-11557-01	WASHER (12.2-22-2.9)	1	1		
3-23	92901-12100	WASHER, spring	1	1		
3-24	98801-12200	NUT	1	1		
3-25	146-11545-00	KEY, woodruff	1	1		

Fig. 4 CLUTCH

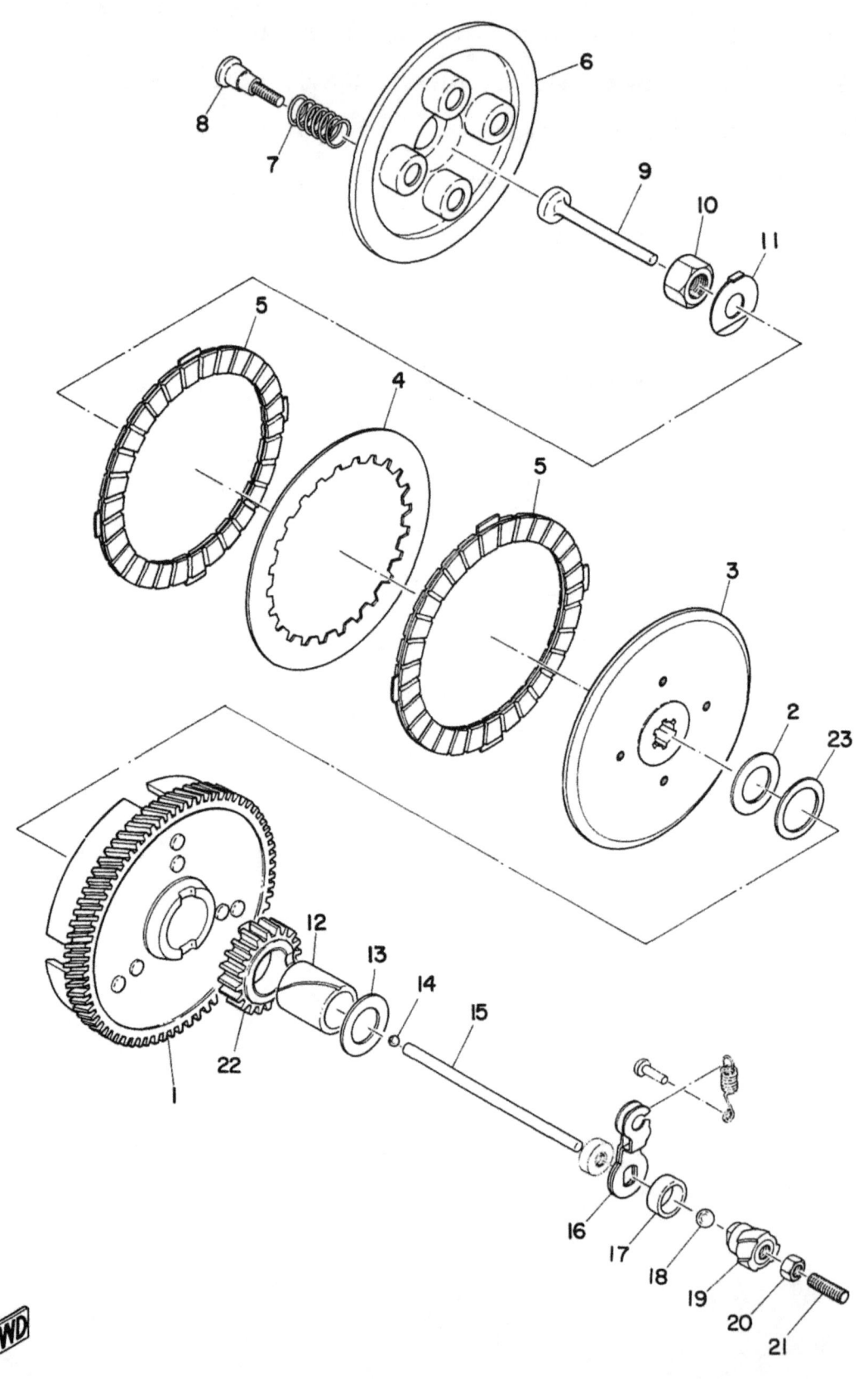

CLUTCH

Ref. No.	Part No.	Description	Q'ty JT	Q'ty MX	Applicable Machine No.	Remarks
4- 0-1	257-16301-01	CLUTCH ASS'Y	1	1		
4- 1	257-16150-01	. DRIVEN GEAR COMP. (74T)	1	1		
4- 2	122-16164-00	. PLATE, thrust (17.2-30-2)	1	1		
4- 3	257-16371-00	. BOSS, clutch	1	1		
4- 4	257-16324-00	. PLATE, clutch	1	1		
4- 5	131-16321-00	. PLATE, friction	2	2		
4- 6	257-16351-00	. PLATE, pressure	1	1		
4- 7	137-16333-00	. SPRING, clutch	4	4		
4- 8	137-16337-01	. SCREW, spring	4	4		
4- 9	137-16356-00	ROD, push 1	1	1		
4-10	137-16377-00	NUT, clutch boss	1	1		
4-11	137-16378-00	WASHER, clutch boss	1	1		
4-12	257-16181-00	SPACER	1	1		
4-13	122-16164-00	PLATE, thrust (17.2-30-2)	1	1		
4-14	93503-16010	BALL (3/16 inch)	1	1		
4-15	257-16357-00	ROD, push 2	1	1		
4-16	257-16342-00	LEVER, push	1	1		
4-17	93108-15001	OIL SEAL (OSO-15-22-7)	1	1		
4-18	93501-04011	BALL (1/4 inch)	1	1		
4-19	257-16341-00	SCREW, push	1	1		
4-20	92801-06300	NUT	1	1		
4-21	257-16343-00	SCREW, adjusting	1	1		
4-22	164-15631-01	GEAR, kick pinion (19T)	1	1		
4-23	116-16153-00	WASHER, thrust (23-30-1.5)	1	1		

Fig. 5 TRANSMISSION

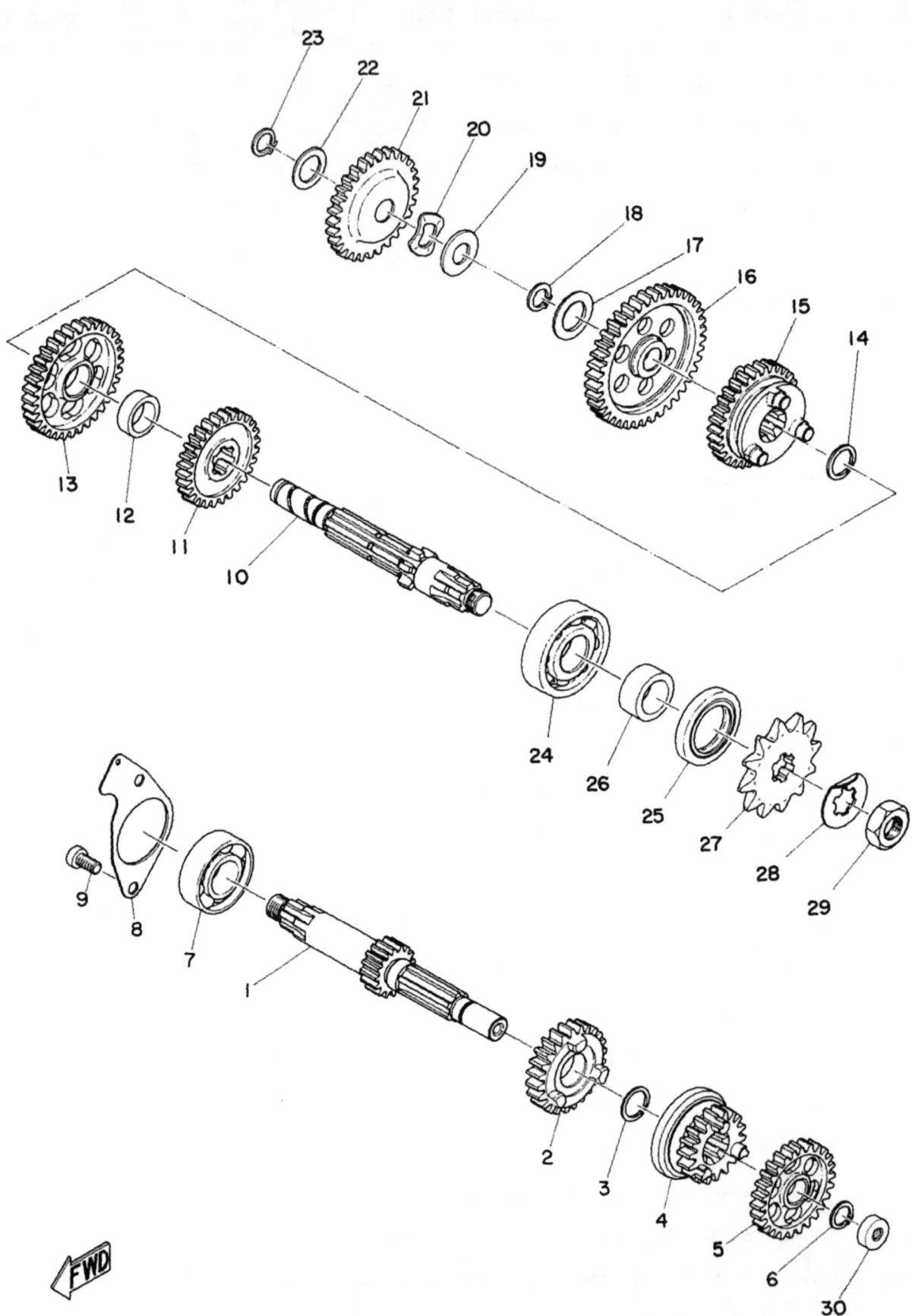

TRANSMISSION

Ref. No.	Part No.	Description	Q'ty JT	Q'ty MX	Applicable Machine No.	Remarks
5-1	257-17411-01	AXLE, main (13T)	1	1		
5-2	257-17131-01	GEAR, 3rd pinion (23T)	1	1		
5-3	257-17414-00	CLIP	1	1		
5-4	257-17121-00	GEAR, 2nd pinion (18T)	1	1		
5-5	257-17141-00	GEAR, 4th pinion (26T)	1	1		
5-6	93410-13004	CIRCLIP (S-13)	1	1		
5-7	93306-20303	BEARING (6203Z)	1	1		
5-8	257-17471-01	PLATE, bearing cover	1	1		
5-9	92501-06012	SCREW, pan head	2	2		
5-10	257-17421-01	AXLE, drive	1	1		
5-11	257-17241-00	GEAR, 4th wheel (27T)	1	1		
5-12	257-17258-00	COLLAR, distance	1	1		
5-13	257-17221-01	GEAR, 2nd wheel (34T)	1	1		
5-14	257-17414-00	CLIP	1	1		
5-15	257-17231-00	GEAR, 3rd wheel (30T)	1	1		
5-16	257-17211-00	GEAR, 1st wheel (40T)	1	1		
5-17	257-17219-00-06	SHIM (13.2-24-0.6)	1	1		
5-18	93410-13004	CIRCLIP (S-13)	1	1		
5-19	201-15653-00	WASHER, thrust (13.2-23-1)	1	1		
5-20	137-15643-00	WASHER, wave	1	1		
5-21	257-15651-00	GEAR, kick idle (28T)	1	1		
5-22	132-15653-00-10	WASHER, thrust (13.3-22-1.0)	U.R 1	U.R 1		
	132-15653-00-12	WASHER, thrust (13.3-22-1.2)				
	132-15653-00-14	WASHER, thrust (13.3-22-1.4)				

TRANSMISSION

Ref. No.	Part No.	Description	Q'ty JT	MX	Applicable Machine No.	Remarks
5-23	93410-13004	CIRCLIP (S-13)	1	1		
5-24	93306-30305	BEARING (6303)	1	1		
5-25	93102-25017	OIL SEAL (SD-25-40-5)	1	1		
5-26	257-17462-00	COLLAR, distance	1	1		
5-27	257-17461-20	SPROCKET, drive (12T)				
	257-17461-30	SPROCKET, drive (13T)				STD
	257-17461-40	SPROCKET, drive (14T)	1	1	U.R U.R	
	257-17461-50	SPROCKET, drive (15T)				
5-28	257-17464-00	WASHER, lock	1	1		
5-29	257-17463-00	NUT, lock	1	1		
5-30	257-15389-00	SEAL, push rod	1	1		

Fig. 6   SHIFTER A

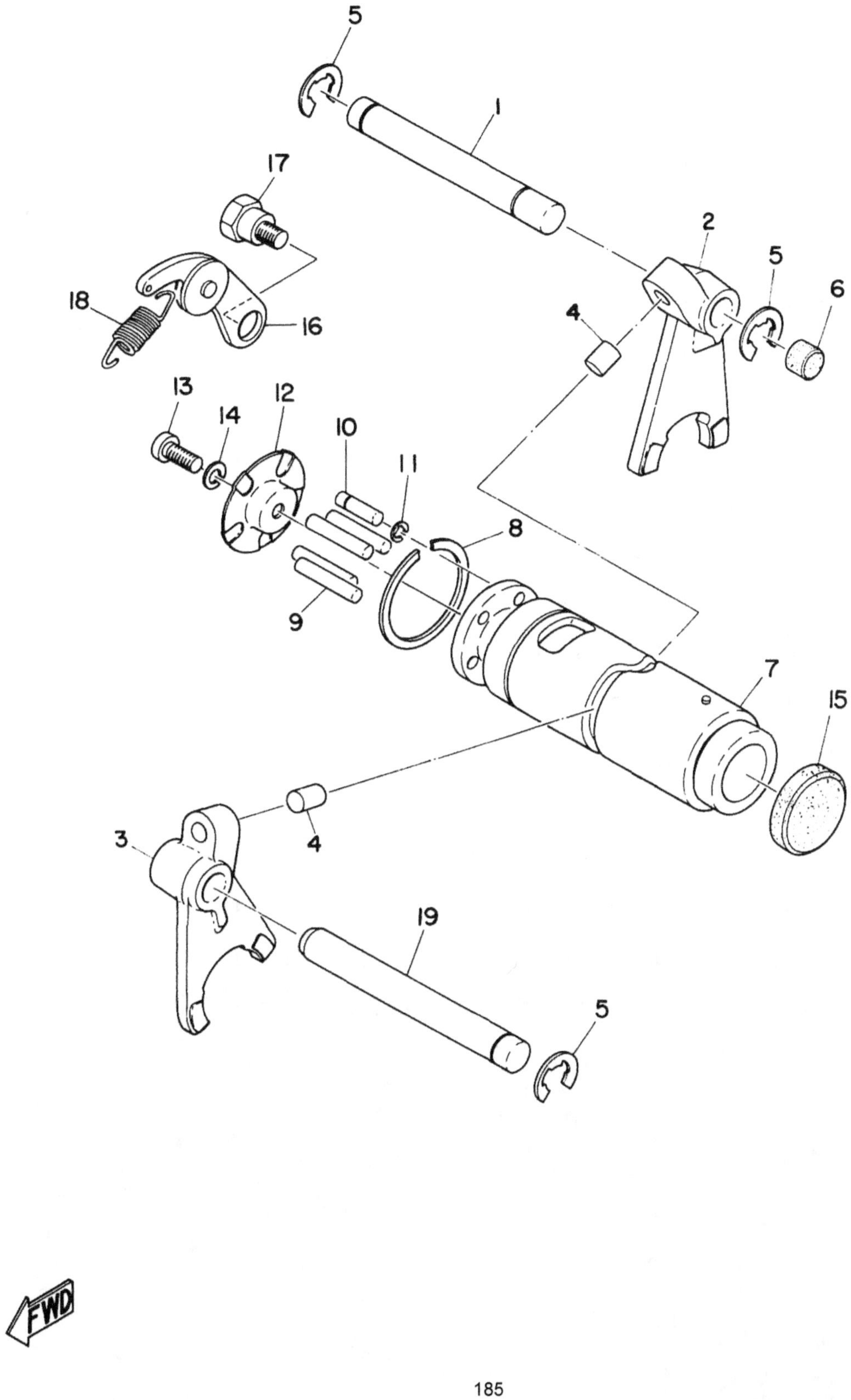

SHIFTER A

Ref. No.	Part No.	Description	Q'ty JT	Q'ty MX	Applicable Machine No.	Remarks
6- 1	257-18534-00	BAR, shift fork guide	1	1		
6- 2	259-18511-01	FORK, shift 1	1	1		
6- 3	257-18512-01	FORK, shift 2	1	1		
6- 4	257-18552-00	PIN, cam follower	2	2		
6- 5	93430-08006	CIRCLIP (E-8)	3	3		
6- 6	150-18328-00	PLUG, blind	1	1		
6- 7	257-18541-61	CAM, shift	1	1		
6- 8	93440-32017	CIRCLIP	1	1		
6- 9	93604-22050	PIN, dowel (4-21.8)	4	4		
6-10	174-18544-00	PIN, locating	1	1		
6-11	93430-03014	CIRCLIP (E-2.5)	1	1		
6-12	164-18561-00	PLATE, side	1	1		
6-13	98501-05012	SCREW, pan head	1	1		
6-14	92901-05100	WASHER, spring	1	1		
6-15	257-18589-00	PLUG, blind	1	1		
6-16	132-18140-00	STOPPER LEVER ASS'Y	1	1		
6-17	132-18177-00	BOLT, stopper	1	1		
6-18	132-18143-00	SPRING, stopper	1	1		
6-19	257-18531-00	BAR, shift fork guide	1	1		

Fig. 7 SHIFTER B

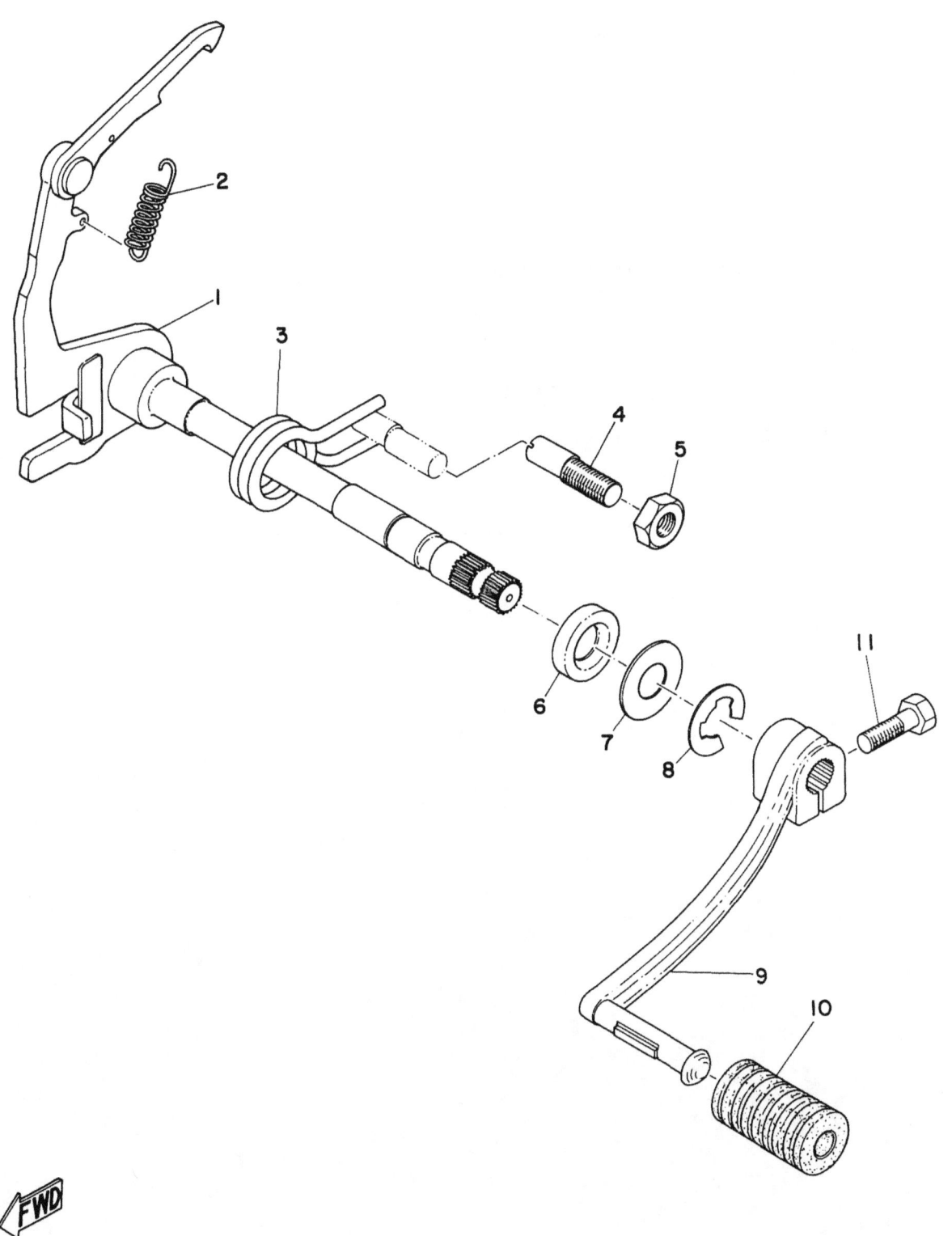

SHIFTER B

Ref. No.	Part No.	Description	Q'ty JT	Q'ty MX	Applicable Machine No.	Remarks
7-1	257-18101-00	CHANGE SHAFT ASS'Y	1	1		
7-2	132-18123-00	. SPRING, shift arm	1	1		
7-3	132-18124-00	SPRING, shaft return	1	1		
7-4	132-18133-00	SCREW, adjusting	1	1		
7-5	98801-08100	NUT	1	1		
7-6	93101-12004	OIL SEAL (S-12-22-5)	1	1		
7-7	132-18137-00	WASHER, change axle (14.1-28-1.6)	1	1		
7-8	93430-10016	CIRCLIP (E-10)	1	1		
7-9	248-18111-00-93	PEDAL, change	1	1		
7-10	132-18113-01	COVER, change pedal	1	1		
7-11	91201-06020	BOLT	1	1		

Fig. 8 STARTER

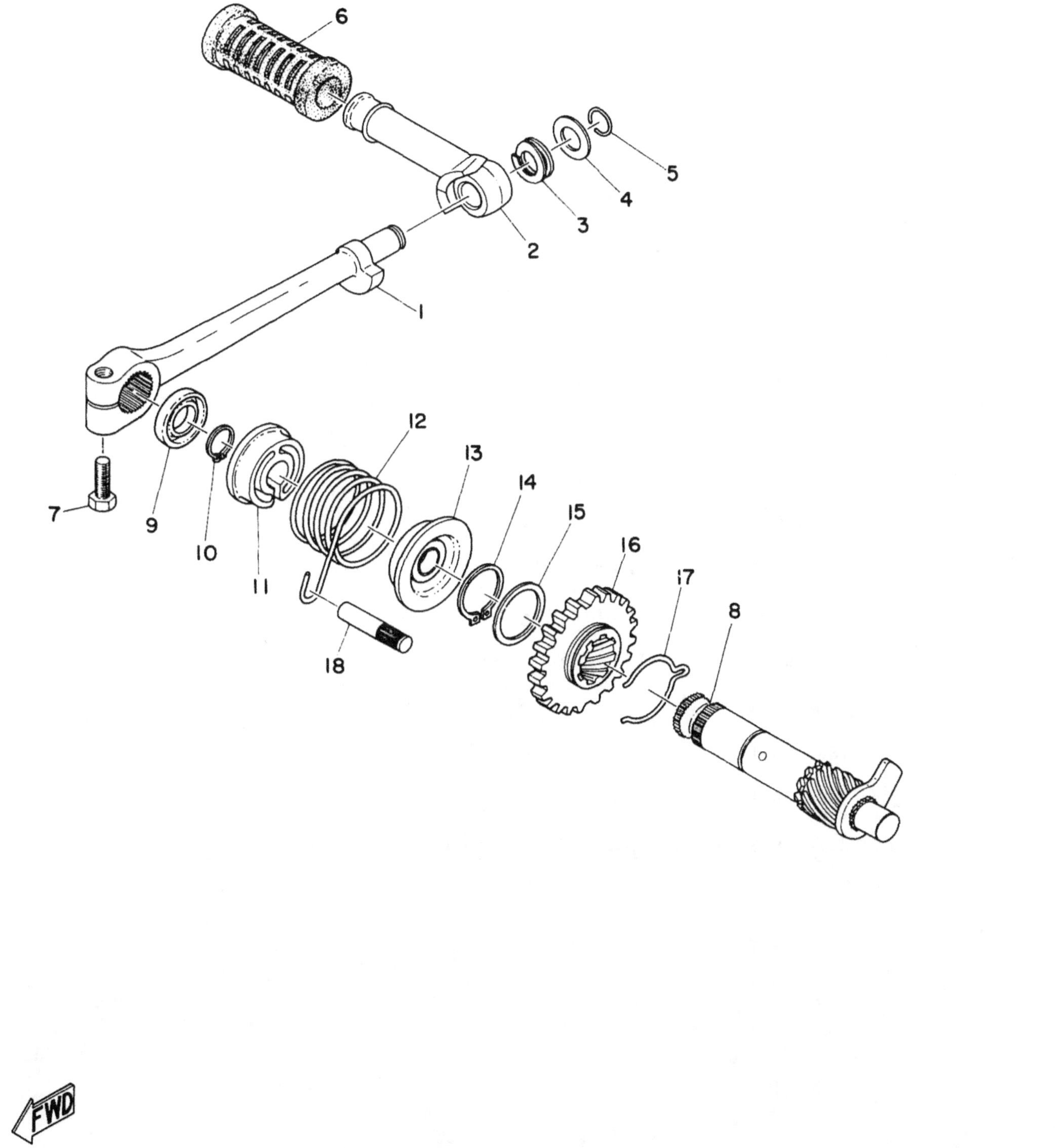

STARTER

Ref. No.	Part No.	Description	Q'ty JT	Q'ty MX	Applicable Machine No.	Remarks
8- 0-1	276-15610-00-93	KICK CRANK ASS'Y	1	1		
8- 1	276-15611-00	. CRANK, kick	1	1		Not for sale
8- 2	122-15612-02	. LEVER, kick	1	1		
8- 3	214-15625-00	. SPRING, kick crank	1	1		
8- 4	132-15616-01	. WASHER, kick lever	1	1		
8- 5	132-15617-00	. CLIP, kick lever	1	1		
8- 6	156-15618-01	COVER, kick lever	1	1		
8- 7	91101-06020	BOLT	1	1		
8- 8	180-15660-00	KICK AXLE ASS'Y	1	1		
8- 9	93109-15001	OIL SEAL (SDO-15-26-6)	1	1		
8-10	93410-15005	CIRCLIP (S-15)	1	1		
8-11	132-15676-00	COVER, kick spring	1	1		
8-12	132-15665-00	SPRING, kick	1	1		
8-13	304-15664-00	GUIDE, kick spring	1	1		
8-14	93410-25017	CIRCLIP (S-25)	1	1		
8-15	117-15644-00	SHIM (25.1-32-1)	1	1		
8-16	180-15641-00	GEAR, kick (28T)	1	1		
8-17	180-15687-00	CLIP, kick	1	1		
8-18	257-15668-00	STOPPER, kick spring	1	1		

Fig. 9 AIR CLEANER

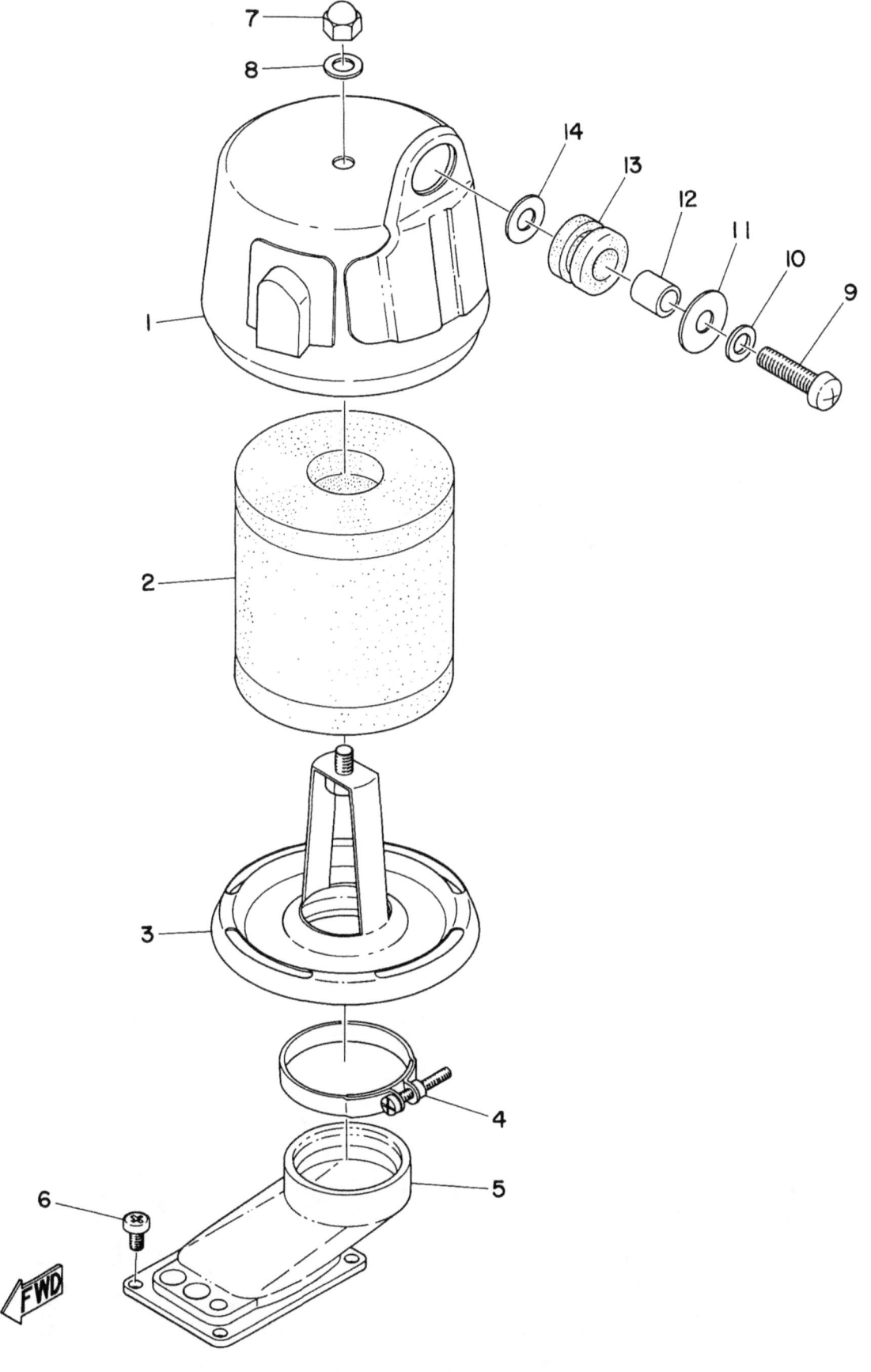

AIR CLEANER

Ref. No.	Part No.	Description	Q'ty JT	Q'ty MX	Applicable Machine No.	Remarks
9- 1	288-14412-01-35	CAP, cleaner case	1	1		
9- 2	288-14451-01	ELEMENT, air cleaner	1	1		
9- 3	288-14411-01-35	CASE, air cleaner	1	1		
9- 4	194-14455-00	BAND	1	1		
9- 5	288-14453-01	JOINT, air cleaner	1	1		
9- 6	98501-04008	SCREW, pan head	4	4		
9- 7	98803-06700	NUT, crown	1	1		
9- 8	178-14766-00	WASHER	1	1		
9- 9	92501-06025	SCREW, pan head	1	1		
9-10	92901-06100	WASHER, spring	1	1		
9-11	116-28324-00	WASHER, leg shield 2	1	1		
9-12	214-21717-00	DAMPER, battery box	1	1		
9-13	214-21633-00	COLLAR, fender mount	1	1		
9-14	148-27219-00	WASHER, brake shaft	1	1		

Fig. 10 CARBURETOR

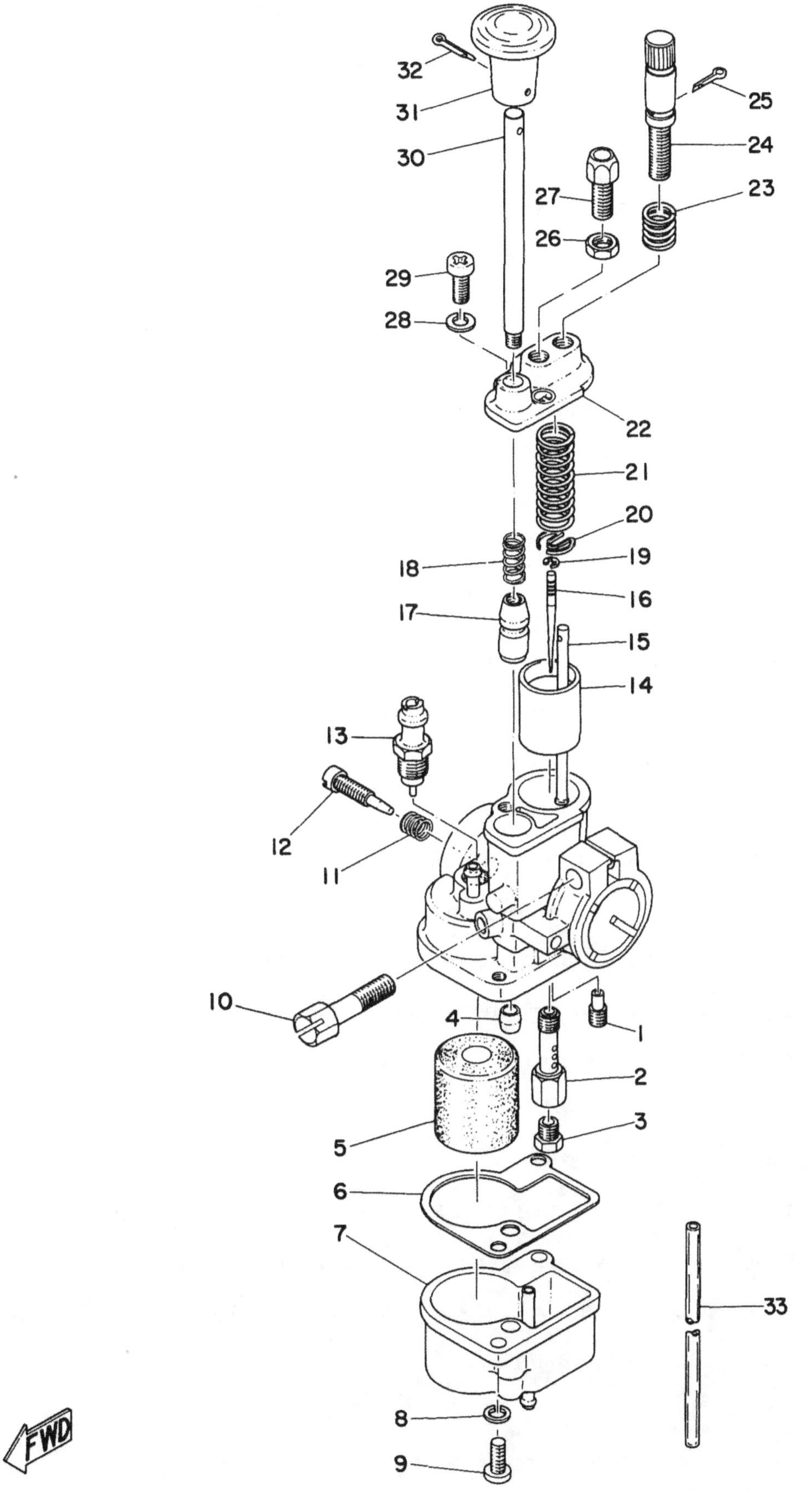

CARBURETOR

Ref. No.	Part No.	Description	Q'ty JT	MX	Applicable Machine No.	Remarks
10- 0-1	288-14301-60	CARBURETOR ASS'Y	1	1		
10- 1	288-14342-38	. JET, pilot (#38)	1	1		
10- 2	288-14341-01	. NOZZLE, main	1	1		
10- 3	288-14343-39	. JET, main (#78)	1	1		
	288-14343-40	. JET, main (#80)	1	1		STD
	288-14343-41	. JET, main (#82)	1	1		
10- 4	288-14344-25	. JET, starter (#50)	1	1		
10- 5	288-14385-00	. FLOAT	1	1		
10- 6	288-14384-00	. GASKET	1	1		
10- 7	288-14381-00	. BODY, float chamber	1	1		
10- 8	92901-04100	. WASHER, spring	2	2		
10- 9	98501-04010	. SCREW, pan head	2	2		
10-10	288-14125-00	. SCREW, body fitting	1	1		
10-11	288-14334-00	. SPRING, air adjusting	1	1		
10-12	288-14323-00	. SCREW, air adjusting	1	1		
10-13	288-14390-10	. VALVE SEAT ASS'Y (#1.0)	1	1		
10-14	288-14312-15	. VALVE, throttle (#1.5)	1	1		
10-15	288-14314-00	. BAR, throttle	1	1		
10-16	288-14336-01	. NEEDLE	1	1		
10-17	288-14371-00	. PLUNGER STARTER ASS'Y	1	1		
10-18	288-14335-00	. SPRING, plunger	1	1		
10-19	288-14137-00	. CLIP	1	1		
10-20	288-14136-00	. SEAT, spring	1	1		
10-21	288-14331-00	. SPRING, throttle valve	1	1		

CARBURETOR

Ref. No.	Part No.	Description	Q'ty JT	Q'ty MX	Applicable Machine No.	Remarks
10-22	288-14158-00	. TOP, mixing chamber	1	1		
10-23	288-14333-00	. SPRING, throttle stop	1	1		
10-24	288-14321-00	. SCREW, throttle	1	1		
10-25	91401-12010	. PIN, cotter	1	1		
10-26	288-14161-00	. NUT, wire adjusting	1	1		
10-27	288-14124-00	. SCREW, wire adjusting	1	1		
10-28	92901-04100	. WASHER, spring	1	1		
10-29	98501-04010	. SCREW, pan head	1	1		
10-30	288-14379-00	. ROD, starter	1	1		
10-31	288-14118-00	KNOB, starter	1	1		
10-32	91401-16012	PIN, cotter	1	1		
10-33	288-14197-00	PIPE, air vent	1	1		

Fig. 11 EXHAUST

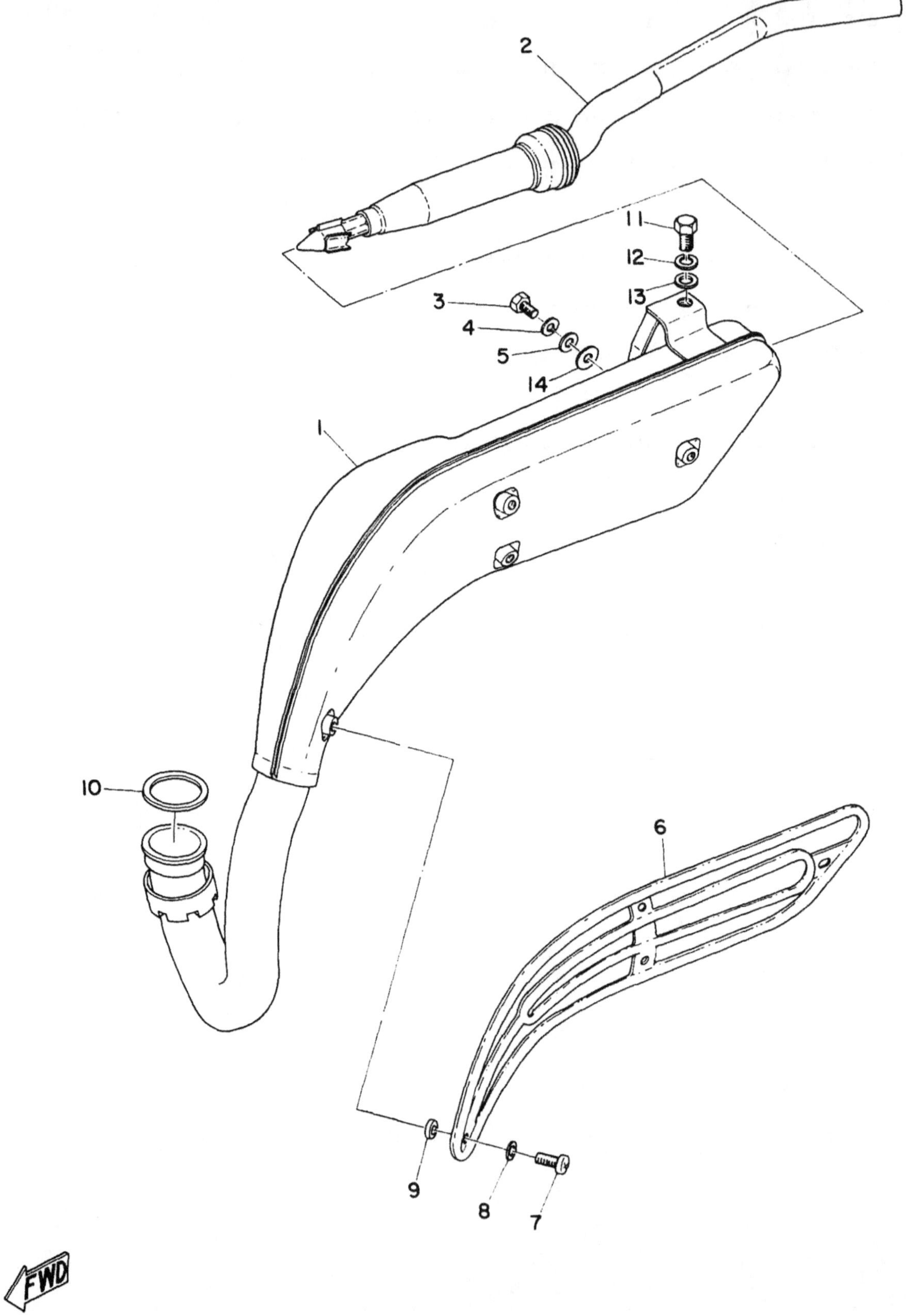

EXHAUST

Ref. No.	Part No.	Description	Q'ty JT	Q'ty MX	Applicable Machine No.	Remarks
11- 1	288-14610-30	EXHAUST PIPE ASS'Y	1	1		
11- 2	288-14752-31	. PIPE, outlet	1	1		
11- 3	91201-06015	. BOLT	1	1		
11- 4	92901-06100	. WASHER, spring	1	1		
11- 5	136-22316-00	. WASHER, chain case (6.5-15-1.2)	1	1		
11- 6	290-14718-10	PROTECTOR, muffler	1	1		
11- 7	91903-06010	SCREW, bind	4	4		
11- 8	178-14766-00	WASHER, protector (6.2-12-3.0)	4	4		
11- 9	214-14766-00	WASHER, protector (6.2-12-1.5)	4	4		
11-10	132-14613-00	GASKET, exhaust	1	1		
11-11	97201-08012	BOLT	1	1		
11-12	92901-08100	WASHER, spring	1	1		
11-13	92901-08200	WASHER, plain	1	1		
11-14	288-14623-00	GASKET	1	1		

Fig. 12 OIL PUMP

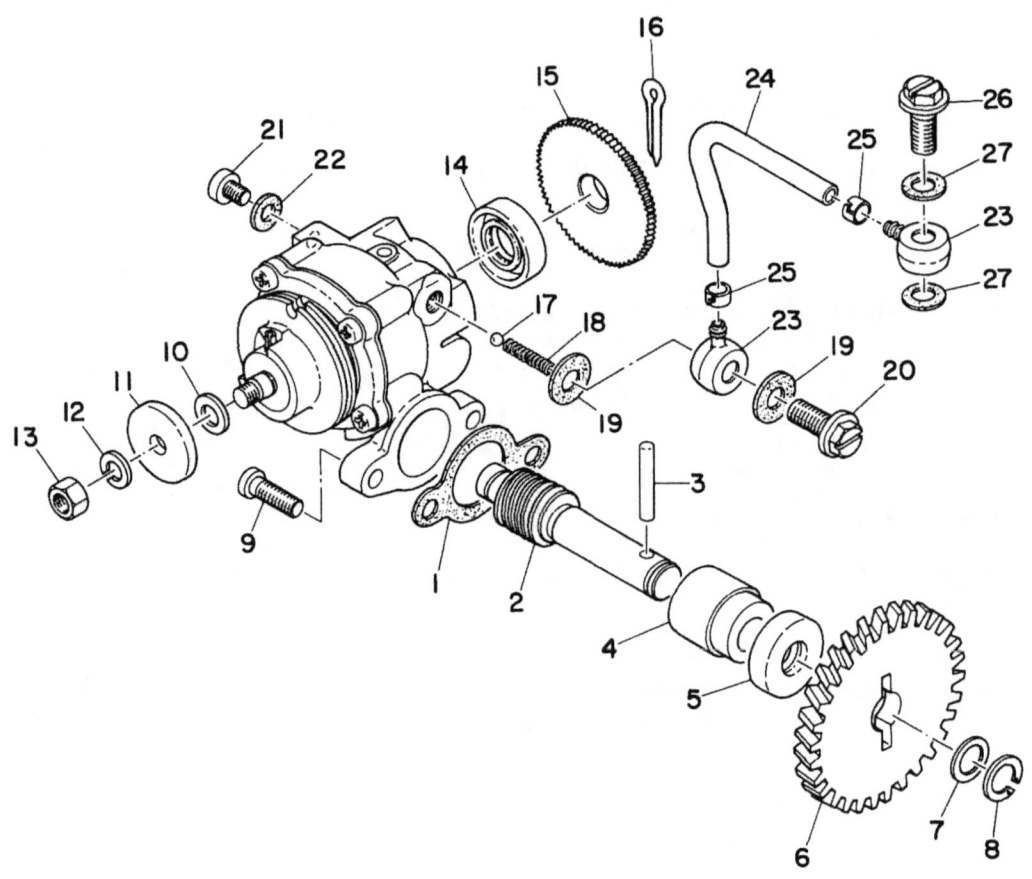

OIL PUMP

Ref. No.	Part No.	Description	Q'ty JT	Q'ty MX	Applicable Machine No.	Remarks
12- 1	126-13116-00	GASKET, pump case	1	1		
12- 2	257-13175-00	SHAFT, worm	1	1		
12- 3	93603-22028	PIN, dowel	1	1		
12- 4	137-13176-00	METAL, worm shaft outer	1	1		
12- 5	93101-10001	OIL SEAL (S-10-21-5)	1	1		
12- 6	257-13178-00	GEAR, drive (30T)	1	1		
12- 7	101-18137-00	WASHER (10.5-20-1.0)	1	1		
12- 8	93440-08001	CIRCLIP	1	1		
12- 9	98501-05015	SCREW, pan head	2	2		
12- 0-1	257-13101-00	OIL PUMP ASS'Y	1	1		
12-10	137-13137-00	. SHIM, plunger (5.8-10-0.1)	1	1		
12-11	137-13138-01	. PLATE, adjusting	1	1		
12-12	92901-05100	. WASHER, spring	1	1		
12-13	98801-05200	. NUT	1	1		
12-14	93101-10001	. OIL SEAL (S-10-21-5)	1	1		
12-15	137-13128-00	. PLATE, starter	1	1		
12-16	91401-12018	. PIN, cotter	1	1		
12-17	93505-32002	. BALL (5/32 inch)	1	1		
12-18	137-13169-00	. SPRING, check ball	1	1		
12-19	137-13167-00	. GASKET, banjo bolt	2	2		
12-20	137-13165-00	. BOLT, banjo	1	1		
12-21	98901-04008	. SCREW, bind	1	1		
12-22	137-13187-00	. GASKET, breather	1	1		
12-23	214-13162-00	. BANJO	2	2		

OIL PUMP

Ref. No.	Part No.	Description	Q'ty JT	Q'ty MX	Applicable Machine No.	Remarks
12-24	257-13161-00	. PIPE, delivery	1	1		
12-25	214-13164-00	. CLIP, delivery pipe	2	2		
12-26	137-13165-00	BOLT, banjo	1	1		
12-27	137-13167-00	GASKET, banjo	2	2		

Fig. 13 FLYWHEEL MAGNETO

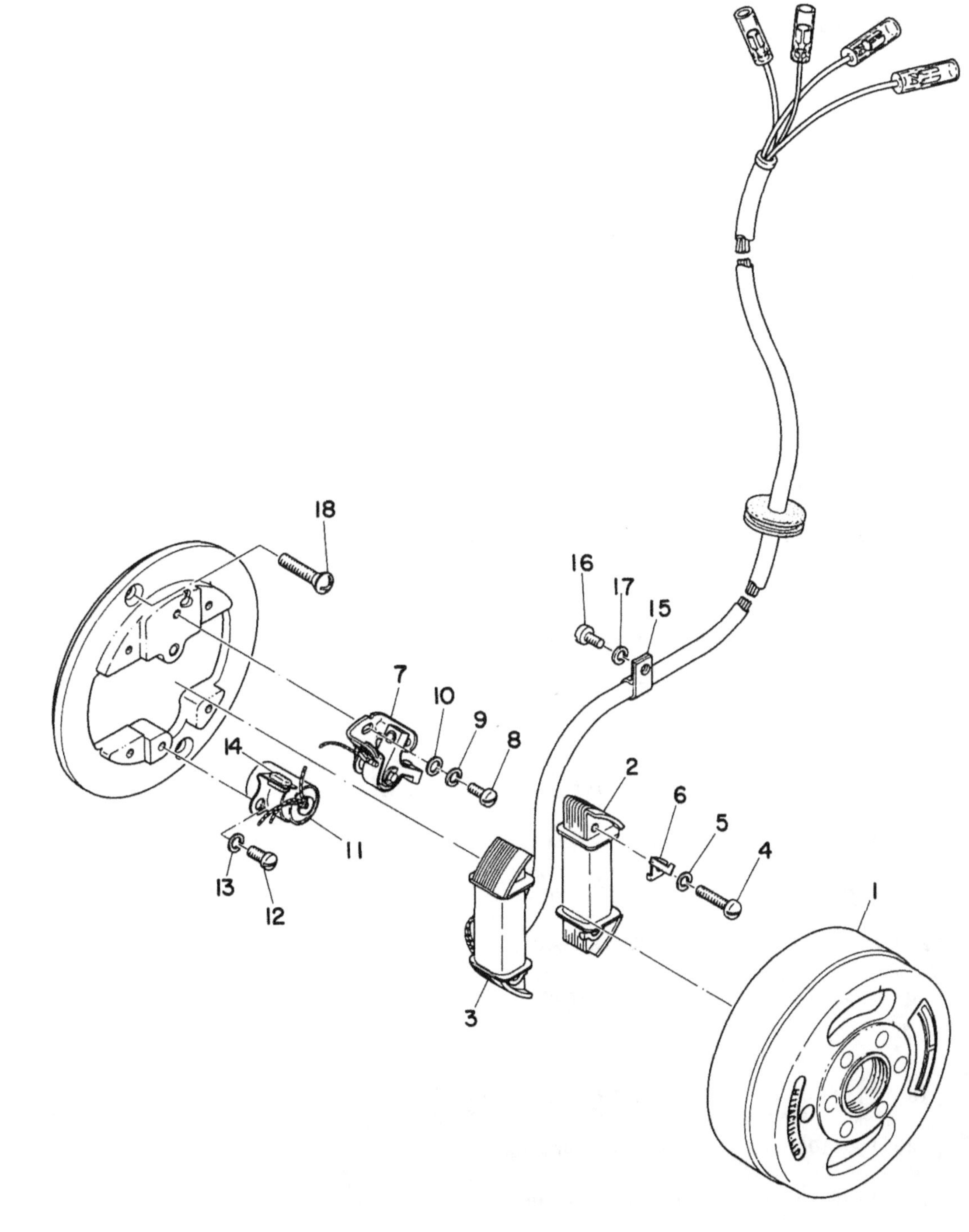

FLYWHEEL MAGNETO

Ref. No.	Part No.	Description	Q'ty JT	Q'ty MX	Applicable Machine No.	Remarks
13- 0-1	338-81300-10	FLYWHEEL MAGNETO ASS'Y	1			
	288-81300-11	FLYWHEEL MAGNETO ASS'Y		1		
13- 1	207-81350-10	. ROTOR ASS'Y	1	1		
13- 2	225-81312-10	. COIL source	1			
	207-81312-10	. COIL, source		1		
13- 3	338-81313-10	. COIL, lighting	1			
	288-81313-11	. COIL, lighting		1		
13- 4	110-81348-20	. SCREW, panhead	4	4		
13- 5	92901-04100	. WASHER, spring	4	4		
13- 6	296-81332-10	. PLATE, timing	1			
	257-81332-10	. PLATE, timing		1		
13- 7	207-81321-10	. CONTACT BREAKER ASS'Y	1	1		
13- 8	110-81347-20	. SCREW, panhead	1	1		
13- 9	92901-04100	. WASHER, spring	1	1		
13-10	92901-04200	. WASHER, plain	1	1		
13-11	207-81326-10	. CONDENSER	1	1		
13-12	110-81346-20	. SCREW, panhead	1	1		
13-13	92901-04100	. WASHER, spring	1	1		
13-14	207-81331-10	. LUBRICATOR	1	1		
13-15	109-81328-10	. CLAMP, lead	1			
13-16	165-81145-21	. SCREW, panhead (4-8)	1	1		
13-17	92901-04100	. WASHER, spring	1	1		
13-18	98701-05015	SCREW, flathead	2	2		

Fig. 14 FRAME

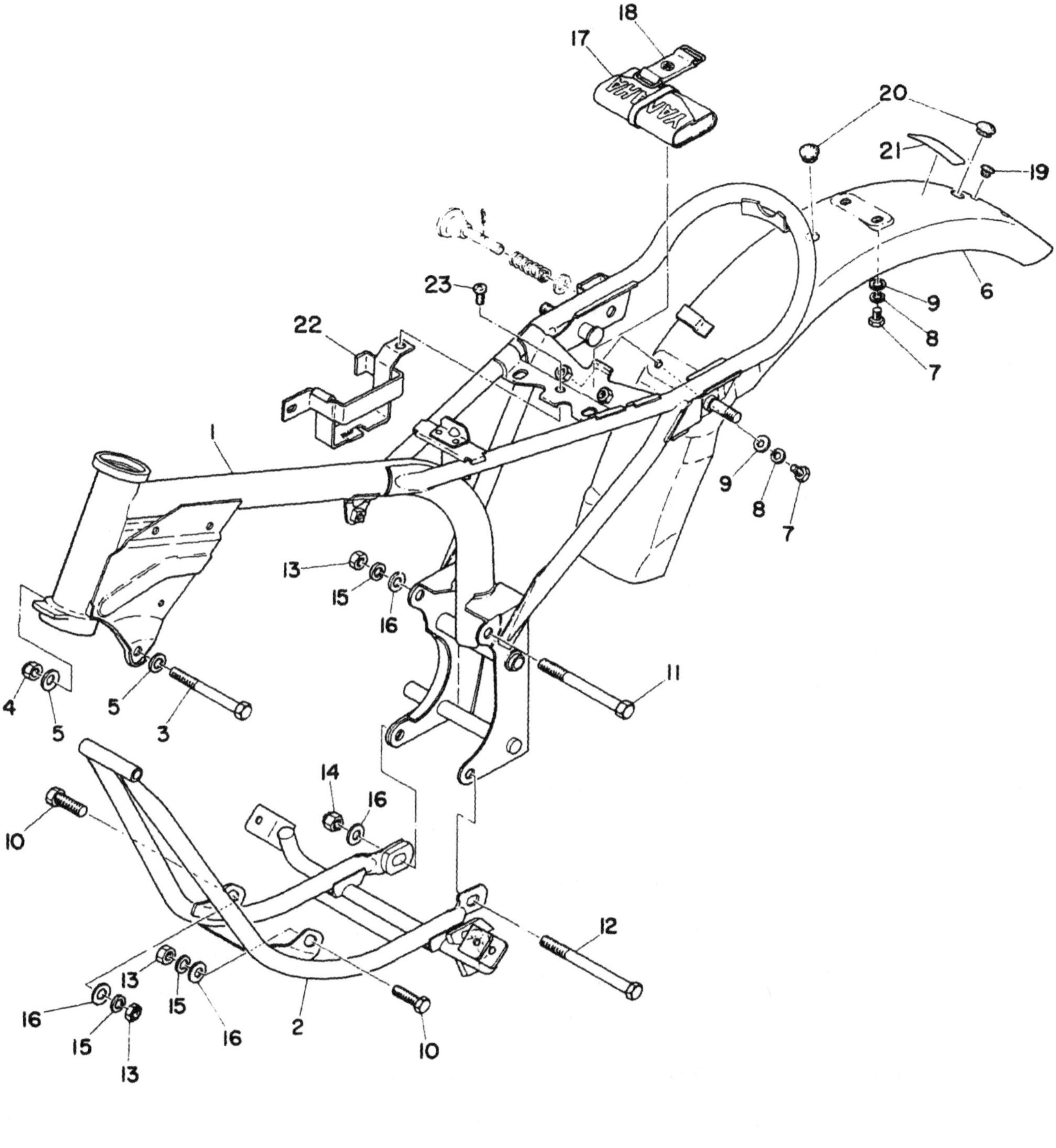

18
17
20
21
19
23
9
6
22
8
7
1
9
8
7
13
15
16
11
4
5
5
3
14
16
10
12
13
13
15
16
15
16
2
10
15
13
FWD

FRAME

Ref. No.	Part No.	Description	Q'ty JT	Q'ty MX	Applicable Machine No.	Remarks
14- 1	288-21110-02-33	FRAME COMP.	1	1		
14- 2	288-21280-00-33	DOWN TUBE COMP.	1	1		
14- 3	288-21481-00	BOLT, special	1	1		
14- 4	183-22143-00	NUT	1	1		
14- 5	92901-08200	WASHER, plain	2	2		
14- 6	338-21610-00-01	REAR FENDER COMP.	1			Mandarin Orange
	288-21610-01-02	REAR FENDER COMP.		1		Competition Yellow
14- 7	91201-06012	BOLT	4	4		
14- 8	92901-06100	WASHER, spring	4	4		
14- 9	92901-06200	WASHER, plain	4	4		
14-10	97201-08030	BOLT	2	2		
14-11	97201-08100	BOLT	1	1		
14-12	97201-08115	BOLT	1	1		
14-13	98801-08100	NUT	3	3		
14-14	183-22143-00	NUT	1	1		
14-15	92901-08100	WASHER, spring	3	3		
14-16	92901-08200	WASHER, plain	4	4		
14-17	207-28100-10	TOOL ASS'Y	1	1		
14-18	288-21376-00	BAND, tool cover	1	1		
14-19	288-83319-00	PLUG, blind	3	3		
14-20	214-84154-60	GROMMET	2	2		

FRAME

Ref. No.	Part No.	Description	Q'ty JT	Q'ty MX	Applicable Machine No.	Remarks
14-21	338-21659-00	LABEL, street warning	1			
	288-21659-00	LABEL, warning		1		
14-22	290-21240-00	BATTERY BOX COMP.	1			
14-23	92501-06012	SCREW, pan head	1			

Fig. 15 REAR ARM · REAR CUSHION

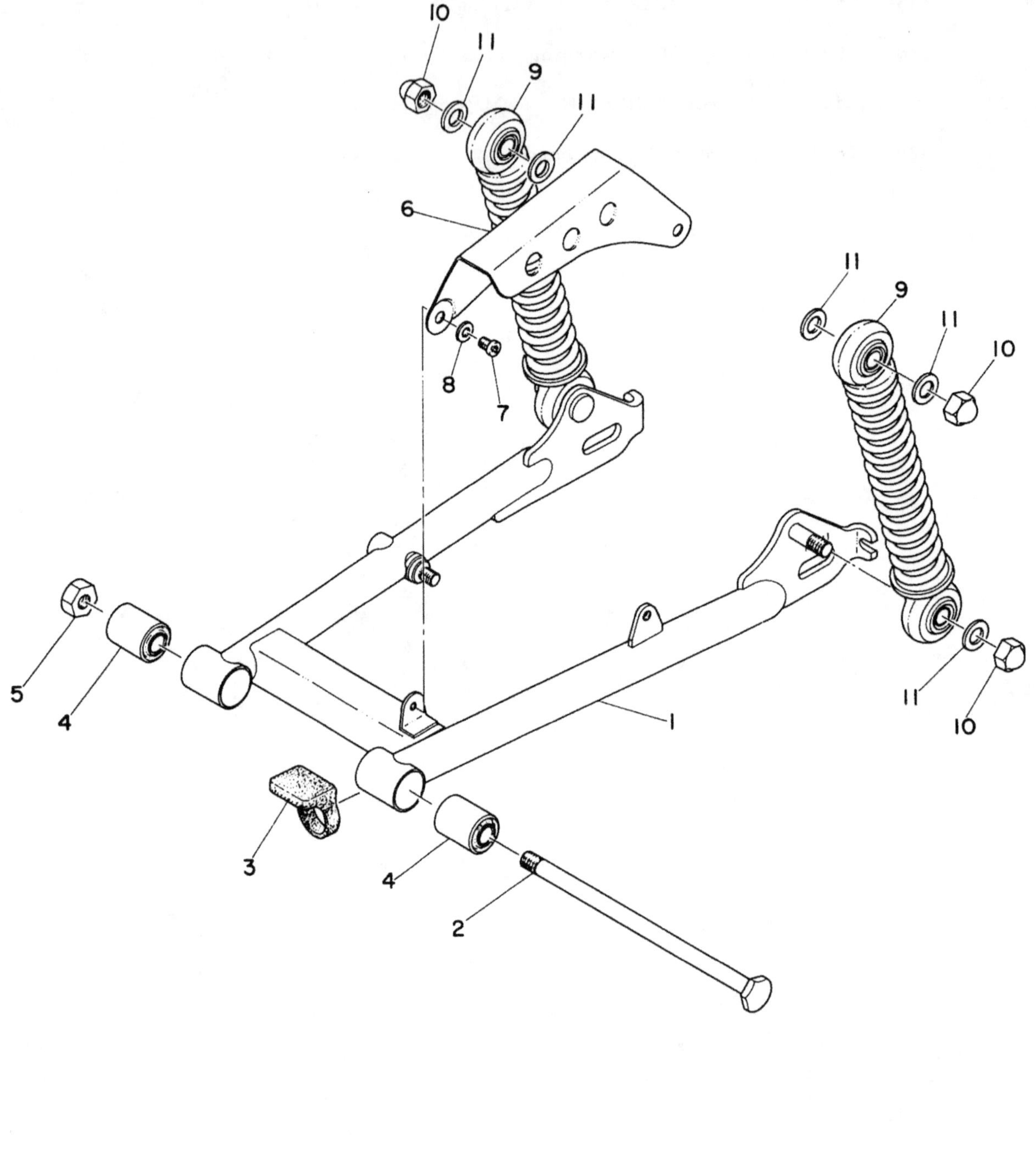

REAR ARM · REAR CUSHION

Ref. No.	Part No.	Description	Q'ty JT	Q'ty MX	Applicable Machine No.	Remarks
15- 1	288-22110-00-33	REAR ARM COMP.	1	1		
15- 2	288-22141-00	SHAFT, pivot	1	1		
15- 3	183-22151-00	SEAL, guard	1	1		
15- 4	102-22123-00	BUSHING, rear arm	2	2		
15- 5	98801-10100	NUT	1	1		
15- 6	288-22311-00-35	CHAIN CASE, half	1	1		
15- 7	98501-05008	SCREW, pan head	2	2		
15- 8	92901-05100	WASHER, spring	2	2		
15- 9	288-22210-20	REAR CUSHION ASS'Y	2	2		
15-10	98804-10700	NUT, crown	4	4		
15-11	102-22243-00	WASHER, rear cushion (10-25-2)	6	6		

Fig. 16 STAND · BRAKE PEDAL

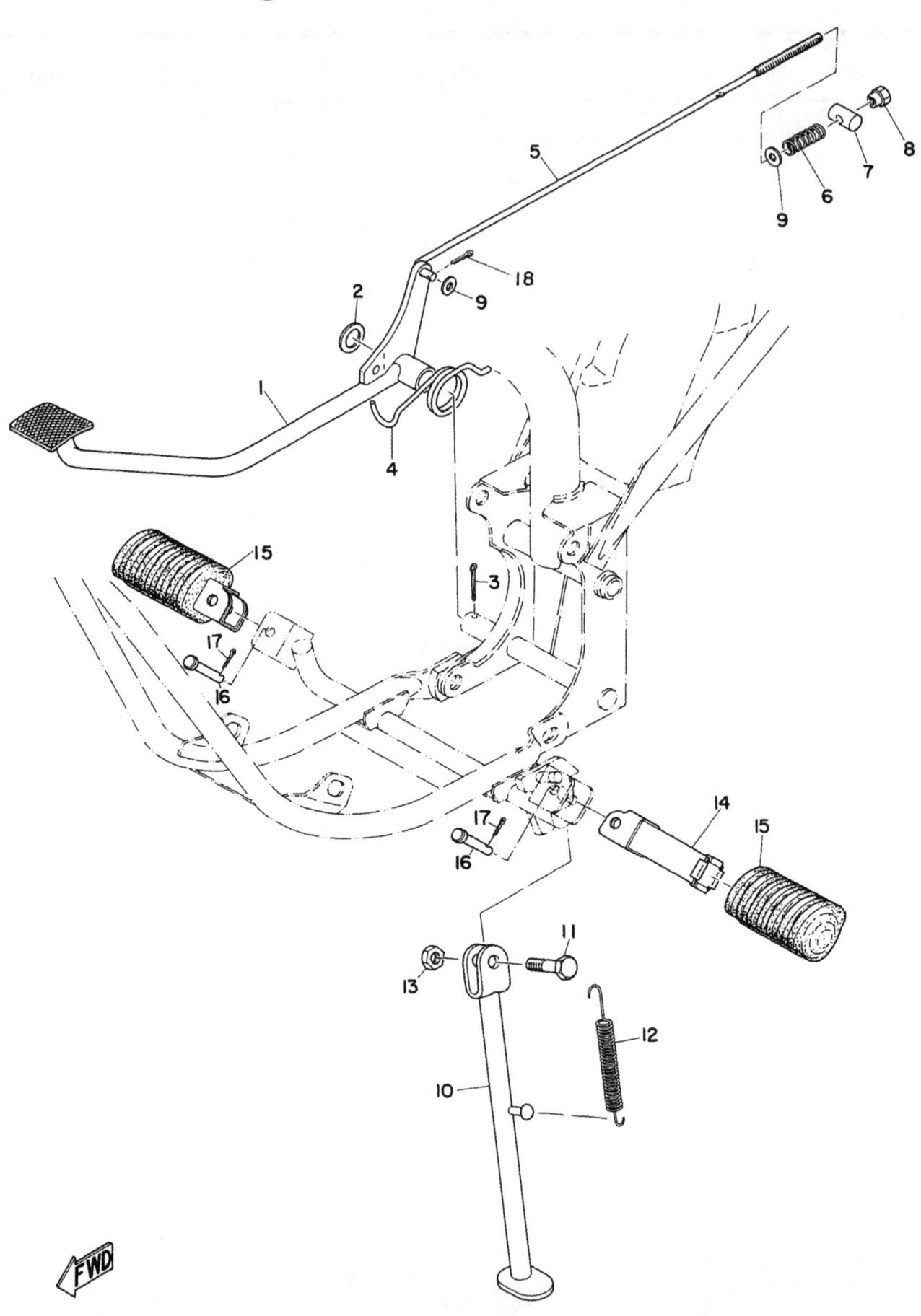

STAND · BRAKE PEDAL

Ref. No.	Part No.	Description	Q'ty JT	MX	Applicable Machine No.	Remarks
16- 1	288-27211-01-91	PEDAL, brake	1	1		
16- 2	135-22243-00	WASHER, rear cushion (14.8-27-2)	1	1		
16- 3	91401-30020	PIN, cotter	1	1		
16- 4	183-27216-00	SPRING, return	1	1		
16- 5	288-27231-00	ROD, brake	1	1		
16- 6	180-27236-00	SPRING, rod	1	1		
16- 7	156-27237-00	PIN, clevis	1	1		
16- 8	206-27238-00	NUT, adjusting	1	1		
16- 9	92901-06200	WASHER, plain	2	2		
16-10	288-27311-00	STAND, side	1	1		
16-11	137-27317-00	BOLT, side stand	1	1		
16-12	150-27316-00	SPRING, side stand	1	1		
16-13	98801-08300	NUT	1	1		
16-14	214-27421-00	FOOTREST	2	2		
16-15	214-27413-00	COVER, footrest	2	2		
16-16	91501-08038	PIN, clevis	2	2		
16-17	91401-20015	PIN, cotter	2	2		
16-18	91401-20012	PIN, cotter	1	1		

Fig. 17 FRONT FORK · FRONT FENDER

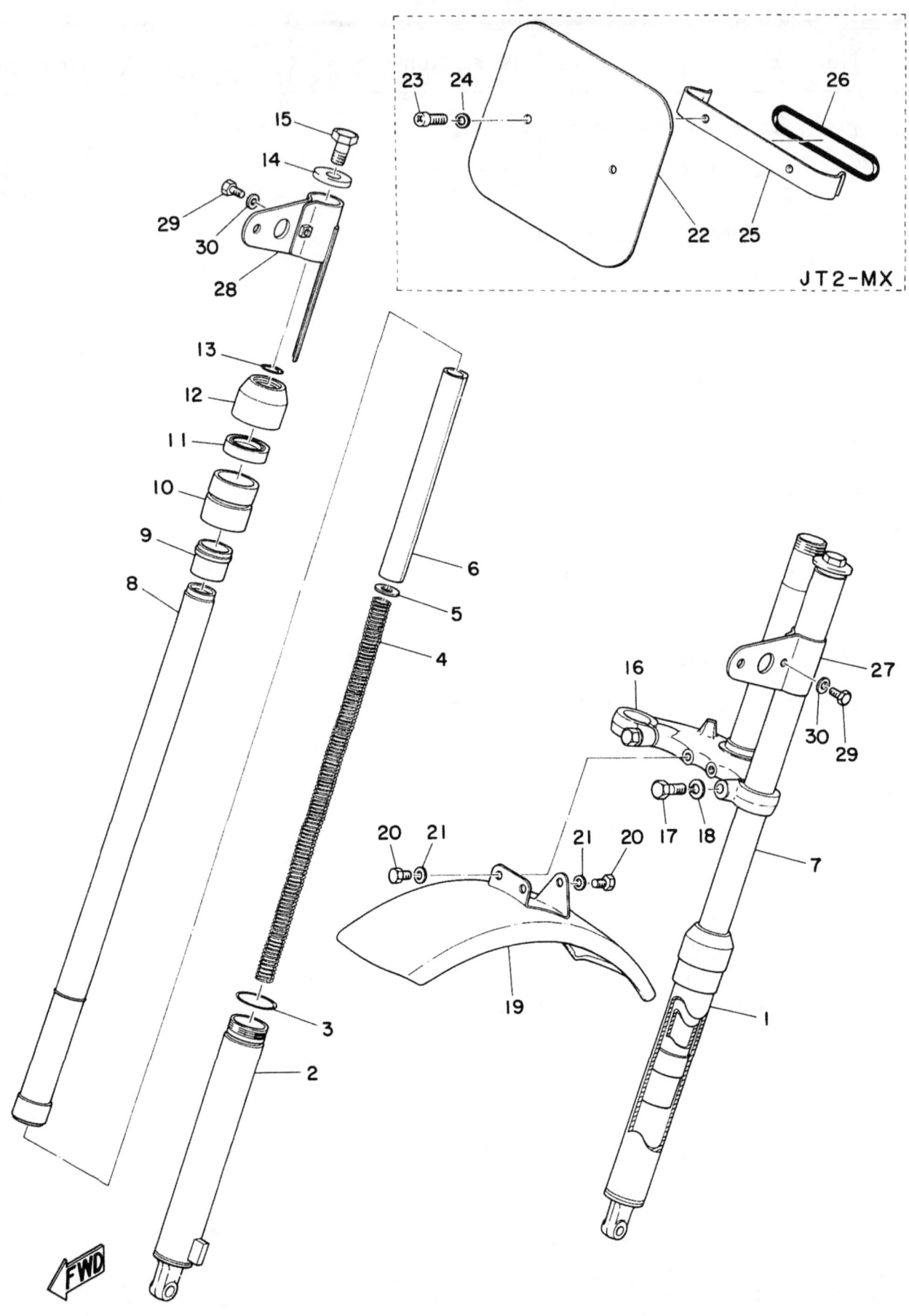

FRONT FORK · FRONT FENDER

Ref. No.	Part No.	Description	Q'ty JT	Q'ty MX	Applicable Machine No.	Remarks
17- 0-1	338-23100-00-35	FRONT FORK ASS'Y	1			Silver
	288-23100-02-35	FRONT FORK ASS'Y		1		Silver
17- 1	288-23126-00-35	. TUBE, outer left	1	1		Silver
17- 2	288-23136-00-35	. TUBE, outer right	1	1		Silver
17- 3	207-23147-00	. O-RING	2	2		
17- 4	290-23141-00	. SPRING, fork	1	1		
17- 5	290-23149-00	. WASHER, spring upper (10-18.5-1.6)	1	1		
17- 6	290-23118-00	. SPACER	1	1		
17- 7	290-23124-00	. TUBE, inner left	1	1		
17- 8	290-23134-00	. TUBE, inner right	1	1		
17- 9	109-23125-00	. METAL, side	2	2		
17-10	290-23150-00	. OUTER NUT COMP.	2	2		
17-11	290-23145-00	.. OIL SEAL	2	2		
17-12	290-23144-00	. SEAL, dust	2	2		
17-13	122-23114-00	. PACKING	2	2		
17-14	207-23112-00	. WASHER, cap	2	2		
17-15	260-23111-40	. BOLT, cap	2			
	205-23111-00	. BOLT, cap		2		
17-16	290-23340-01	. UNDER BRACKET COMP.	1	1		
17-17	122-23346-01	. BOLT, under bracket	2			
	122-23346-00	. BOLT, under bracket		2		
17-18	92901-10100	. WASHER, spring	2	2		
17-19	288-21510-00-03	FRONT FENDER COMP.	1			Mandarin Orange
	288-21510-00-02	FRONT FENDER COMP.		1		Competition Yellow

FRONT FORK · FRONT FENDER

Ref. No.	Part No.	Description	Q'ty JT	Q'ty MX	Applicable Machine No.	Remarks
17-20	91201-06010	BOLT	3	3		
17-21	92901-06200	WASHER, plain	3	3		
17-22	288-23485-00	PLATE, number		1		
17-23	92501-06010	SCREW, pan head		2		
17-24	92901-06200	WASHER, plain		2		
17-25	288-23486-00	STAY, plate		1		
17-26	288-23489-00	BAND		1		
17-27	290-84118-01	STAY, head lamp left	1			
17-28	290-84119-01	STAY, head lamp right	1			
17-29	289-85119-00	BOLT	2			
17-30	92901-06200	WASHER, plain	2			

Fig. 18 STEERING

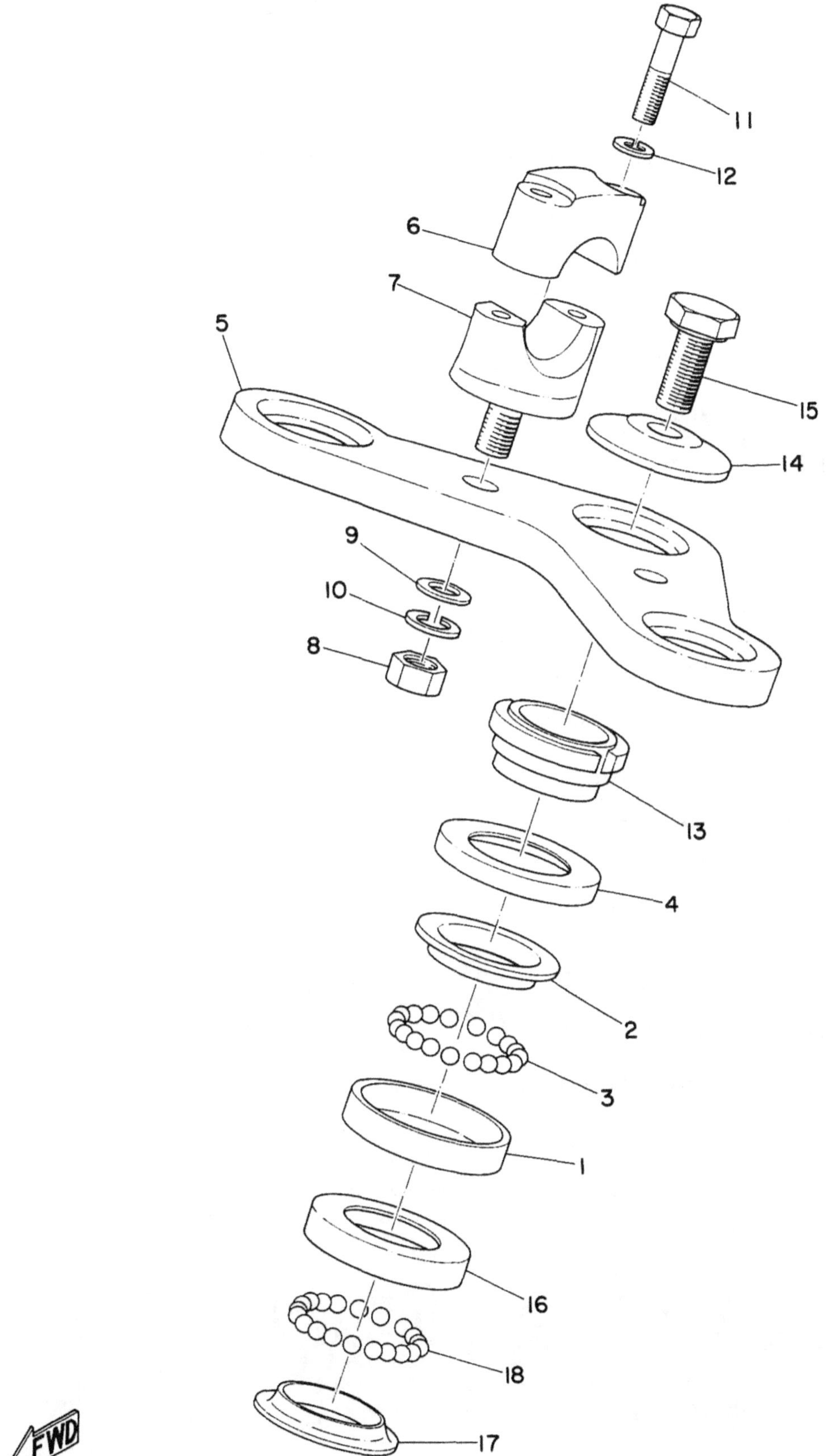

STEERING

Ref. No.	Part No.	Description	Q'ty JT	Q'ty MX	Applicable Machine No.	Remarks
18-1	122-23412-00	RACE, ball 2	1	1		
18-2	122-23411-00	RACE, ball 1	1	1		
18-3	93503-16010	BALL (3/16 inch)	22	22		
18-4	122-23416-00	COVER, ball race	1	1		
18-5	185-23435-00-35	CROWN, handle	1	1		
18-6	122-23441-00	HOLDER, handle upper	2	2		
18-7	122-23442-02	HOLDER, handle under	2	2		
18-8	98801-10100	NUT	2	2		
18-9	92901-10200	WASHER, plain	2	2		
18-10	92901-10100	WASHER, spring	2	2		
18-11	91103-06035	BOLT	4	4		
18-12	92901-06100	WASHER, spring	4	4		
18-13	122-23453-00	NUT, fitting	1	1		
18-14	122-23443-00	WASHER, crown	1	1		
18-15	122-23451-00	BOLT, fitting	1	1		
18-16	156-23412-00	RACE, ball 2	1	1		
18-17	156-23411-00	RACE, ball 1	1	1		
18-18	93501-04011	BALL (1/4 inch)	19	19		

Fig. 19 HANDLE · WIRE

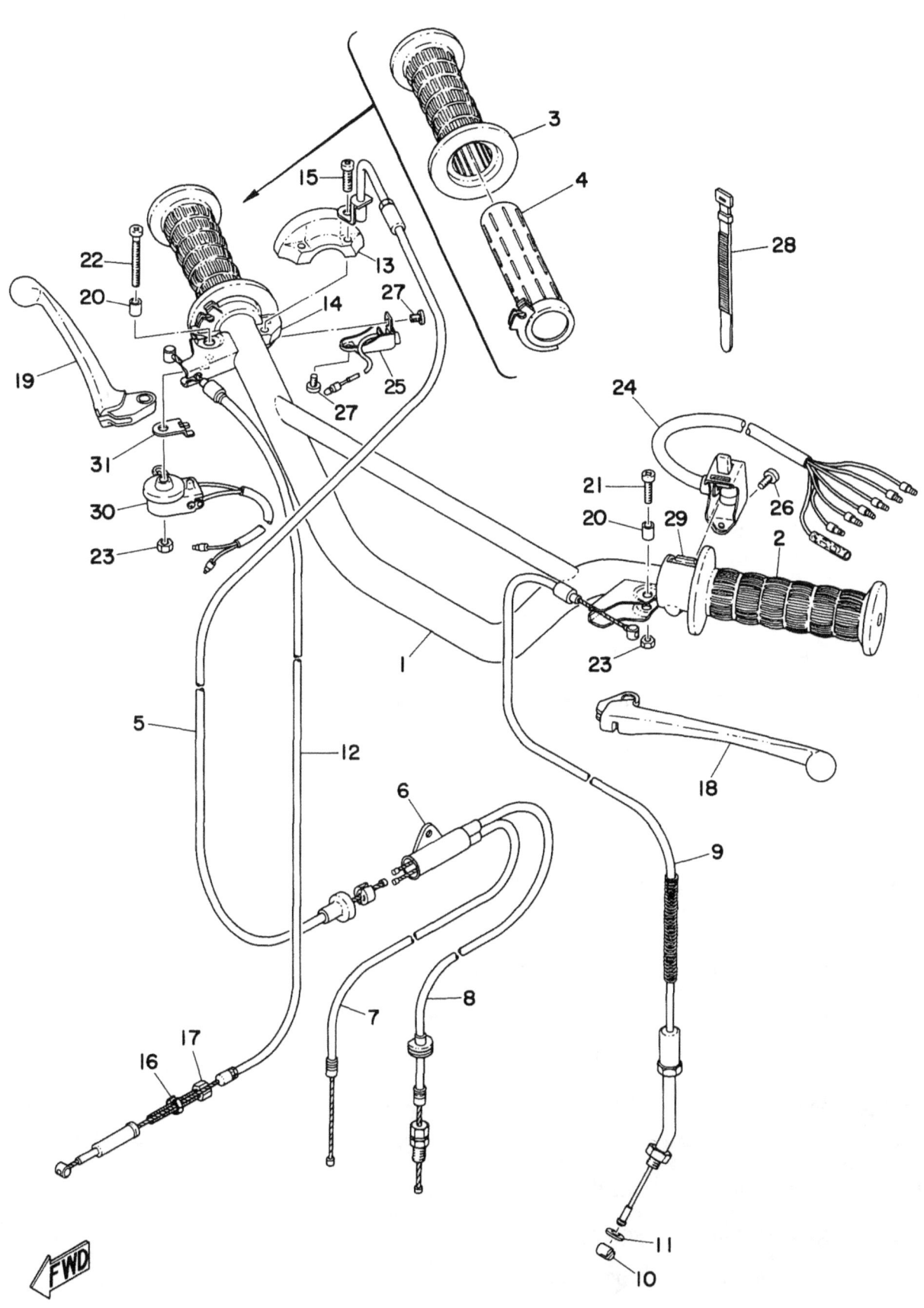

HANDLE · WIRE

Ref. No.	Part No.	Description	Q'ty JT	Q'ty MX	Applicable Machine No.	Remarks
19- 1	288-26111-01	HANDLE	1	1		
19- 2	214-26241-00	GRIP, left	1	1		
19- 3	214-26242-00	GRIP, right	1	1		
19- 4	214-26243-00	TUBE, guide	1	1		
19- 5	288-26311-00	WIRE, throttle	1	1		
19- 6	266-26261-00	CYLINDER	1	1		
19- 7	288-26312-00	WIRE, throttle 2	1	1		
19- 8	288-26321-00	WIRE, pump	1	1		
19- 9	288-26335-00	WIRE, clutch	1	1		
19-10	164-26363-00	. END, wire	1	1		
19-11	92901-06200	WASHER, plain	1	1		
19-12	288-26341-00	WIRE, brake	1	1		
19-13	214-26281-01	CAP, grip upper	1	1		
19-14	248-26282-00	CAP, grip under	1	1		
19-15	98501-05018	SCREW, pan head	2	2		
19-16	109-26344-00	NUT, wire adjusting	1	1		
19-17	109-26345-00	BOLT, wire adjusting	1	1		
19-18	137-83912-01	LEVER, left	1	1		
19-19	137-83922-01	LEVER, right	1			
	137-83922-01	LEVER, right		1		
19-20	288-83913-00	COLLAR, lever	2	2		
19-21	98501-05018	SCREW, pan head	1	2		
19-22	338-83915-00	SCREW, lever fitting	1			
19-23	98801-05100	NUT	2	2		

HANDLE · WIRE

Ref. No.	Part No.	Description	Q'ty JT	Q'ty MX	Applicable Machine No.	Remarks
19-24	289-83975-00	SWITCH, handle 2	1			
19-25	261-83976-00	SWITCH, handle 1		1		
19-26	98503-05018	SCREW, pan head	1			
19-27	98501-05005	SCREW, pan head		2		
19-28	168-83936-01	BAND, siwtch cord	1	1		
19-29	214-83974-00	HOLDER, handle switch	1			
19-30	233-83980-30	FRONT STOP SWITCH ASS'Y ...	1			
19-31	338-83983-00	BRACKET, front stop switch ...	1			

Fig. 20 FUEL TANK

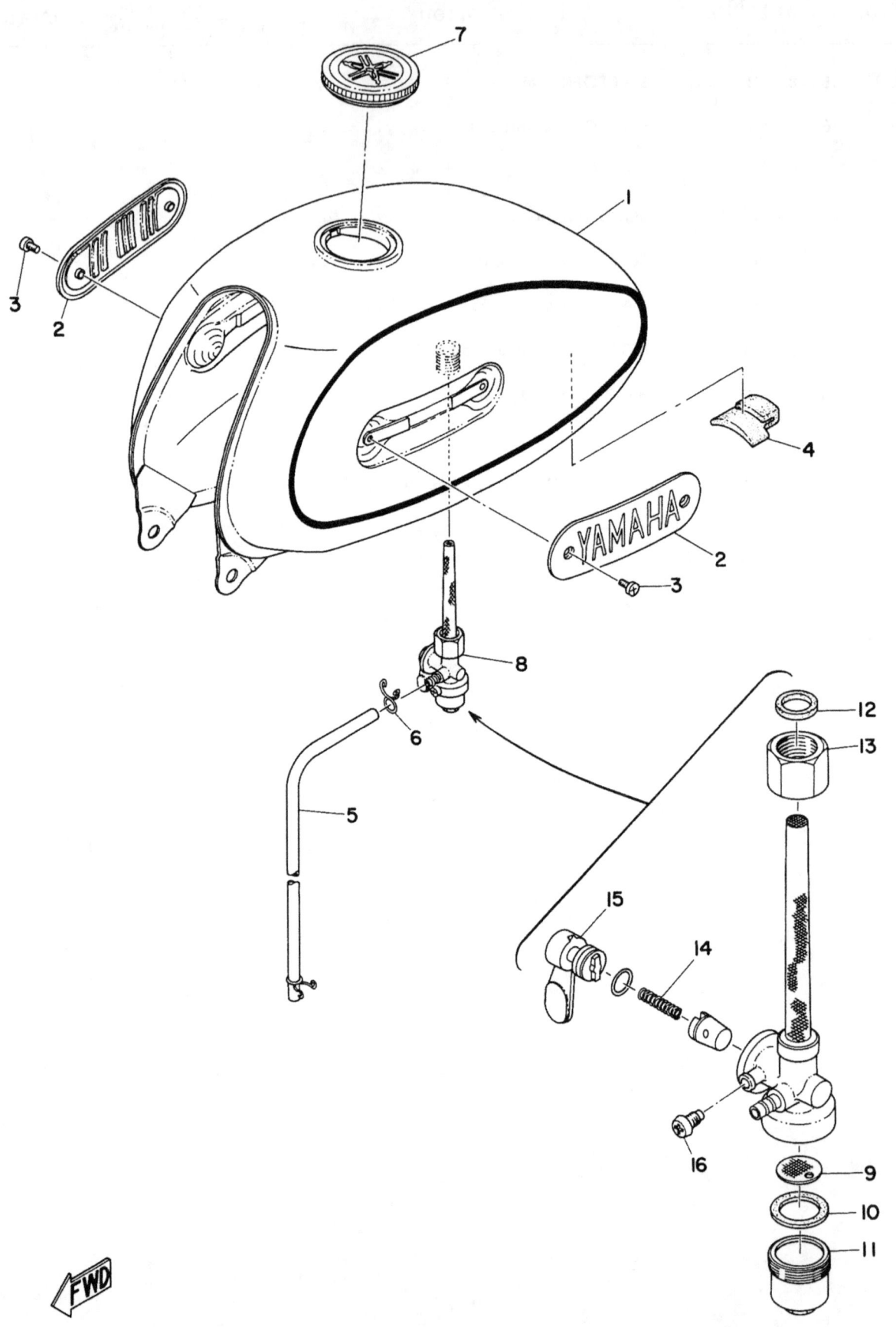

FUEL TANK

Ref. No.	Part No.	Description	Q'ty JT	Q'ty MX	Applicable Machine No.	Remarks
20-1	288-24110-01-05	FUEL TANK COMP.	1			Mandarin Orange
	288-24110-01-03	FUEL TANK COMP.		1		Competition Yellow
20-2	276-24161-00	EMBLEM	2	2		
20-3	98501-04008	SCREW, pan head	4	4		
20-4	288-24181-00	DAMPER, locating	1	1		
20-5	612-24311-00	PIPE (5-250)	1	1		
20-6	101-24356-00	CLIP, pipe	2	2		
20-7	122-24610-01	CAP ASS'Y	1	1		
20-8	127-24500-00	FUEL COCK ASS'Y	1	1		
20-9	122-24515-00	. NET, filter	1	1		
20-10	102-24522-00	. GASKET, filter	1	1		
20-11	122-24521-00	. CUP, filter	1	1		
20-12	122-24532-00	. GASKET, nut	1	1		
20-13	122-24531-00	. NUT	1	1		
20-14	102-24529-00	. SPRING	1	1		
20-15	122-24524-00	. LEVER, cock	1	1		
20-16	127-24535-00	. SCREW, lever fitting	1	1		

Fig. 21 OIL TANK

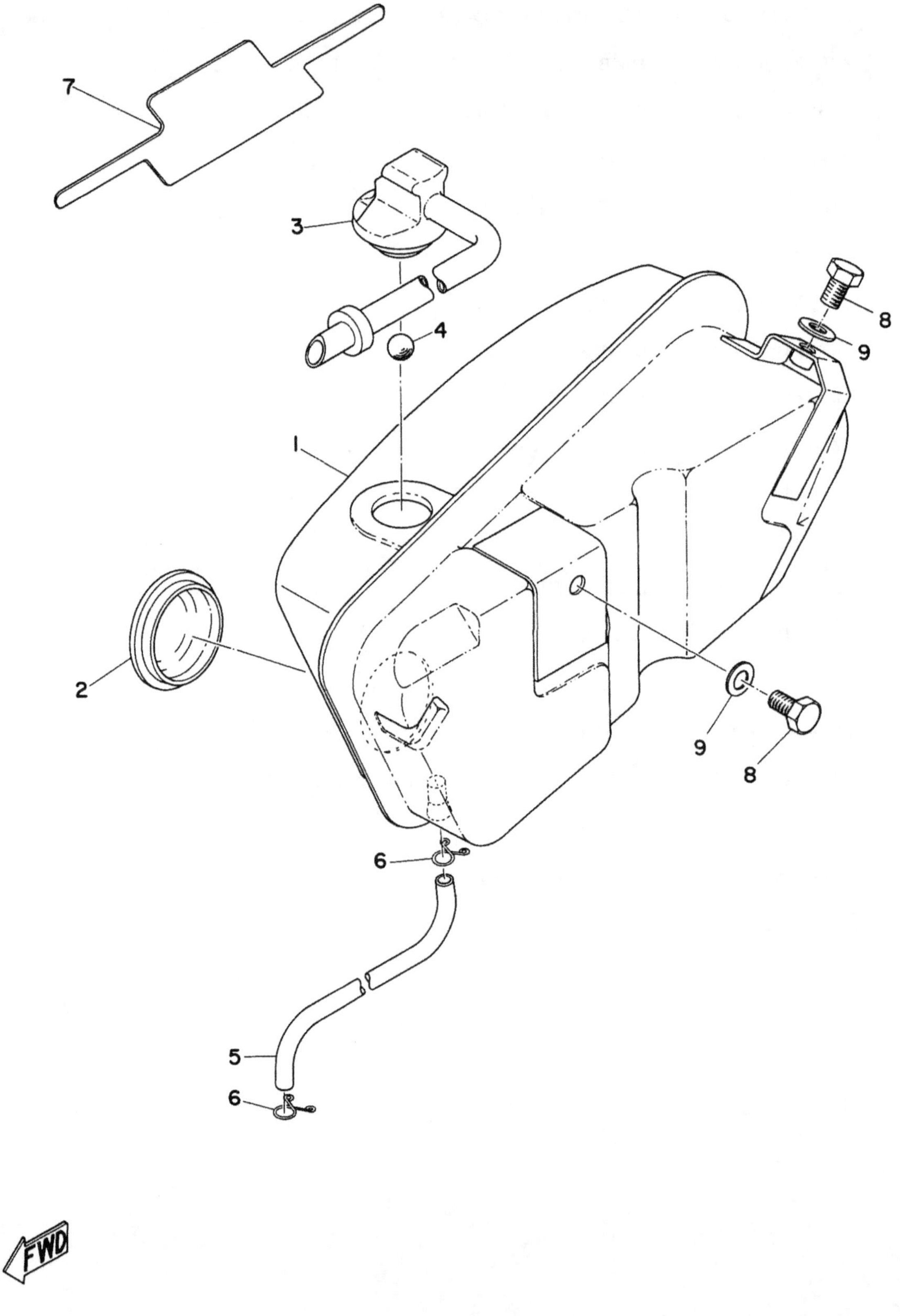

OIL TANK

Ref. No.	Part No.	Description	Q'ty JT	Q'ty MX	Applicable Machine No.	Remarks
21-1	288-21705-00-71	OIL TANK ASS'Y	1			Mandarin Orange
	288-21705-00-26	OIL TANK ASS'Y		1		Competition Yellow
21-2	214-21761-00	. GAUGE, level	1	1		
21-3	288-21771-00	BODY, cap	1	1		
21-4	288-24684-00	BALL	1	1		
21-5	132-24319-01	PIPE, oil (5-380)	1	1		
21-6	101-24356-00	CLIP, oil	2	2		
21-7	288-21787-00	EMBLEM, enduro	1	1		
21-8	91201-06012	BOLT	2	2		
21-9	92901-06200	WASHER, plain	2	2		

Fig. 22 SEAT

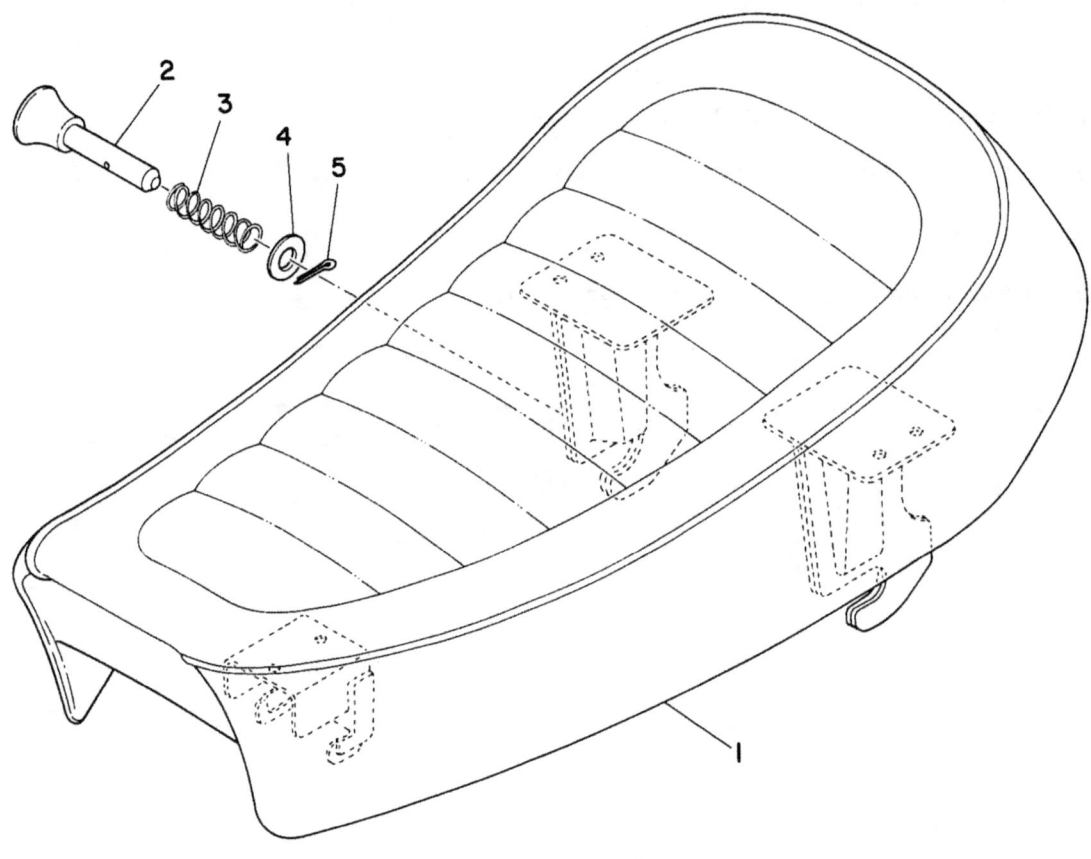

SEAT

Ref. No.	Part No.	Description	Q'ty JT	MX	Applicable Machine No.	Remarks
22- 1	288-24770-01	SEMI-DOUBLE SEAT ASS'Y	1	1		
22- 1-1	288-24771-01	. COVER, seat	1	1		
22- 2	288-24727-00	PIN, seat fitting	1	1		
22- 3	288-24781-00	SPRING, seat	1	1		
22- 4	156-27226-00	WASHER (8.2-13-0.6)	1	1		
22- 5	91401-20012	PIN, cotter	1	1		

Fig. 23 FRONT WHEEL

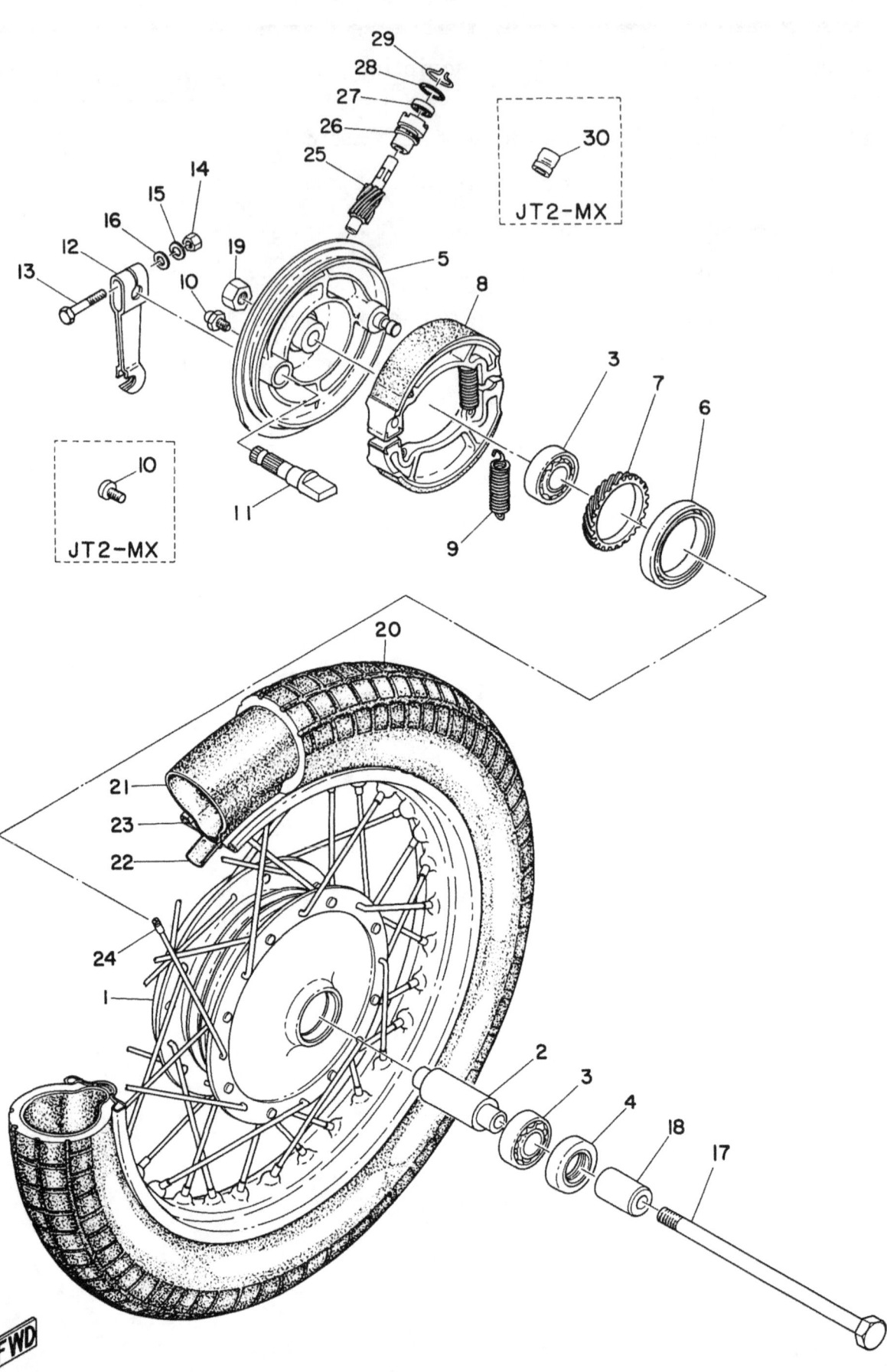

FRONT WHEEL

Ref. No.	Part No.	Description	Q'ty JT	MX	Applicable Machine No.	Remarks
23- 1	288-25111-00	HUB, front	1	1		
23- 2	102-25117-00	SPACER, bearing	1	1		
23- 3	93306-20203	BEARING (6202)	2	2		
23- 4	93106-20001	OIL-SEAL (DD20-35-7)	1	1		
23- 5	109-25121-01-35	PLATE, brake shoe	1	1		
23- 6	93107-42001	OIL-SEAL (OS 42-52.5-7)	1	1		
23- 7	290-25135-00	GEAR, drive	1			
23- 8	122-25330-00	BRAKE SHOE COMP.	2	2		
23- 9	102-25333-00	SPRING, return	2	2		
23-10	93700-06001	NIPPLE, grease	1			
	92501-06010	SCREW, pan head		1		
23-11	122-25351-01	CAM SHAFT	1	1		
23-12	109-25155-00	LEVER, cam shaft	1	1		
23-13	91201-06030	BOLT	1	1		
23-14	98801-06100	NUT	1	1		
23-15	92901-06100	WASHER, spring	1	1		
23-16	92901-06200	WASHER, plain	1	1		
23-17	128-25181-00	SHAFT, wheel	1	1		
23-18	128-25183-00	COLLAR, wheel shaft	1	1		
23-19	98801-10100	NUT	1	1		
23-20	94125-15091	TIRE (2.50-15-4PR)	1	1		
23-21	94225-15036	TUBE (2.50-15)	1	1		
23-22	94325-15028	BAND, rim (2.50-15)	1	1		
23-23	94414-15058	RIM, (1.40-15)	1	1		

FRONT WHEEL

Ref. No.	Part No.	Description	Q'ty JT	MX	Applicable Machine No.	Remarks
23-24	288-25104-00	SPOKE SET	1s	1s		
23-25	290-25138-00	GEAR, meter	1			
23-26	109-25136-00	BUSHING	1			
23-27	93104-07003	OIL SEAL (S07-14-4)	1			
23-28	93210-14104	O-RING (2.4-13.4)	1			
23-29	102-25137-00	RING, stop	1			
23-30	288-25139-00	PLUG, blind		1		

Fig. 24 REAR WHEEL

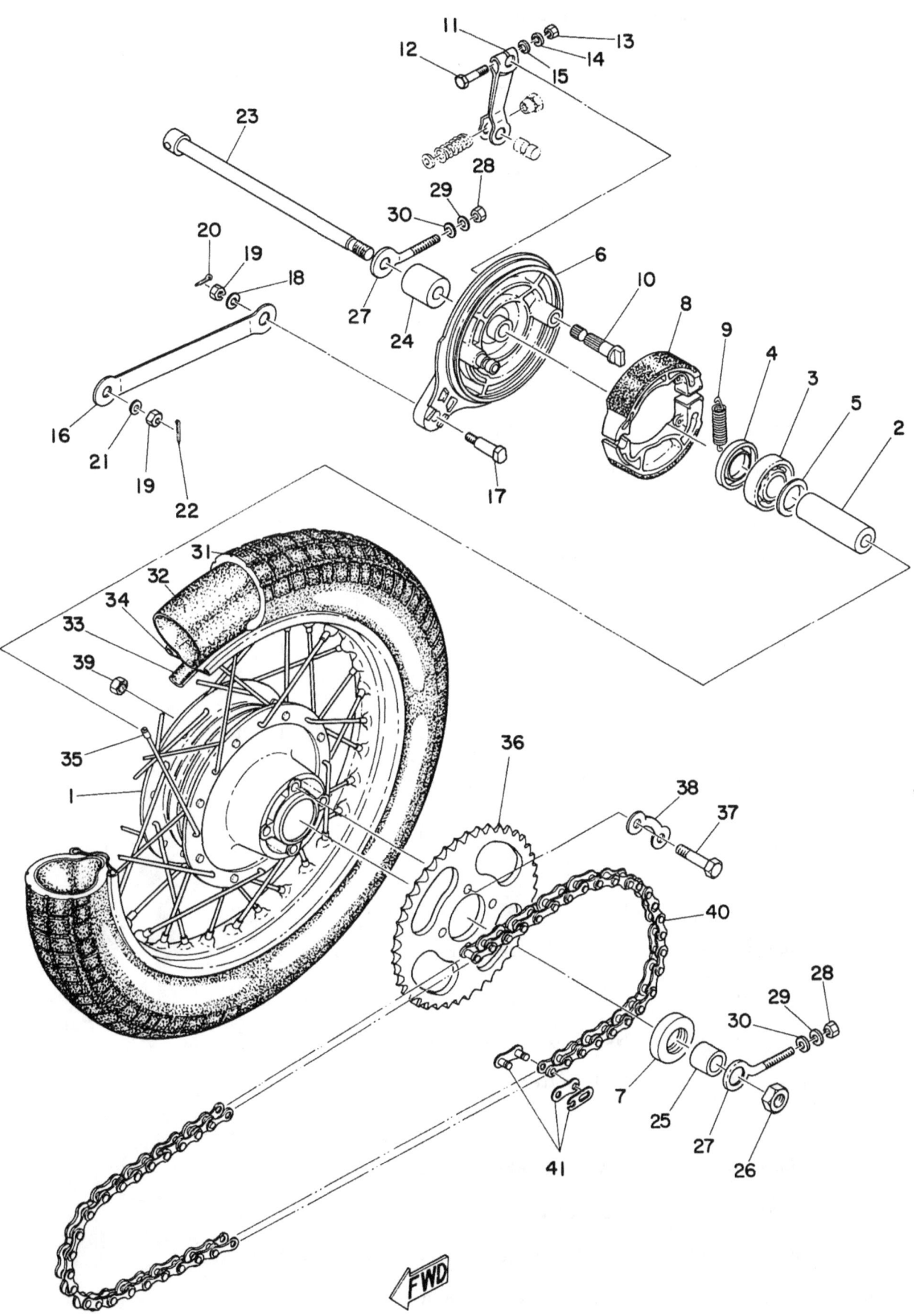

REAR WHEEL

Ref. No.	Part No.	Description	Q'ty JT	Q'ty MX	Applicable Machine No.	Remarks
24- 1	288-25311-00	HUB, rear	1	1		
24- 2	109-25317-00	SPACER, bearing	1	1		
24- 3	93306-30101	BEARING (6301)	1	1		
24- 4	93106-20002	OIL SEAL (DD-20-37-8)	1	1		
24- 5	102-25315-00	FLANGE, spacer	1	1		
24- 6	109-25321-01-35	PLATE, brake shoe	1	1		
24- 7	93104-18006	OIL SEAL (SO-18-37-8)	1	1		
24- 8	122-25330-00	BRAKE SHOE COMP.	2	2		
24- 9	102-25333-00	SPRING, return	2	2		
24-10	122-25351-01	CAM SHAFT	1	1		
24-11	122-25355-00	LEVER, cam shaft	1	1		
24-12	91201-06030	BOLT	1	1		
24-13	98801-06100	NUT	1	1		
24-14	92901-06100	WASHER, spring	1	1		
24-15	92901-06200	WASHER, plain	1	1		
24-16	102-25371-00	BAR, tension	1	1		
24-17	109-25373-00	BOLT, tension bar	1	1		
24-18	92901-08100	WASHER, spring	1	1		
24-19	98801-08300	NUT	2	2		
24-20	91401-20012	PIN, cotter	1	1		
24-21	92901-08200	WASHER, plain	1	1		
24-22	91401-20012	PIN, cotter	1	1		
24-23	288-25381-00	SHAFT, wheel	1	1		
24-24	102-25383-00	COLLAR, wheel shaft	1	1		

REAR WHEEL

Ref. No.	Part No.	Description	Q'ty JT	Q'ty MX	Applicable Machine No.	Remarks
24-25	109-25377-01	COLLAR, shaft	1	1		
24-26	183-25182-00	NUT, shaft	1	1		
24-27	102-25389-00	PULLER, chain	2	2		
24-28	98801-06100	NUT	2	2		
24-29	92901-06100	WASHER, spring	2	2		
24-30	92901-06200	WASHER, plain	2	2		
24-31	94125-15091	TIRE (2.50-15-4PR)	1	1		
24-32	94225-15036	TUBE (2.50-15)	1	1		
24-33	94325-15028	BAND, rim (2.50-15)	1	1		
24-34	94414-15058	RIM (1.40-15)	1	1		
24-35	288-25304-00	SPOKE SET	1s	1s		
24-36	288-25441-10	GEAR, sprocket wheel (41T)	1	1		
24-37	109-25411-00	BOLT, fitting	4	4		
24-38	101-25412-00	WASHER, lock	2	2		
24-39	98801-08300	NUT	4	4		
24-40	94504-20090	CHAIN (DK420-90L)	1	1		
24-41	94604-20001	. JOINT, chain	1	1		

Fig. 25 HEAD LAMP · SPEEDOMETER

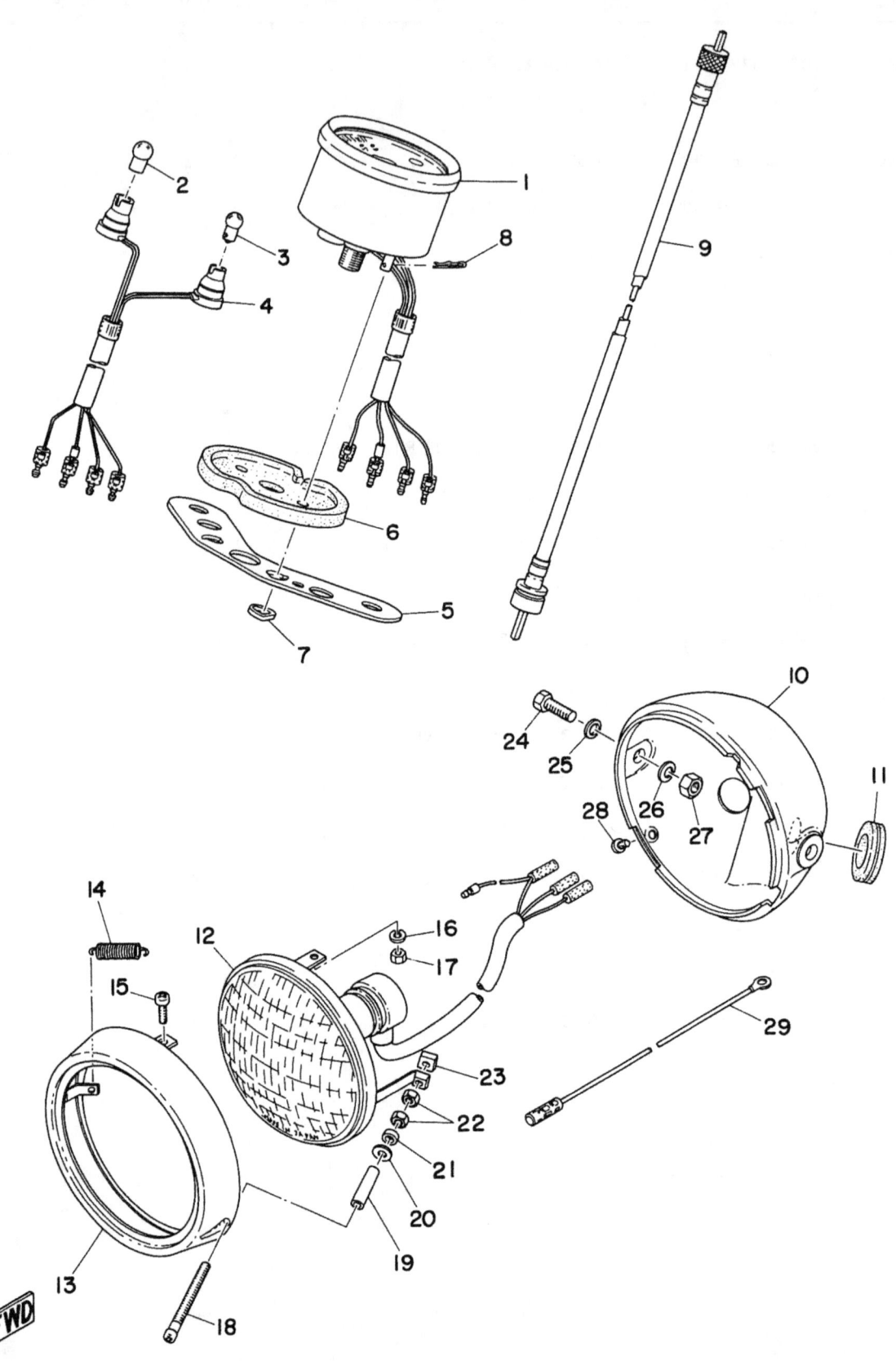

HEAD LAMP · SPEEDOMETER

Ref. No.	Part No.	Description	Q'ty JT MX	Applicable Machine No.	Remarks
25- 1	338-83510-30	SPEEDO METER ASS'Y 1			
25- 2	188-83517-10	. BULB (6V/1.5W) 1			For light
25- 3	122-83516-10	. BULB (6V/3W) 1			For highbeam
25- 4	338-83520-30	. SOCKET ASS'Y 1			
25- 5	290-83519-00-35	BRACKET, speedo meter 1			
25- 6	237-83523-00	DAMPER 1			
25- 7	214-83524-00	WASHER, special 2			
25- 8	156-83525-00	CLIP 2			
25- 9	290-83550-00	SPEEDOMETER CABLE ASS'Y . 1			
25-10	338-84130-60-71	BODY ASS'Y 1			Mandarin Orange
25-11	150-84153-00	. GROMMET 2			
25- 0-1	338-84110-60	HEAD LAMP UNIT ASS'Y 1			
25-12	338-84120-60	. LENS ASS'Y (6V/15W) 1			
25-13	261-84315-61	. RIM, head lamp 1			
25-14	132-84335-60	. SPRING, lens adjust 1			
25-15	98501-04010	. SCREW, pan head 2			
25-16	92901-04100	. WASHER, spring 2			
25-17	802-84126-00	. NUT 2			
25-18	198-84331-60	. SCREW, rim adjusting 1			
25-19	233-84133-60	. COLLOR, adjust screw 1			
25-20	92901-04200	. WASHER, plain 1			
25-21	132-84328-60	. SPACER 1			
25-22	802-84126-00	. NUT 2			
25-23	198-84334-60	. NUT, adjust 1			

HEAD LAMP · SPEEDOMETER

Ref. No.	Part No.	Description	Q'ty JT MX	Applicable Machine No.	Remarks
25-24	97204-08020	BOLT	2		
25-25	92903-08200	WASHER, plain	2		
25-26	92901-08100	WASHER, spring	2		
25-27	98801-08100	NUT	2		
25-28	195-84325-00	SCREW, rim fitting	1		
25-29	173-84313-00	WIRE, earth	1		

Fig. 26 TAIL LAMP

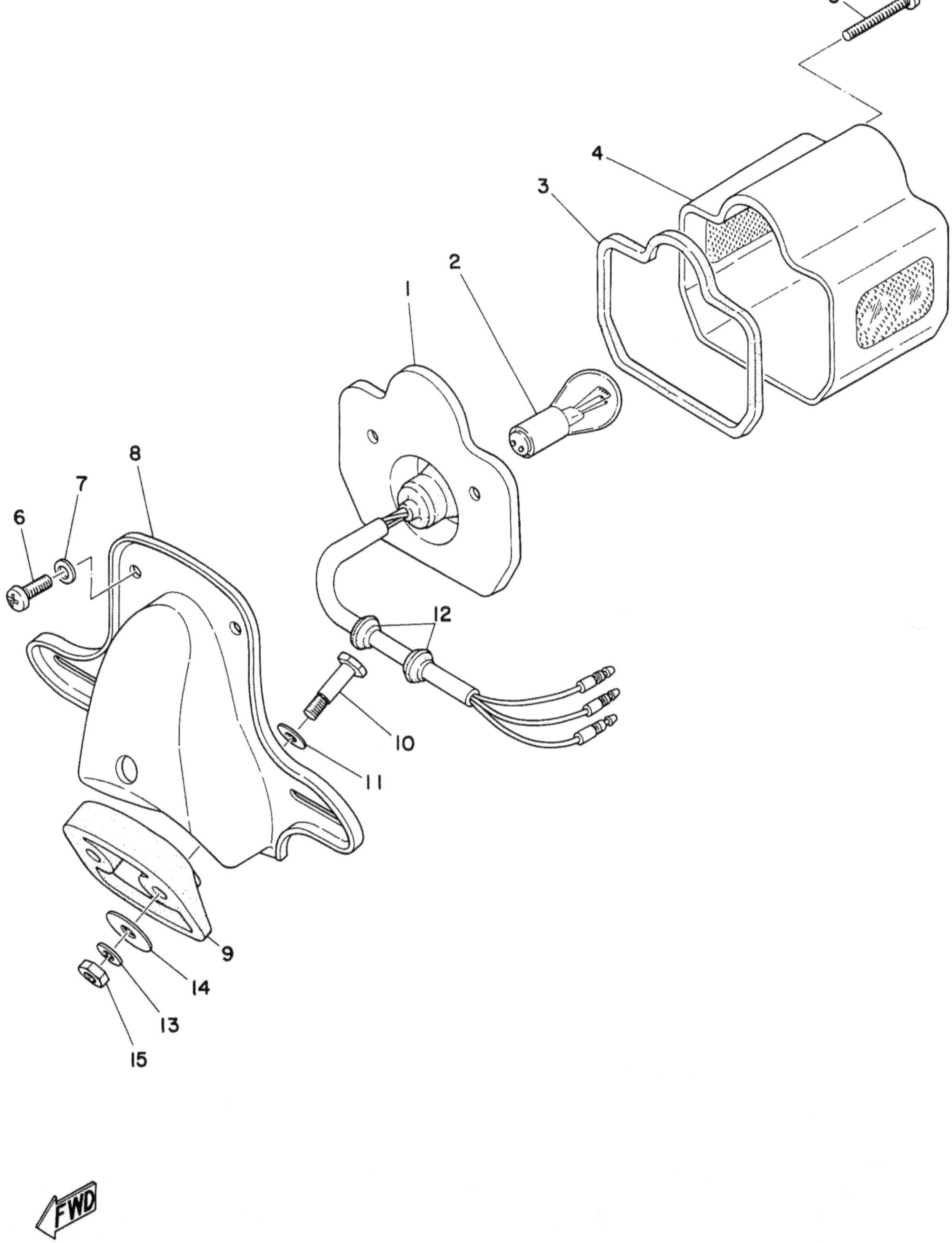

TAIL LAMP

Ref. No.	Part No.	Description	Q'ty JT MX	Applicable Machine No.	Remarks
26- 0-1	338-84510-60	TAIL LAMP UNIT ASS'Y 1			
26- 1	338-84511-60	. BASE, tail lamp 1			
26- 2	124-84514-60	. BULB (6V/5.3W) 1			
26- 3	168-84712-60	. SEAT, base 1			
26- 4	168-84721-60	. LENS, tail lamp 1			
26- 5	193-84724-00	. SCREW, lens fitting 2			
26- 6	92503-06010	SCREW, pan head 2			
26- 7	92901-06100	WASHER, spring 2			
26- 8	168-84751-00-35	BRACKET, licence 1			
26- 9	338-84553-00	DAMPER 1			
26-10	338-84552-00	BOLT 2			
26-11	92901-06200	WASHER, plain 2			
26-12	152-84518-00	GROMMET 2			
26-13	92901-06100	WASHER, spring 2			
26-14	156-24186-00	WASHER, special 2			
26-15	98801-06100	NUT 2			

Fig. 27 ELECTRICAL

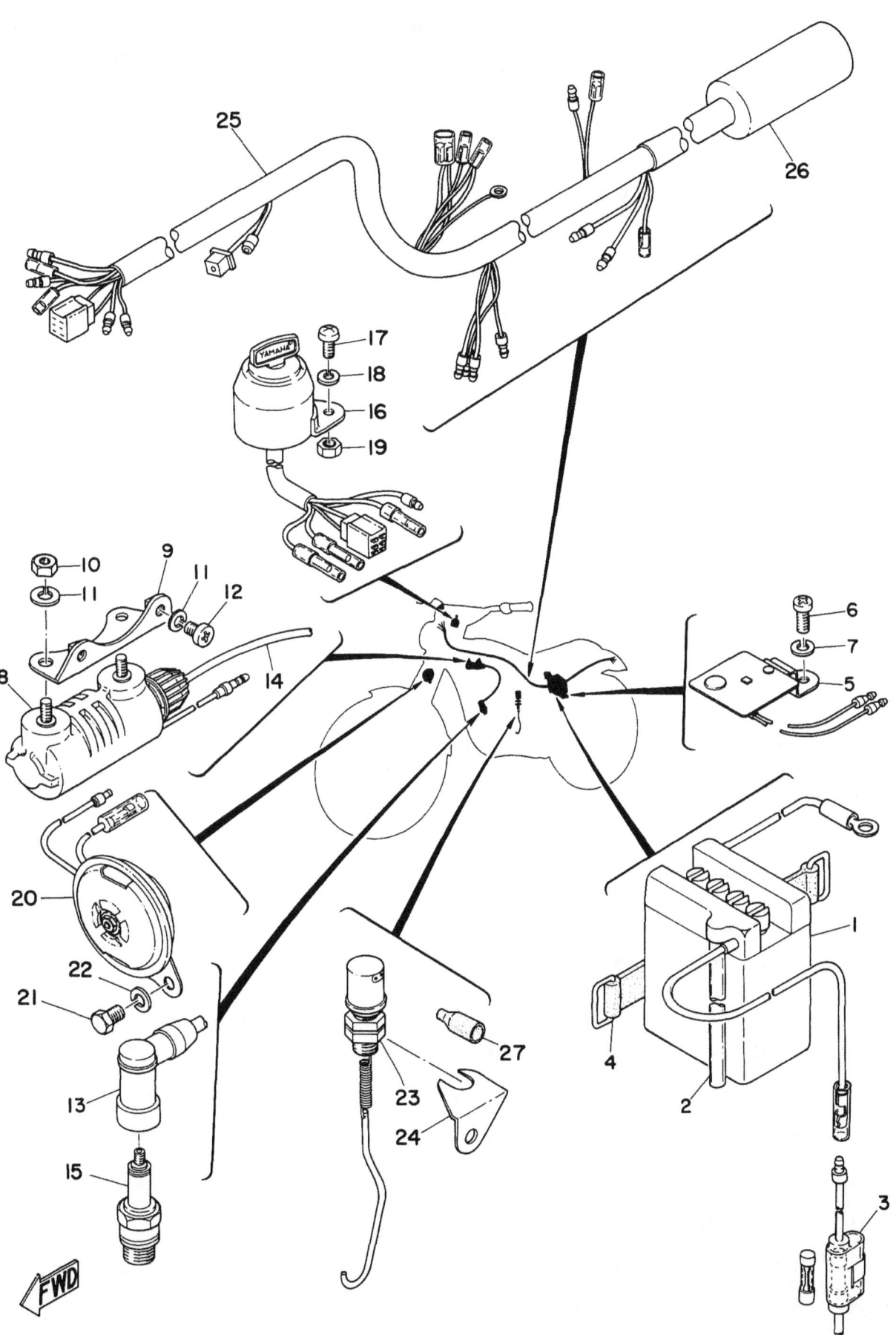

ELECTRICAL

Ref. No.	Part No.	Description	Q'ty JT	MX	Applicable Machine No.	Remarks
27- 1	116-82110-11	BATTERY ASS'Y	1			U.R
	116-82110-21	BATTERY ASS'Y				
27- 2	123-82112-00	PIPE, breather	1			
27- 3	116-82150-00	FUSE HOLDER ASS'Y	1			
27- 4	133-82131-00	BAND, battery	1			
27- 5	812-81970-41	RECTIFIER ASS'Y	1			
27- 6	98501-06012	SCREW, pan head	1			
27- 7	92901-06100	WASHER, spring	1			
27- 8	248-82310-11	IGNITION COIL ASS'Y	1	1		
27- 9	248-82316-00	BRACKET, ignition coil	1	1		
27-10	98801-06100	NUT	2	2		
27-11	92901-06100	WASHER, spring	4	4		
27-12	92501-06012	SCREW, pan head	2	2		
27-13	117-82370-20	PLUG CAP ASS'Y	1	1		
27-14	183-82341-00	CORD, high tension	1	1		
27-15	94700-00040	PLUG, spark (B-7HS)	1	1		
27-16	338-82508-20	MAIN SWITCH ASS'Y	1			
27-17	92501-06012	SCREW, pan head	1			
27-18	92901-06100	WASHER, spring	1			
27-19	98801-06100	NUT	1			
27-20	290-83371-10	HORN	1			
27-21	91201-06015	BOLT	2			
27-22	92901-06200	WASHER, spring	2			
27-23	290-82530-00	STOP SWITCH ASS'Y	1			

ELECTRICAL

Ref. No.	Part No.	Description	Q'ty JT MX	Applicable Machine No.	Remarks
27-24	290-82539-00	STAY, stop switch 1			
27-25	338-82590-20	WIRE HARNESS ASS'Y 1			
27-26	290-82599-00	COVER, conector 1			
27-27	248-82599-00	COVER, conector 1			

VELOCEPRESS MANUALS - MOTORCYCLE

1930'S BRITISH MOTORCYCLE CARBS & ELEC COMPONENTS (BOOK OF)
1930'S BRITISH MOTORCYCLE ENGINES (OVERHAUL & MAINTENANCE)
1930'S BRITISH MOTORCYCLE GEARBOXES & CLUTCHES (BOOK OF)
AJS 1932-1948 SINGLES & TWINS 250cc THRU 1000cc (BOOK OF)
AJS 1945-1960 SINGLES 350cc & 500cc MODELS 16 & 18 (BOOK OF)
AJS 1955-1965 SINGLES 350cc & 500cc (BOOK OF)
ARIEL UP TO 1932 (BOOK OF)
ARIEL 1932-1939 PREWAR MODELS (BOOK OF)
ARIEL 1933-1951 (WORKSHOP MANUAL)
ARIEL 1939-1960 4 STROKE SINGLES (BOOK OF)
ARIEL 1958-1964 LEADER & ARROW (BOOK OF)
BMW R26 R27 (1956-1967) FACTORY WORKSHOP MANUAL
BMW R50 R50S R60 R69S (1955-1969) FACTORY WORKSHOP MANUAL
BRIDGESTONE 90 SERIES FACTORY WSM & PARTS CATALOGUE
BRIDGESTONE 175 SERIES FACTORY WSM & PARTS CATALOGUE
BSA BANTAM ALL MODELS FROM 1948 ONWARDS (BOOK OF)
BSA SINGLES & V-TWINS UP TO 1927 (BOOK OF)
BSA SINGLES & V-TWINS UP TO 1930 (BOOK OF)
BSA SINGLES & V-TWINS UP TO 1935 (BOOK OF)
BSA SINGLES & V-TWINS 1936-1939 (BOOK OF)
BSA OHV & SV SINGLES 250-600cc 1945-1959 (BOOK OF)
BSA OHV & SV SINGLES 250cc (ONLY) 1954-1970 (BOOK OF)
BSA OHV SINGLES 350 & 500cc 1955-1967 (BOOK OF)
BSA TWINS 1948-1962 (BOOK OF)
BSA TWINS 1962-1969 (SECOND BOOK OF)
CYCLEMOTOR (BOOK OF)
DOUGLAS 1929-1939 PREWAR ALL MODELS (BOOK OF)
DOUGLAS 1948-1957 POSTWAR ALL MODELS FACTORY SHOP MANUAL
DUCATI 160cc, 250cc & 350cc OHC MODELS FACTORY SHOP MANUAL
HONDA 50 ALL MODELS UP TO 1970 INC MONKEY & TRAIL (BOOK OF)
HONDA 90 ALL MODELS UP TO 1966 (BOOK OF)
HONDA 125-150cc TWINS C/CS/CB/CA FACTORY WORKSHOP MANUAL
HONDA 250-305 TWINS C/CS/CB FACTORY WORKSHOP MANUAL
HONDA 450 CB/CL 1965-1974 K0 TO K7 WORKSHOP MANUAL
HONDA C100 SUPER CUB FACTORY WORKSHOP MANUAL
HONDA C110 SPORT CUB 1962-1969 FACTORY WORKSHOP MANUAL
HONDA TWINS & SINGLES 50cc THRU 305cc 1960-1966 (BOOK OF)
HONDA TWINS ALL MODELS 125cc THRU 450cc UP TO 1968 (BOOK OF)
J.A.P. ENGINES 1927-1952 & MOTORCYCLES 1934-1952 (BOOK OF)
LAMBRETTA 1947-1957 ALL 125 & 150cc MODELS (BOOK OF)
LAMBRETTA 1957-1970 LI & TV MODELS (SECOND BOOK OF)
MATCHLESS 1931-1939 ALL MODELS 250cc THRU 990cc (BOOK OF)
MATCHLESS 1945-1956 350 & 500cc SINGLES (BOOK OF)
MATCHLESS 1955-1966 350 & 500cc SINGLES (BOOK OF)
NEW IMPERIAL ALL SV & OHV FROM 1935 ONWARDS (BOOK OF)
NORTON 1932-1939 PREWAR MODELS (BOOK OF)
NORTON 1932-1947 (BOOK OF)
NORTON 1938-1956 (BOOK OF)
NORTON 1955-1963 MODELS 19, 50 & ES2 (BOOK OF)
NORTON 1955-1965 DOMINATOR TWINS (BOOK OF)
NORTON 1957-1970 TWINS FACTORY WORKSHOP MANUAL
NSU PRIMA 1956-1964 ALL MODELS (BOOK OF)
NSU QUICKLY 1953-1963 ALL MODELS (BOOK OF)
PANTHER 1932-1958 LIGHTWEIGHT MODELS 250 & 350cc (BOOK OF)
PANTHER 1938-1966 HEAVYWEIGHT MODELS 600 & 650cc (BOOK OF)
RALEIGH MOPEDS 1960-1969 (BOOK OF)
RALEIGH MOTORCYCLES 1919-1933 (BOOK OF)
ROYAL ENFIELD 1934-1946 SINGLES & V TWINS (BOOK OF)
ROYAL ENFIELD 1937-1953 SINGLES & V TWINS (BOOK OF)
ROYAL ENFIELD 1946-1962 SINGLES (BOOK OF)
ROYAL ENFIELD 1958-1966 250cc & 350cc SINGLES (SECOND BOOK OF)
ROYAL ENFIELD 736cc INTERCEPTOR FACTORY WORKSHOP MANUAL
RUDGE 1933-1939 (BOOK OF)
SUNBEAM 1928-1939 (BOOK OF)
SUNBEAM 1946-1957 S7 & S8 (BOOK OF)
SUZUKI 50cc & 80cc UP TO 1966 (BOOK OF)
SUZUKI T10 1963-1967 FACTORY WORKSHOP MANUAL
SUZUKI T20 & T200 1965-1969 FACTORY WORKSHOP MANUAL
SUZUKI TWINS 1962 ONWARDS 125-500cc WORKSHOP MANUAL
TRIUMPH 1935-1939 PREWAR MODELS (BOOK OF)
TRIUMPH 1935-1949 (BOOK OF)
TRIUMPH 1937-1951 (WORKSHOP MANUAL)
TRIUMPH 1945-1955 FACTORY WORKSHOP MANUAL
TRIUMPH 1945-1958 TWINS (BOOK OF)
TRIUMPH 1956-1969 TWINS (BOOK OF)
VELOCETTE 1925-1970 ALL SINGLES & TWINS (BOOK OF)
VESPA 1951-1961 (BOOK OF)
VESPA 1955-1963 125 & 150cc & GS MODELS (SECOND BOOK OF)
VESPA 1955-1968 GS & SS (BOOK OF)
VESPA 1963-1972 90, 125 & 150cc (THIRD BOOK OF)
VILLIERS ENGINE UP TO 1959 INC. 3 WHEELERS (BOOK OF)
VILLIERS ENGINE UP TO 1969 (BOOK OF)
VINCENT 1935-1955 (WORKSHOP MANUAL)
YAMAHA 1971-1972 JT1& JT2 (WORKSHOP MANUAL & ILL PARTS LIST)

VELOCEPRESS TECHNICAL BOOKS – MOTORCYCLE

CATALOG OF BRITISH MOTORCYCLES (1951 MODELS)
INDIAN PONYBIKE, BOY RACER & PAPOOSE ILL PARTS LIST & SALES LIT
MOTORCYCLE ENGINEERING (P.E. Irving)
SPEED AND HOW TO OBTAIN IT (Motor Cycle Magazine UK)
TUNING FOR SPEED (P.E. Irving)

VELOCEPRESS MANUALS - THREE WHEELER'S

BSA THREE WHEELER (BOOK OF)
VINTAGE MORGAN THREE WHEELER (BOOK OF)

VELOCEPRESS MANUALS - AUTOMOBILE

ALFA ROMEO GIULIA WORKSHOP MANUAL 1300 TO 2000cc 1962-1975
ALFA ROMEO GIULIA TECH MANUAL CARBURETED CARS FROM 1962
ALFA ROMEO GIULIA TECH MANUAL FUEL INJECTED CARS FROM 1969
AUSTIN-HEALEY 6-CYLINDER WORKSHOP MANUAL
AUSTIN-HEALEY SPRITE & MG MIDGET WORKSHOP MANUAL 1958-1971
BMW 600 LIMOUSINE FACTORY WORKSHOP MANUAL
BMW 600 LIMOUSINE OWNERS HAND BOOK & SERVICE MANUAL
BMW 2000 & 2002 1966-1976 WORKSHOP MANUAL
BMW ISETTA FACTORY WORKSHOP MANUAL
CORVAIR 1960-1969 WORKSHOP MANUAL
CORVETTE V8 1955-1962 WORKSHOP MANUAL
FIAT 500 FACTORY WORKSHOP MANUAL 1957-1973
FIAT 600, 600D & MULTIPLA FACTORY WORKSHOP MANUAL 1955-1969
JAGUAR E-TYPE 3.8 & 4.2 SERIES 1 & 2 WORKSHOP MANUAL
JAGUAR MK 7, 8, 9 & XK120, 140, 150 WORKSHOP MANUAL 1948-1961
METROPOLITAN FACTORY WORKSHOP MANUAL
MGA & MGB OWNERS HANDBOOK & WORKSHOP MANUAL
MG MIDGET TC, TD, TF & TF1500 WORKSHOP MANUAL
PORSCHE 356 1948-1965 WORKSHOP MANUAL
PORSCHE 911 2.0, 2.2, 2.4 LITRE 1964-1973
PORSCHE 912 WORKSHOP MANUAL
TRIUMPH TR2, TR3, TR4 1953-1965 WORKSHOP MANUAL
VOLKSWAGEN TRANSPORTER, TRUCKS & WAGONS 1950-1979 WSM
VOLVO 1944-1968 ALL MODELS WORKSHOP MANUAL

VELOCEPRESS TECHNICAL BOOKS - AUTOMOBILE

FERRARI 250/GT SERVICE AND MAINTENANCE
FERRARI GUIDE TO PERFORMANCE
FERRARI OWNER'S HANDBOOK
FERRARI TUNING TIPS & MAINTENANCE TECHNIQUES
HOW TO BUILD A FIBERGLASS CAR
HOW TO BUILD A RACING CAR
HOW TO RESTORE THE MODEL 'A' FORD
MASERATI OWNER'S HANDBOOK
OBERT'S FIAT GUIDE
PERFORMANCE TUNING THE SUNBEAM TIGER
SOUPING THE VOLKSWAGEN
SOLEX CARBURETORS (EMPHASIS ON UK & EU AUTOMOBILES)
SU CARBURETORS (EMPHASIS ON UK AUTOMOBILES)
WEBER CARBURETORS (EMPHASIS ON ALFA & FIAT)

VELOCEPRESS BOOKS & GUIDES - AUTOMOBILE

ABARTH BUYERS GUIDE
COMPLETE CATALOG OF JAPANESE MOTOR VEHICLES
FERRARI 308 SERIES BUYER'S AND OWNER'S GUIDE
FERRARI BERLINETTA LUSSO
FERRARI BROCHURES AND SALES LITERATURE 1946-1967
FERRARI BROCHURES AND SALES LITERATURE 1968-1989
FERRARI OPP, MAINTENANCE & SERVICE H/BOOKS 1948-1963
FERRARI SERIAL NUMBERS PART I - ODD NUMBERS TO 21399
FERRARI SERIAL NUMBERS PART II - EVEN NUMBERS TO 1050
FERRARI SPYDER CALIFORNIA
HENRY'S FABULOUS MODEL "A" FORD
MASERATI BROCHURES AND SALES LITERATURE

VELOCEPRESS BOOKS – RACING

CARRERA PANAMERICANA - MEXICAN ROAD RACE (BOOK OF)
DIALED IN - THE JAN OPPERMAN STORY
IF HEMINGWAY HAD WRITTEN A RACING NOVEL
VEDA ORR'S NEW REVISED HOT ROD PICTORIAL

AUTOBOOKS WORKSHOP MANUALS & BROOKLANDS ROAD TEST PORTFOLIOS

FOR A COMPLETE LISTING OF THE AUTOBOOKS & BROOKLANDS TITLES THAT WE CURRENTLY HAVE AVAILABLE, PLEASE VISIT OUR WEBSITE.